Praise for Silver Linings

"Bishop Fairley's memoir paints a harsh, yet profound, picture of the realities of poverty and racism while embracing the enduring qualities of loyalty, family, devotion, perseverance, love, and faith. This is a journey of hope and healing, inspiring us to embrace the God-given relationships that shape our lives and help us recognize how we might overcome the polarization that too often divides us."
United Methodist Bishop Paul L. Leeland

"Seldom have I read a memoir written with such clarity that I feel like I'm the character de-scribed by the author. Empathy flows from the pages to your heart. You cry, laugh, and wonder with the author. Captivated, you can't wait to read about the Creator of *Silver Linings*, who guides the memoirist's hand. This memoir of Leonard's life reveals glimpses of what it was like to grow up poor with black skin. Ponder *Silver Linings*, imagine the author's pain and joy as he feels the touch of a Living Father reaching out to still the storm, and spread the clouds inviting Leonard to look up and discover Son-rays of hope shining through. Read about Leonard and his adventures growing up. As you read *Silver Linings*, you will sense God reaching down, touching, and bearing Leonard's pain. You will feel God reaching down and bearing your pain, too! Pick up this book, and you won't be able to put it back down. Savor Leonard's way of sharing sacred stories. Discover, claim, and share your sacred stories, too."
Rev. Dr. Bart W. Milleson
Author's college roommate, kindred spirit, fellow follower of Jesus, and United Methodist minister

"Leonard Fairley has every reason to be bitter. Born into a world of racism, poverty, injustice, and crushing circumstances, in *Silver Linings*, Leonard shows us how something altogether different took root in his life, shaping him to see and feel God in everything. From his birth story, the apartment he called 'the coffin in Queens,' his grandma's back porch bathtub, and beyond, Leonard leads us through his remarkable life with authenticity, truth, and loving care. As you read it, take heart. You are headed into deep waters that may very well pull you under and spit you out in a different place. Trust Leonard's story to lead you where you need to go, then invite it to take root in your life as well."

Susan Newton Graebe
Residency in Ordained Ministry Coordinator
North Carolina Conference of The United Methodist Church

SILVER LININGS

SILVER LININGS

A Memoir

Leonard E. Fairley

AdvocatePress

Advocate Press, Columbia, South Carolina

Copyright © 2025 by Advocate Press

All scripture quotations are taken from the Revised Standard Version of the Bible, copyright © 1946, 1952, and 1971 the Division of Christian Education of the National Council of the Churches of Christ in the United States of America. Used by permission. All rights reserved.

All rights reserved. No part of this book may be reproduced or transmitted in any form or by any means, electronic or mechanical, including photocopying, recording, or by any information storage and retrieval system, without permission in writing from the publisher.

First published in the United States of America in 2025.

Library of Congress Cataloging-in-Publication Data
Silver Linings
p. cm.

ISBN 978-1-966237-10-5

Contents

Preface ix
Chapter 1: Dying to Live 1
Chapter 2: Deadman's Creek 49
Chapter 3: Lessons of Nature 69
Chapter 4: The Pine Street Patriots 85
Chapter 5: Family Circle 96
Chapter 6: Rummie 108
Chapter 7: The Kenny Pool 123
Chapter 8: First Love 137
Chapter 9: Fields of Dreams 156
Chapter 10: Fire 182
Chapter 11: Out of the Fire and into the Frying Pan 212
Chapter 12: Explosion 239
Chapter 13: Healing Dreams 277
Chapter 14: Trailer Park Trash 297
Chapter 15: Salvation 339
About the Author 383

Preface

After reading the Table of Contents of this book and scanning its pages, one may conclude that the work is simply a collection of random short stories that romanticize small-town poverty. But the stories shared in these pages are my attempt to present life as viewed through the eyes of a young boy who discovers that even the unpredictable nature of everyday life is a woven tapestry held together by God's providence.

The experiences of our lives can appear to be random, unfair, and disconnected, seeming to forever scream the eternal question, "Why?" Why me? Why couldn't I have been born in a different place, under different circumstances? Why was I born on the wrong side of the tracks? Why are some people rich and others poor? Why is the world content to leave it that way, to let the poor get poorer and the rich get richer?

There is indeed nothing romantic about poverty and oppression, but there is something liberating in the journey through suffering when one is constantly forced to look for the light at the end of the tunnel.

I did not ask to be born under the circumstances that became a part of my life, but I learned that I could find ways to straighten out the question marks into the exclamation points of purpose. This book describes my attempt to walk through the difficult task of transforming those question marks. The process of writing the book has clarified for me the sense of purpose I ultimately discovered in my journey through life as a boy. The title, *Silver Linings*, refers to a familiar saying that became my life's mission statement from the cradle onward. Thanks to this amazing mantra, which always sustained me in the darkest of nights, I would be able to face the challenges of life's injustices—not by becoming bitter, but by increasing my focus on the prize of the high calling that is Christ Jesus. And somehow I trust that it will carry me for the rest of my life: Remember that there is always a silver lining behind every dark cloud.

It is my hope that readers will find places in their own lives where the dark threads of life's ups and downs have been woven together by a God who often does his best work in the midst of chaos. God does not discard any of the experiences we encounter but has the ability to use all of life to create wholeness.

It may often appear that the city of Laurinburg, the geographic setting of *Silver Linings*, is no more than a backward town, and that many of the characters in the book have no redeeming qualities. However, this would be a gross misreading of the book. Laurinburg has been and will always be my home. I was nurtured in the warmth of its slow summer days, which gave me wonderful moments for reflection. The water of Laurinburg quenched my thirst, and the blood of its people runs through my veins. Like any city, it has its shortcomings, but perfection is not a requirement for raising a native son. I owe all that I am or hope to become to the many people and places of Laurinburg that challenged me to always walk toward the light. The events recounted in *Silver Linings* helped me to focus on the light in spite of the darkness that was all around me. I give thanks to God for the places and people who shaped my dreams. I give thanks to God for the many times in my journey when God nurtured me. I guess that is why I can remember places and people with such ease. I drank deeply from the wells of those experiences and was able to find hope and purpose in each one of them.

I will never accept injustices such as poverty, oppression, and racism as natural realities of life. I have gleaned wonderful lessons through the joys, laughter, tears, heartaches, trials, and friendships shared in these pages. It is, was, and will be these lessons that remind me never to allow the unfairness of life to strip me of a hope that is rooted in God's desire to make life worth living for all his children. I hope that this work will be of help to people who have allowed darkness to blind them to the many threads of light that make life worth living. It is my desire that it will restore hope in those who have lost the ability to believe in silver linings.

A disclaimer: The dialogue in this memoir is written from memory as I both felt and remembered living each event. I have tried from memory to re-create events, locations, and conversations that were shared with me, especially about my birth and earlier years. When imagination meets memory, the results can be amazingly liberating and inspiring. The day I started writing *Silver Linings*, I liberated my story. In some cases, I have taken literary license with the dialogue to make it fit the actual event. I have had to convince myself in choosing to publish this memoir that perfect verbatim recall was not necessary.

What is and was most important is how each event transformed my life and helped shape who I am today, and that is always a risk worth taking in telling and sharing your own story.

Leonard E. Fairley
October 2025

Chapter 1

Dying to Live

There I stood—face to face with the clerk of records at Scotland County Courthouse. As I asked the clerk for a copy of my birth certificate, I was certainly unaware of the events that would unfold.

"What was your mother's maiden name?" the clerk matter-of-factly asked.

"Her name was Fairley," I answered with apparent anxiety. I had learned as a young child to be afraid of the courthouse, because that was where they locked you up. I was fifteen now, but the fear of being locked up in jail still existed in my mind.

"What is your father's name?" she continued her questioning.

"My father's name was Sylvester McLeod, but he's dead now."

The clerk took this information and walked into the room where all the certificates of birth were stored. It seemed to take such a long time for the clerk to come back with mine. During the eternity of the search, I began to suspect the police were being summoned to come lock me up.

Once, as a young child, I had been caught playing in the unfinished courthouse building. My mind drifted back to that frightening experience.

Exploring every inch of the new courthouse building had been the adventure of the day. "Let me go," I'd begged my cousin Jimmy. "I want to play in that courthouse with y'all."

"No, you're too little and you might get hurt," Jimmy scolded.

"Well if I can't go, I'll tell on y'all!" I shouted.

"All right, come on, boy," Jimmy said, finally yielding. "But if you get hurt, don't start crying."

Once inside the courthouse, we began playing and hiding from each other in the unfinished building. Suddenly, we heard the loud ringing of what we knew to be the alarm system.

"Somebody tripped the alarm!" Jimmy screamed. "Come on, let's get out of here!"

Before we could make it out, we heard the thundering voice of a policeman calling through a bullhorn.

"All right you kids, get out of there!" the voice blasted, echoing throughout the empty cement building.

"Come on here, Leonard! We've got to jump or the police will lock us up!" Jimmy cried.

In one fluid leap, our Black bodies were airborne and out of the exit. Then we were running as fast as we could to get back home.

"Come on, boy, you've got to run faster if you don't want to go to jail!" Jimmy yelled.

Before I had time to say, "I can't run any faster," I felt his hands grip my arm with almost superhuman strength.

"Jimmy, you're about to drag me in the dirt!" I whimpered.

"What do you want—to be drug in the dirt or locked up?" Jimmy answered.

The black and white police car was speeding down the road with its red light twirling—hurrying to cut us off at the edge of the woods. Jimmy would have easily made it if I hadn't been there to slow him down.

"You wanted to come; now you've got to run because here comes that policeman!" Jimmy said, trying to catch his breath.

But we couldn't get away; the policeman finally chased us down and handcuffed us. Our fear was so great that neither Jimmy nor I spoke.

"Now what I ought to do is take y'all boys straight to jail and lock you up," the policeman said.

I had never known real fear until I heard those words. I had heard stories of what happened to Black boys who found themselves on the wrong side of the law, especially "White Law."

He continued, "But I'm not going to do that. I'm going to take you home now, but if I ever catch you in this or any other courthouse, I'm going to lock you up and throw away the key."

The policeman had spoken our salvation.

"Son, are you sure you gave me the right information?" the clerk said loudly to me now as I stood before her, waiting for my birth certificate. She had to ask me twice because I was lost in the thought of being locked up for daring to go into the courthouse again.

"Yes, ma'am, that's the right information," I answered with relief, realizing I wasn't going to jail. I was at the courthouse because I was ready to take the driver's education course at the local junior high school, and the only way I could take the course was to get my birth certificate and prove I was old enough.

"Let me look again," the clerk replied.

I had risked coming back to the courthouse despite my fear. No matter what it cost, I wanted my driver's license just like all my friends.

But the clerk soon returned. "I'm sorry, son, but we don't seem to have a copy of your birth certificate."

I could hear it in her voice. This clerk understood how important this was to me. I had been afraid of the law, but in this voice, I heard and felt compassion. Old ways die hard, and I was still afraid to press the law any further.

As I turned to walk out of the office, the clerk called after me. "Talk to your mother and see if she can help you," she said. "Tell her to come with you next time."

I turned and slowly walked out of the door of the courthouse. I had overcome my fear only to be confronted with new ones. I thought every living person had a birth certificate—how could I be living with no record of my birth?

Still unaware of the significance of what had just happened, I began the long walk home.

Walking with water in your eyes is a difficult thing to do. I couldn't keep the tears out of my eyes so I could see where I was going. I don't know which came faster—the tears or the questions.

"What is happening?" I sobbed. "Am I even alive? There is no record of my ever being born."

There appeared to be no answers.

"What are you crying about?" my mama asked as I reached the front door.

"They told me I didn't have a birth certificate," I moaned through the tears.

"Wait a minute. Slow down and tell me—who told you that?" my mama asked.

"I went to the courthouse to get my birth certificate and the lady told me I didn't have one," I answered.

I had never seen my mama's facial expression change so quickly. Her sudden change of body language let me know I had said something that struck a nerve. After a long period of silence, my mama started to speak in a calm manner. She seemed to be struggling as she tried to find the right words for explaining the missing birth certificate.

She sat down beside me on the sofa and began her long, difficult story.

"Now, Leonard," she started. "There's something I must tell you, but you must promise to listen and try to understand."

"Is it about my missing birth certificate?" I asked before she could compose herself.

Although my mind was still preoccupied with getting a driver's license, I could sense the unfolding drama of some deep dark secret.

"I don't want you to say anything. Just listen," my mama reiterated. "I'm going to tell you how you were born, and that will answer why you don't have a birth certificate."

With each new word my mama's struggle became more intense.

I could not believe what I heard come from her lips. By the time my mama and daddy reached twenty-five years of age, they'd had seven children. He and my mama worked together on the same farm from sunup to sundown, picking cotton for twenty-five cents a sack. That was all he was allowed to do. He owed his life to the farm owner, and that farm owner refused to release him from the bondage of the dirt farm. What could he do? My father had been molded and shaped to be a nobody. He had no other skills, and he had nothing to call his own.

Being twenty-five, Black, and the father of seven children was a death sentence for a man with no job skills. For my daddy, it was a slow death caused by alcoholism. This was a sentence that could not only lead to physical death but would almost certainly mean abuse for the mother and children.

"He would come in and almost beat me to death if I didn't do as he told me," my mama said.

Because he had been a nobody in society, his only self-worth came from whipping his family into submission. His dignity and self-esteem had been so severely stripped that he had to get drunk even to gain the courage to do what he called "running his own house."

"He couldn't love me." The tears began to run down my mama's face. I wished that I had never needed to know this terrible secret—this secret of struggle and suffering. I was the third of their seven children. My mama gave me the unbelievable news that my conception came as a result of my father's drunken demand for sex.

"I tried to tell him that I wasn't well," my mama continued.

"What do you mean you were not well?" I asked.

"I had just given birth to your brother Curtis, and it was too early to get pregnant again." It was as if the light had gone out in my mama's face as she sat there on the sofa with tears staining her cheeks.

The taste of salt made me realize that I was crying as well. Was it because I would have to accept the fact that I was the product of a drunken man's desire for dignity? In a dusty sharecropper's shack in Marston, North Carolina, I had become the physical reality of a drunken husband's demands.

Mama told me that when she started having birth pains, my grandma called a midwife, Mrs. Ruth Monroe, to deliver me.

"It ain't no use in y'all going through the trouble of getting a birth certificate for that child. He ain't going to live through the night. He'll be dead before morning," Mama quoted Mrs. Monroe as saying.

Mrs. Monroe had probably seen many babies die in the night; she had brought most of the Black children born in Marston into the world.

Mrs. Monroe's hands were the first that felt Black flesh born into the hostile world we lived in. Hers were the hands that brought life into the world, only to watch it be snuffed out in the slow death of poverty. Mrs. Monroe saw beyond the physical signs of probable death. Yes, she knew my mama's young body had suffered the burden of trying to successfully carry another child when it wasn't ready. She knew I had been forced into the world too soon, but that wasn't all she saw. In her heart, she knew that society had already written and signed my death certificate. There must have been countless times when Mrs. Monroe subconsciously wished that the shivering wet Black flesh in her hands would die before it had the chance to suffer the hate, poverty, and rejection that awaited it.

"Why did she say that?" I asked.

A million questions were now racing through my bewildered brain. I was becoming consumed by this mystery.

"You were born three months premature," my mama answered.

"That means I was born in six months rather than nine," I knowingly answered.

"Yes, that's right," Mama reaffirmed.

Although the question of the missing birth certificate was being answered, there were now many new questions: How had I lived without being taken to the hospital and placed in an incubator? What did I look like? Why did I survive when most babies born that early die?

I began to see that this was not a mystery but a miracle.

"You were so small that we could hide you underneath a baby's diaper." My mama was now willing to tell me all the details of my peculiar birth. "You see those scars on my legs," she said, pointing to the large areas of dark spots on the front of her plump legs. "I got those from sitting too close to the fireplace. I scorched my legs trying to keep you warm. We had to guess when you were hungry. Your vocal cords weren't developed, which meant that you couldn't cry. So we guessed when to feed you and change your diaper."

I could only sit there, awestruck. *How could this be true?* Grandma had often said that God saved my life, but I never knew what she meant until I learned these details. I learned that it was Grandma who took over the duties of taking care for me while I was a baby. The midwife and even my mama had given up on me ever living past that first night.

It was my grandma's religious zeal and hope that enabled her to see the circumstances through different eyes. The midwife could only see through the eyes of her many years of experience in birthing babies.

It ain't no use in getting a birth certificate for this child. He ain't going to live through the night. Mrs. Ruth Monroe's words echoed through my mind as I remembered my grandma's hope.

"Your grandma said 'Doretha, you're too young to kill yourself taking care of this child,'" Mama continued. According to Mama, Grandma Gladys would not let anybody, including her, come near me. "Your grandma said 'Let me and the Lord take care of him, and he'll make it through.'"

Those were the words my grandma used to counter Mrs. Monroe's pessimism.

My grandma's "mother-wit" had kept me alive. My incubator was a drawer covered with blankets surrounded by mason jars of hot water that helped regulate my temperature, especially at night.

It was these two opposing views of whether I would survive that caused still more questions. *Had God really saved my life? What kind of God was he to save a life, only to watch it suffer slowly in the degradation of poverty?*

It was this intense struggle that would give me a "why" to live.

Grandma Gladys never failed to remind me that it was God who had saved my life. "God's got his hands on you, boy, and don't you ever forget," she would always tell me.

Deep inside my heart, I believed Grandma Gladys. It was my belief in this strange God that gave me the drive to live.

After hearing my mama's story of my birth, my life took on a new meaning. I was determined to see God's hand in all my experiences. In poverty, I was determined to see the hand of the God who had saved my life. In the pain of being told by a stranger that I had no birth certificate, I was determined to live life and not let it live me. If society had indeed signed my death certificate, then, thanks to my grandma, I was going to be dying to live.

There I stood, face to face with the clerk of records again, but unlike the first time, my head was held high.

"Yes, may I help you?" the clerk asked.

With no fear, I answered. "Yes, I would like to get a delayed birth certificate for Leonard Fairley."

Despite Mrs. Ruth Monroe's prophecy, I was alive. Despite my status in society, I was alive. God had saved my life, and nothing could take that away.

I was trying to make myself go to sleep there in the pew, but before my eyelids were closed, I felt a sharp poke to my ribs.

"Wake up, boy." I don't know if it was Grandma McLeod's voice or her elbow that caused me to instantly jump. If it wasn't my grandma's poking, it was my mama's pinching.

The preacher's rich bass voice thundered so loud that it caused the wooden church to vibrate. "The Lord is too wise to make a mistake."

I was only ten years old, but I knew what a mistake was. I began to wonder if the preacher knew what he was talking about. He certainly wasn't there when my father threw me against the wall. Now, that was what I called a mistake. I thought it was a mistake the night my father almost bit my mama's thumb off during one of their many fights. Mistakes were made when my father tried to starve us to death because he wouldn't or couldn't find work.

How could a man of God stand there preaching about mistakes? I could give him a lesson or two about mistakes.

The preacher continued his eulogy. *Could he be talking about the same man I had grown up fearing?*

"The Lord has called one of his children home, and we must accept God's will," Reverend Joseph intoned.

A chorus of "Amen" and "Have mercy, Lord" rose from the sea of people that packed the country church. I think most of the people had come on such a hot day in order to see how my mama would react.

People were already beginning to say, "He died because that girl took his children away from him."

"Yeah!"

The whispers grew.

"She took that poor boy's children and moved down to Laurinburg."

"Ain't that a shame."

Reverend Joseph's eulogy had now reached that point where he and the people were one.

"Fix it, preacher!"

"Make it plain!"

"Say so!"

The more they called, the stronger Reverend Joseph's voice got. If eulogies determined whether a person entered heaven, the way Reverend Joseph was preaching, my father would have no trouble passing through the pearly gates. The funeral seemed to last forever.

There was no comfort in trying to sleep now.

"Get up boy," I heard my mama's voice whisper in my ear.

The church choir was singing, "When we all get to heaven, what a day of rejoicing that will be."

"Amen!" the voices cried out.

The choir continued with more emotion, "When we all see Jesus, we'll sing and shout the victory."

While the singing continued, two men wheeled the silver metallic casket that held my father's body to the rear of the church. From where I sat, I could see that they were opening the casket for viewing. I really wished I were asleep now.

It takes much more than just passing on biological genes to be a father. The things I remembered about my father were not at all good. His drinking made our lives a living hell. My mama finally decided enough was enough, so we moved and left him in New York nursing his drinking habit. But his hard drinking and living had caught up with him, and now here we were to see him one last time.

I didn't want to see him.

"Mama, do I have to go look at him?" I cried.

The answer was the one I knew was coming.

"Yeah, you've got to. That's your daddy. Get up so we can go." My mama's tone let me know I had no choice.

Before I knew what was happening, Grandma McLeod took my hand and jerked me from my seat. We walked down the narrow aisle of Silver Hill Presbyterian Church toward my father's open casket. The closer we got, the louder my grandma began to cry. The funeral attendant gave her tissue and fanned her tear-stained face.

"I hope she lets go of my hand," I prayed, but even in her grief Grandma McLeod still held my hand like a vise grip.

"My poor son, my poor baby," she cried. "Lord, why did you take my baby from me so soon?"

No matter how close we got to the casket, none of those words of sorrow came from my lips. It was only when we reached the open casket that my grandma let go of my stinging hand. Grandma McLeod proceeded to reach into the casket, slowly starting to caress my father's lifeless face.

"Go on and look." I heard my mama's voice call from behind us. "There are other people waiting to pay their last respects."

Is that what they call it, "last respects"? I didn't know what I was doing here if these were my last respects. My father had done nothing for me to respect him. When I looked into my father's still face, I felt no emotional attachment. I thought that at least I would be frightened, but there was no fear. I had forgotten what he looked like.

"Mama, I don't know that man," I said.

Truly, my father had died before this funeral. He died long before the preacher's words. Walking by his open casket gave me visions of what a true living father would be like.

"Will I ever know a living father?" I whispered under my breath.

It was at the gravesite that I finally felt some emotional attachment to that lifeless body. The casket was suspended over its final resting place.

"Ashes to ashes, dust to dust," the preacher said, exhausted and with sweat running down his glistening face.

Three roses were placed on the casket. I felt sorry for my father. He didn't know me, and all I knew about him was pain and suffering. He must have wanted to be a good father, but there were too many things standing in his way.

His fight to be a father was over now as they lowered him into the ground.

I never realized what effect the poverty of New York had on me until the train ride south.

"Come on, y'all. Get your stuff together. We're moving to Laurinburg," my mama shouted. With train tickets in hand and seven children in tow, the journey began.

On the way, we saw many things we had never seen before.

"Look at those big dogs," a small voice spoke in excitement.

Every nose pressed immediately against the window of our train compartment.

"Yeah, they look big to me," another voice chimed.

"Those ain't no dogs," Mama corrected us as we stared at the cows in the pasture.

Living in the concrete tenements of Queens, New York, we rarely got to go outside. The only animals we were ever acquainted with in Queens were two dogs, Dot and Charlie.

We shared our two-room apartment in New York with Mrs. Sally and her pet dogs. The one-bathroom, one-kitchen dungeon was more like a prison. It was illegal to keep pets in the building. This rule puzzled me a great deal, because there were always rats and cockroaches. The only thing that kept them from being pets was the simple fact that they were not tame.

Mrs. Sally was able to keep Dot and Charlie without breaking the rules because she listed the dogs as her children. I would soon discover that she took this literally. Dot and Charlie were often dressed in baby's clothes and paraded down the city sidewalks in a baby carriage. One of the few ways we got to see the sun was by sitting on the windowsill of our high-rise cage.

Once, while sitting on that windowsill, I had the opportunity to see how serious Mrs. Sally was about Dot and Charlie being her children. From my caged perch, I could see Mrs. Sally pushing her familiar carriage down the sidewalk.

"Are those your babies?" a lady asked.

"Yes, they are," Mrs. Sally proudly answered.

The lady reached down toward the carriage covers in order to get a closer look at the two angels. When she pulled the covers back, I heard a scream—and out jumped Dot followed by Charlie. The astonished lady just stood there with her mouth wide open.

"You frightened my babies!" Mrs. Sally yelled.

"What do you mean, babies?" the lady asked after gaining her composure.

Mrs. Sally went running after her two dogs, calling, "Come back, babies! Please, come back! The mean lady didn't mean it."

The last I saw of Dot and Charlie that day was their legs as they ran around the corner, still dressed in baby clothes.

With experiences like that, one should not wonder why we thought cows were dogs. What little common sense we did have, Mrs. Sally tried to scald out of us. Mrs. Sally was our babysitter while my mama did domestic work in the city.

Among the many things we hated about Mrs. Sally was the way in which she gave us baths. She would fill the bathtub with scalding hot water, and then call, "Now you two come and get in the water."

"Mrs. Sally, the water is too hot!" we would cry to no avail.

"That means it will get all of the dirt off you," she would justify.

It was beyond me as to why she worried about all of us getting clean, especially for those who followed the first two kids. The first bathers would get scalded while the last two would nearly freeze to death. Mrs. Sally never changed the water until everybody was finished.

Leaving New York was like being released from prison. The excitement of moving to North Carolina overwhelmed us all.

"What are you going to do when you get to Grandma's?" I asked Curtis.

"I'm going to stay outside all day long," he answered.

We heard stories of Grandma Gladys's big backyard. All we thought about during the long train ride was getting to Grandma's house and playing outside.

"When are we going to get there?"

"Are we almost there?"

My mama must have answered these questions a million times. After being squeezed and suffocated by the concrete coffin in Queens, it was all we could do to sit still on the train. I'm sure the other passengers thought we were wild animals just freed from the zoo.

Even as children, we could read the eyes of disgust and disdain. One of the things that poverty had done was to sensitize us. Maybe that is why my mama never took us shopping with her. She could ignore the whispers. She could withstand the looks of rejection and harsh words, but she would never allow what little self-esteem we had to be damaged.

But it didn't matter now what people on the train thought or said. This was our Exodus from poverty to the promised land of fresh air and freedom.

"Next stop, Laurinburg, North Carolina!" the porter cried.

"Wake up, Calvin! We're here," I said shaking the sleep from my brother's body.

The pushing match began as soon as the train wheels came to a screeching halt.

"Move, Curtis!" The scream echoed through the compartment.

"No, boy, I was in line first." Curtis used his status as the oldest brother to assert his right to the front of the line, despite my piercing scream.

I felt the back of my mama's hand fall across the nape of my exposed neck with such force that it pushed me into a shocked Curtis.

"Y'all stop that pushing and screaming," Mama commanded. "Everybody is going to get off this train together."

The first thing I noticed as I stepped down from the train was the absence of the tall condemned high-rise housing projects. There was nothing to obstruct the view of the rising sun. The only things standing tall were the trees. The early morning sunlight filtered through the blowing green leaves.

It was hard to believe that I had been born just fifteen miles from here in a small town called Marston. I had forgotten what North Carolina looked like. Living in the Borough of Queens had all but erased what little memory there was of North Carolina. I couldn't imagine why anyone would ever want to leave this place.

"You're going to get left behind if you don't get in this car." Mama's voice broke the spell that captivated me.

Frank, my mama's older brother, had come to carry us to Grandma Gladys's house.

Once we were packed into my uncle's station wagon, I asked, "Mama, why did we ever move to New York?"

"We moved because we thought we could do better up north," she explained.

I have since learned that poverty is still poverty no matter the name or size of the city. Poverty knows no geographical boundaries.

We were on our way to Grandma Gladys's house, and that's all that mattered. Grandma's address was 226 Center Street.

"Look for the street name," Curtis said.

"Boy, you can't even read," Calvin reminded us.

But that didn't keep us from looking anyway.

"We know what the house looks like," Curtis countered.

Frank explained the details of the living arrangements for my mama.

"I don't think you're going to be able to live with Mama for a long time. She's already taking care of Esther Mae's two children, Jimmy and Audrey," he said.

"I know Mama is having a hard time," Mama answered. "I can help her out with the welfare check I'll be getting. That will help stretch the money she's getting for Odessa."

This was grown folks' talk, so we just listened with no questions asked.

I was beginning to wonder if it was going to be like New York all over again, with fourteen people living in the same house. My aunts, Beulah and Viola, along with Beulah's child, were also living with Grandma. We should have stayed in New York, I thought.

Remembering previous conversations with my mama helped explain why so many people were living in Grandma's house. Mama would often gather us around her and reminiscence about the "good ole days."

Mama's father, Simuel Fairley, raised thirteen children as a tenant farmer. Naturally, all the children worked on the farm.

"We didn't have anything fancy to eat, but we always had plenty," she told us.

We loved my mama's stories about cotton picking in the field, and how she and her other brothers and sisters would get into dirt clod throwing contests.

"We never got any work done," she would laughingly recount.

I was proud when I heard stories about my Grandfather Simuel.

"He was a hard-working Christian man," my mama remembered reverently. "He would often sacrifice things he needed to make sure we were taken care of."

I wished my father had been like Grandpa Simuel. I vowed that when I grew up and had a family, I would be like Grandpa.

I tried to visualize what Grandpa looked like, how he talked, and how he walked. In my mind, he was a tall, strong, Black man, with a voice like thunder and a smile like an angel. Before I ever heard of Superman, my grandpa was my Superman. He was the Superman who instead of wearing a cape wore bib overalls and an old dusty hat. He was the Superman who stood behind a plow and mule from sunup until sundown. He was the Superman who was often cheated by the landowner, but never let it keep him from making a way for his family.

There must have been an unspoken covenant between my grandma and my grandpa to keep the family together, especially the girls. Upon my grandpa's death, the family became a matriarchy headed by my strong-willed grandma. There was nothing she wouldn't do in order to keep her family together.

So here we were—headed back home. My brain hurt as I tried to figure out how Grandma was going to make room for all of us. "That house must be mighty big," I reasoned. But if anybody could make it work, Grandma Gladys Fairley could.

It took what seemed to be forever for us to reach Grandma's house.

"We're here!"

Those were the most beautiful words I had heard Frank say during the entire ride from the train station.

"Boy, look at that big yard!" Curtis yelled.

I didn't even bother to answer. My mouth wouldn't have worked anyway. My eyes told the story. When I finally gained control of my senses, the words flowed out like a waterfall.

"I don't care if I have to sleep outside. This is better than Queens!"

It was early summer, and children were outside playing in the warmth of the southern summer sunshine. With the possibility of playing outside, we piled out of the crowded station wagon pushing, biting, and scratching. The whole neighborhood appeared to be watching us as if we were wild animals being set free.

"We don't have to worry about finding somebody to play with around here," Calvin said as he picked himself up from the ground where he had been pushed.

"You better get to know them first," Mama cautioned.

Grandma Gladys, as usual, was prepared for our arrival. We could smell the traditional Friday southern dinner of fish, cabbage, and corn bread. It only took a couple of whiffs from our noses to remind us that we hadn't eaten.

"We must have died and gone to heaven," I whispered to Curtis as the two of us tried to go through the door at the same time. We would have never noticed our cousins, Jimmy and Audrey, if they had not shouted at us as soon as we walked in.

"Close that door," they yelled in unison. "Can't you see we're watching television?"

Audrey turned back and became engrossed in whatever they were watching. Jimmy made another remark that let us know he had no intentions of making us feel welcome.

"Where were y'all born at, in a barn?" he quipped.

"They don't seem to be happy to see us," I told Calvin.

"Shh, boy, can't you see we trying to watch *Flipper*?"

I soon learned that this show, along with the meal, was a part of Friday's ritual—fish for supper and fish on television.

"Jimmy, you and Audrey get up and help Doretha and her children get their stuff out of Frank's car." The voice came from the direction of the heavenly smell.

"I hope this don't take long," Audrey growled.

She didn't have to worry about it taking too long; we didn't have much. The car was quickly unloaded of our meager belongings, and Jimmy and Audrey were back to their stations in front of the television set.

The charming voice of summer's spell immediately began calling me outside.

"Come on, Jimmy. Let's go outside and play," I begged.

"Boy, you better get out of my face before I knock you into next week."

There seemed to be nothing I could do to pull Jimmy away from *Flipper*.

"Is that any way to treat your cousin who's come all the way from New York?" my mama came to my defense.

This, too, proved to be useless, as Jimmy reacted as if my mama had said nothing.

"Go on, take him outside until it's time to eat," my mama persisted.

"Let him go by himself." Jimmy finally acknowledged.

"Now, you know that boy don't know nobody out there."

My mama was right. I didn't know anybody, and I didn't want to get in a fight on my first day in North Carolina.

Jimmy lost all patience and began raising his voice to my mama. "Can't he wait until *Flipper* goes off?"

It was clear to me that nothing my mama or I said was going to cause Jimmy to budge from his spot.

The sound of fast-approaching footsteps came from the kitchen. The next thing I saw was a short, stoutly built woman in an apron standing over my cousin. The force of her blow knocked Jimmy off his chair, and he lay on the ground clutching the side of his head.

With eyes flashing like a mongoose through black-framed glasses, Grandma Gladys ordered Jimmy to take me outside.

"Don't ever let me hearing you sassing another grown person like that again! Don't forget you're a child!" Grandma said, pointing her long finger for emphasis.

From that moment on, I knew who was in charge in that house. I had to learn the rules quickly if I was to avoid getting on Grandma's bad side.

After the long train ride, being outside in the warm sunshine was the highlight of the day, but of course Jimmy didn't think so. He showed his anger by not introducing his friends to us as they whispered back and forth to each other. I knew he was talking about me, but who cared. I had gotten what I wanted.

"Come on and eat," a voice called. We had gotten filthy from our play. "Go wash your hands and face before you come to this table," the unmistakable voice of Grandma commanded.

"Grandma, we ain't dirty," I began to say, but the sight of Jimmy lying on the floor quickly changed my mind and I kept my mouth shut.

Once again, I thought I'd died and gone to heaven. After being half starved in New York, I had to pinch myself to make sure I wasn't dreaming. Grandma loved to buy mullet on Friday and fry them golden brown in cornmeal. I had never seen such big fish, and to go along with that, there was a mountain of golden yellow cornbread and, of course, vegetables. The steamed cabbage would make you hurt yourself just smelling it, and nothing goes better with cabbage than fatback.

I was ready to dive into this sea of food, but before I could reach my hand out, a familiar voice ordered us to pray. In Grandma Gladys's house, the children said the grace. Today it was Audrey's turn.

Audrey prayed so slowly. If I didn't know better, I would say she was trying to torture us.

"God is great," she began, stopping to add emphasis on each word. "God is good. Let us thank him for our food."

When Audrey paused this time, I opened my eyes to make sure the food hadn't disappeared.

"Close your eyes, boy," Grandma said. "If you open them one more time, you won't get nothing to eat."

That was another thing I learned about Grandma Gladys. She had eyes like a hawk, even while we were praying.

Audrey continued her prayer without interruption. "By his hands we all are fed. Thank you, Lord, for our daily bread. Amen."

How to feed this army with some order was a task that took the genius of a general.

"It's going to be a long time before we get something to eat," I moaned to Calvin. "I hope we go first. I'm hungry."

Obviously, my grandma and my mama had discussed a plan to feed this small army. My mama would serve us.

"Doretha, get up and fix those children something to eat," Grandma said.

"Grandma, I can fix my own plate," Curtis blurted out.

"No, Grandma, don't let him fix his own plate," I pleaded. "He'll try to eat everything."

Once again, I realized that Grandma was the boss in her house.

"Doretha, I told you to get up and fix plates for those children. You know I don't allow no children in my pots."

At Grandma's house, we were never allowed to serve ourselves.

I was sure to get something to eat now that Grandma Gladys had given the word, much to Curtis's dismay.

Our getting to eat first didn't please my cousin Jimmy. I could see in his eyes that he was keeping score, and once out of Grandma's sight, he would attempt payback. Jimmy was the last thing on my mind. I knew a few tricks, and I would deal with him when the time came. My only concern was feeding my empty stomach.

"Y'all musta ain't had nothing to eat in years," Audrey said after observing us put away helping after helping of food.

"Audrey, leave them alone and let them eat," my mama said, defending us.

Our first day at Grandma Gladys's ended the same way it began—with her in charge. Like a drillmaster, she ordered us to the huge back porch. The porch had a large screened area, which is a luxury during summer nights in the south. The screened porch served as a necessary defense against those dreaded vampires of the insect world, mosquitoes. The mosquitoes seemed to come from everywhere, sometimes before the sun even went down.

During warm summer nights, all children had their baths on the back porch, and if there were holes in the screen, it didn't take long to realize it. We found several washtubs hanging from the wall. Jimmy and Audrey knew instinctively what to do, so we followed their every move.

"I ain't taking no bath outside!" Curtis yelled. "Nobody ain't gonna see me naked."

"Boy, ain't nobody going to be looking at you," answered Grandma as she drew the curtains dividing each washtub.

After being assured that no one would see us, we marched into the house where we found foot-tubs filled with steaming hot water. The waiting tubs of water were carried to their assigned washtub on the back porch. The water was emptied into each tub. The scene was repeated until each tub was filled.

"Come in here and get these wash towels and soap!" Grandma called to the first seven bathers. "Don't y'all go out there playing, neither!"

Testing the water was a necessary part of my bathing ritual, especially after my experience with Mrs. Sally in New York. My toes barely broke the surface of the water, causing ripples to race outward toward the boundary of the washtub.

"Boy, you better go on and get in that water," Jimmy warned. "That's right, you better quit messing around. You don't want Grandma to come out here."

I understood that I needed to heed Jimmy's warning. If I doubted his words, all I had to do was recall the scene I had witnessed earlier that day, which had ended with Jimmy lying on the floor.

After my toes convinced the rest of my body that the water was safe, I slid down into the warm water with assurance.

The summer breeze blew across my face and naked chest with a hypnotic peacefulness. I became aware of things I'd never noticed in New York City.

There were never moments like this in the concrete jungles of the slums. Something spiritual was happening.

For the first time, my ears heard the sounds of crickets and frogs playing their southern summer night's symphony. My eyes saw the tree branches dance with the wind as the moonlight of evening dusk silhouetted their performance. I knew I had probably heard these sounds before, but here was a moment in which they meant something.

Jimmy's voice invaded my moment of peace. "Boy, you better get out of that water," he said as his hand slipped across my still wet shoulders. Water splashed everywhere.

"What do you mean scaring me like that? Are you crazy or something? I could've drowned!" I screamed.

"If you don't get out of that water so somebody else can take their turn, you're really going to know what scared is. Didn't you hear Grandma calling you?" he asked with a sinister grin on his face.

I could tell by his grin that I was coming closer to one of Grandma's notorious whippings.

Sleeping arrangements were made while we completed our baths. Seven "pallet" quilts stuffed with old clothes were arranged near the foot of my grandma's large bed. I wondered if all grandmas have huge beds. Looking at this bed from our pallets was like looking up at a mountain.

"I wonder what that long string tied to the bedpost is for?" I whispered to Darryl.

"I don't know," was Darryl's answer. "But the other end leads up to that light."

Like everything in this house, there was a purpose for this gadget. Instead of standing to turn on the light that stood in the center of the ceiling, all Grandma needed to do was pull the string on the bedpost and the light came on. With seven children sleeping around your bed, I guess it was a necessary piece of ingenuity.

"Y'all say your prayers before I turn this light out," Grandma commanded.

Sleep came easily and with no interruptions. There were no sounds of sirens or gunfire. There were no noises of doors slamming or the laughing of streetwalkers under the window. The only sounds were those of insects, and of course my brothers' snoring, which could be ceased with a quick kick.

"Get up and go look out the window," my mama whispered as she shook the sleep from my body.

The sun was rising through the trees. Its bright orange color seemed to set the leaves on fire. No smog or city filth blocked its strength and brilliance. The sunbeams dancing through the windowpanes were truly like lights from heaven.

For the first time, the size of my grandma's house was revealed to me in the sunlight.

"Mama," I asked with excitement, "Can I go look around?"

"Go ask your grandma. I don't think she'll mind."

As I made my way to the kitchen, I could smell the aroma of breakfast cooking.

"Grandma," I called, "Mama told me to come ask you if it would be all right to look around."

Grandma Gladys answered without taking her eyes away from the sizzling bacon, while at the same time opening the oven door to check baking biscuits.

"You can look around, honey." Her voice was different this morning, and it rung with the sweetness of an angel. But then the angel's voice disappeared and was replaced with her familiar in-charge tone. "Yes, you can look around, but don't you wake up nobody else."

The kitchen was in the rear of the house. Turning left toward the back door, I found myself standing at the end of a long corridor. The sunlight shone brightly through the front screen door.

While walking down the hall toward the door, I realized there were no doors and no windows on the left side of the corridor. In awe and amazement, I continued my journey toward the front door. Grandma Gladys had not given me permission to go outside, but she didn't tell me not to go outside, either.

That's all I needed to get into trouble. Vague instructions were like saying, "Go on, do what you like," and in these cases, I usually did what I wanted.

I made the decision that if I wanted to really see the whole house, I had to take the risk of going outside. I just had to see why there were no windows or doors on one side of the hall. If I got into trouble, I could always dare telling my grandma she'd never said I couldn't go outside.

Upon reaching the front door, I unhooked the locked screen-door latch and walked out into the bright sun. The front porch was huge, but a tall wooden banister divided it. Through the barred woodwork of the banister, I saw a second door for the first time. I recognized why the house was so huge—it was an apartment house.

I dared come this far, I thought to myself. Why not go further?

The right-turn pointed in the direction of the high cement steps. I made my descent to the ground. The grass was wet with summer morning dew. The dew droplets wet the bottom of my bare feet and sluiced between my toes.

What I discovered next was something that would soon become our favorite hiding place in the whole house.

The apartment's foundation sat high off the ground. It was so high that we could walk standing up underneath the house. We played all kinds of games in this secret place. My favorite game was one called "Doodle Bug," which was played with ant lion houses. We would crawl underneath the house where the ground was covered with ant lion houses, and we would compete with each other to see who could catch the most doodle bugs. The trick to winning this game was to find a good spot, then with small twigs to start stirring in the ant lion's trap, and finally to sing the magic words:

Doodle bug,
Doodle bug,
Your house is on fire!
You better come get your meat and bread!

Over and over, this chorus was sung, while stirring the ant lion's trap until the doodle bug would appear. Once it appeared, it would begin snapping at the twigs with its jaws, trying to back under cover into its hole. The object of the game was to get the doodle bug to bite the twig and then, while it held on, to place the insect in a jar as quickly as possible.

The only other game I recall having so much fun playing underneath the house involved hiding and scaring people when they walked down the steps. This particular game sometimes came at a high cost to your backside. If anyone discovered us playing, the result was a good old-fashioned whipping from Grandma Gladys.

That first morning, after satisfying my curiosity, I returned inside just in time to hear Grandma command, "Y'all get up and wash your faces and hands." Her voice rumbled through the big house. "Put on your clothes so you can eat breakfast."

"Grandma, who lives next door?" I asked without thinking.

I asked the question to prove to my brothers that I knew something they did not. The consequences were the last thing on my mind. I saw the jealous look scrawled across their faces.

However, my joy would be short lived. Grandma Gladys immediately turned on me.

"Boy, who told you to go outside? Just for disobeying me, you can stay inside and help me with the dishes."

"But Grandma, you didn't tell me not to go outside," I said.

"Boy, use some common sense," she steamed. "And because you're being smart, you can stay inside for the rest of the day."

By now my brothers' jealously quickly turned into happy vengeance. It was as if Grandma knew this hurt more than a whipping. I knew better than to say anything else. The morning had started out with so much promise, but only a few words destroyed all my discoveries. All the sunlight in the world meant nothing after that.

Grandma went on to tell us who lived on the other side of the house.

"Mrs. Aida Walls lives next door, and y'all don't need to be messing around there," she warned. "That woman has a dog named Fuzzy and anything that's got teeth will bite."

That was warning enough to keep us from becoming too curious about going next door.

I always considered my mama to be a beautiful lady, but her beauty was more inward. Hers was not a catalog or television beauty, the kind that always seemed to persuade you to buy something.

But today, my mama was a catalog beauty. I did not understand why she was so dressed up now, and I certainly didn't understand what she was trying to sell. However, I did know there were two places dressed up people went in Newtown. The first was called "Guster's Store," and the other was called "Marge Douglas."

"Doretha, you know you don't need to be hanging around no juke joint," Grandma said.

"Mama, you know I can't sit in this house and go crazy doing nothing," my mama countered.

"What do you think you're going to find hanging out in a juke joint?" Grandma argued.

It was clear that at least this time, my mama planned on winning an argument with Grandma.

"You let Odessa and Beulah go," Mama triumphantly answered.

I knew Mama had won, because she and I played the same game many times.

I didn't know what a juke joint was.

"Grandma," I asked, "What's a juke joint?"

Suddenly, the palm of Grandma's hand swiftly connected with my face.

"Don't ever let me hear you say that word again," Grandma scolded. "That's a place where people go and do anything and everything. They don't do nothing but cause trouble in them places. If I ever catch you even looking in one, I'll skin your little narrow butt alive."

Despite my grandma's warning, I just had to see what went on in a juke joint. The doors were always open in the summertime, especially when the joint was crowded. It was a whole different world. I peered through the open door of Guster's juke joint, and the faces I saw were not the faces I'd been accustomed to seeing. They were not the faces of worry and anxiety. I looked from face to face and only saw joy and excitement. In that place, it appeared as if burdens were lifted. Bodies that had marched to the beat of hard labor were now free to move wherever the music took them. The voice of Jackie Wilson belting out "Lonely Tear Drops" rose above the hum of the huge fan that stood in the corner. On the dance floor, faces glistened in sweat that poured down as people danced with the precision of world-class ballet dancers. It was as if each dancer were attempting to sweat out every ounce of pain they had suffered during the week.

I could not understand how my grandma could be so adamant in calling these places "dens of trouble." I had never seen people so happy. They danced as if they were floating on air. Even the smell that came from those jerking, swiveling, finger-popping, gyrating bodies was not funky, but oddly seemed like a sweet smell of release.

How could such joy come from a small rickety wooden building that the city should have condemned long ago? The city fathers were never eager to condemn such firetraps, as long as they were in Black neighborhoods. The juke joint smelled of kerosene. That's because kerosene was poured on the wooden floors to prevent splinters from popping up; unfortunately, this made the juke joint even more of a death trap.

Among the others in that crowded room, I saw my mama sitting at a table with a man whose eyes were riveted on her every move. I could see why my mama had dressed up. Everybody in the joint was dressed in their finest outfits. I would have given anything to hear the conversation between my mama and that strange man. However, there was no way that would happen. I had already defied my grandma's orders by even standing at the door of that den of iniquity. Somehow, I was certain that if I stayed there any longer, my grandma would find out about my disobedience.

As I turned to walk away, I wondered if I would ever see the strange man again.

If the way he looked at Mama was any indication, I knew that I would.

I saw many conflicting images in that rickety juke joint. I saw joy, not the danger my grandma spoke of in judgment. My mama's presence in that setting was something I had never seen before. Gone were the worries that had etched premature wrinkles upon her face where none should have been. Gone, if only for a moment, were the familiar expressions of pain and frustration that were beginning to seem almost natural and permanent. I didn't realize that my mama could be at such ease and express such joy. It was amazing to realize how inhuman my mama appeared in New York compared to that moment. The person I saw in the juke joint was a different person altogether. Sitting there was a woman who could express happiness and, yes, love—love for someone besides her children.

Two weeks passed following my trip to the forbidden juke joint, but I was reminded of my revelation there every time I looked into my mama's face.

She still carried that expression of joy, but now it was blended with a sweet mystery.

I wasn't the only one who noticed the change.

"Doretha, what's wrong with you?" Beulah asked.

"Nothing's wrong with me, girl," Mama answered.

"Yes, there is," Beulah replied, unwilling to let my mama off the hook. "You ain't walking round here with that grin on your face for nothing."

If anyone could get to the bottom of my mama's mysterious change of demeanor, my Aunt Beulah could. Although she was younger than my mama, it was Beulah's job to find out about the goings and comings of all her sisters and promptly report them to Grandma Gladys.

"Come on Doretha, you might as well tell me," Beulah said. "You know I'm going to find out sooner or later."

"Well, you won't find it out from me," Mama countered.

I guess my ability to keep things inside came from my mama. She had no intention of telling Beulah anything, but my Aunt Beulah had other means of finding out things.

Despite my grandma's stern judgment of juke joints being dens of iniquity, she allowed Beulah to work at Guster's during the daylight hours. Like most juke joints, Guster's doubled as a community general store during the day. During the daylight hours, you could buy anything necessary for physical use, and at night you could buy anything to make you feel good or forget you were in the world.

Grandma's shrewdness allowed her to make this unholy compromise. She understood that no one would be dancing, courting, or drinking during the day. It was a contradictory arrangement with Beulah in order to keep her daughters in check. They were women, after all, and where there are women you will find men out for the hunt.

Grandma Gladys tried everything within her power to keep her daughters from getting what she called "tied up with no-good men." Because my mama had already been through hell with one man who'd left her with seven children, Grandma instructed Beulah to keep a close eye on her. Beulah relished her job, and she carried it out with the efficiency of a top-notch CIA agent. Absolutely nothing got past Beulah's radar eyes and ears. My grandma chose her spy well.

I received confirmation of my aunt's effectiveness at espionage while playing underneath the porch. It had become a ritual of summer. Jimmy and Audrey would join Curtis, Calvin, me, and anybody else who could stomach getting ashy underneath the house for a game of Doodle Bug. On this particular day, Calvin and I decided to play alone.

We had just settled ourselves into prime doodle bug property when we heard female voices. Instinctively, we grew quiet. I lifted my finger to my lips, signaling Calvin to keep quiet. It's amazing what you can hear under the floor of a wooden porch.

"Doretha, I told you I would find out what was going on." We recognized Beulah's voice as she spoke triumphantly.

"What do you mean, you found out?" Mama answered.

Evidently the two of them were sitting down on the front steps, talking about these new developments. Calvin motioned for me to come closer toward the back of the steps in order to hear better.

"Yeah, I know what you been up to," Beulah replied.

"I don't know what you're talking about," Mama said, attempting to throw Beulah off the trail.

Beulah was having none of that. She was on a hot tip and she was not about to let Mama off the hook.

"You know what I'm talking about—that man you were talking with at Guster's store."

"I've talked with lots of men since I've been back home," Mama said.

"Okay," Beulah said with laughter in her voice. "Since you want to play dumb, I'll go ahead and spill the beans, Miss I-Don't-Know."

I could imagine in my mind Beulah's facial expression as she began to recount what she had learned. I could just see her smiling from ear to ear like the Grinch who stole Christmas.

"His last name is Avery. He lives on Dickson Street near Bright Hopewell Baptist Church," Beulah began rattling off her information. "Everybody calls him 'Stank.'"

The nickname Stank almost caused Calvin and me to lose it right then and there. Somehow, we were able to hold the laughter inside. We were not about to blow the opportunity to hear about this man who had suddenly become a part of our mama's life. We would have plenty of time to discover the origins of the nickname later, but not there, not then.

"How did you find out so fast?" Mama nervously asked.

Beulah gloated in apparent victory. "I told you I would, didn't I? I'll tell you how I found out. I was working yesterday when Koot and his friend came into the store and asked me if I knew the new girl who had just moved into town. I said 'I might know her. What's her name?' When they told me Doretha, I knew right then why you been walking round here grinning so much."

Koot and Stank had told Beulah how they met my mama. They

had asked her to go to the movies with them. Koot was only joking, but not Stank.

Stank. So he was the mystery man I had seen talking to my mama and suspected that I would see again. Now I knew for a fact that I would. After Beulah told Grandma Gladys, my mama would have no other choice but to bring him home for interrogation.

"Well, Beulah," my mama answered like a beaten fighter. "I have to give you credit. I might have known you'd find out. I don't have to guess what you're going to do next."

As I was soon to learn, my mama was not beaten after all; Beulah's victory would be short lived. The minute Mama found Beulah was on the case, she gave Stank instructions about what might happen. She informed him that he would eventually have to meet Grandma Gladys. My mama had also taken the liberty to tell him about us and the death of our father.

The stage was set and the mystery was about to become unraveled—not by Beulah but by my mama, on her terms.

After listening to the conversation between Mama and Beulah, Calvin and I were shocked into an exciting yet subdued daze.

"I hope Mama don't get married again," I selfishly said.

"Me neither," Calvin followed. "I like it right where I am."

"Anyway, our real daddy is dead. What do we need with another one?" I added.

The day did not begin with its usual promise. Something on the inside told me my days of living with Grandma Gladys were numbered.

I forced myself to eat on what had previously been my favorite night, when we had "Fish and Flipper." We were just finishing eating when the knock came. My mama was the first to react, but Grandma quickly took control.

"Sit down, Doretha. I'll get that door."

As Grandma rose from her chair, you could tell in her eyes that something important was about to happen. What she did next removed all doubt.

"Doretha, you expecting somebody?" Grandma's radar eyes seemed to burn right through my mama's deepest secrets.

Had Beulah already said something to Grandma? Was Grandma a prophet? Could she see into the future? Was her intuition that strong? Knowing Grandma, I would have to believe all of the above were somehow true.

It took what appeared to be an eternity for Grandma to reach the door. Anticipatory tension filled the room as we began to hear muffled voices resonating from the front door. I was certain one of the voices belonged to a man. *Could it be that Stank had gotten the courage to finally come and confront Grandma Gladys?*

Mama's eyes nervously danced with the excitement of a schoolgirl waiting to get her first glance at a blind date.

Then we saw him, approaching the kitchen behind Grandma. The top of his head almost touched the top of the kitchen door. You could have heard a pin drop.

Grandma broke the silence as the rest of us sat there with gawking eyes and wide opened mouths.

"Doretha, somebody's here to see you," she said, almost unaware that Stank had already followed her into the kitchen.

For the few minutes that we were allowed to stay, we sized up this intruder. He looked a lot younger than my mama did, and from what I could tell, he was very strongly built. He looked nothing like my father. My father had been only a shell of a man before his untimely death.

One could tell from the way he was dressed that Stank's visit had been planned in order to impress Grandma Gladys. His hair was neatly cut and brushed into a pompadour. It was apparent Mama had told him about Grandma's religious fervor. He looked like he was going to church. I sensed this was all a part of the game of courtship.

Before we could complete our examination, Grandma ordered us outside in her serious "don't play with me" voice. When she spoke like that, it was highly dangerous to disobey.

"Doretha, why don't you and Stank come up here in the living room with me so we can talk," Grandma said.

It always happened like that when grown-ups didn't want you to hear anything. Grandma considered it a sin for children to get into what she called "grown folks' business." Despite her strict rules, we still knew ways of listening.

Before Grandma and Mama, with Stank in tow, left the kitchen, I asked, "Grandma, can I go outside when I'm through eating?"

"Yeah, boy" came the expected answer. "But I better not see you in this front room while grown folks are talking."

"Curtis," I whispered. "Go peek and see where they're sitting."

I knew every child in the house, including Jimmy and Audrey, wanted to know who Stank was. Therefore, I never doubted Curtis would take the risk of getting caught.

After receiving the awaited news from Curtis, we proceeded to plant ourselves outside beneath the windows closest to the action so we wouldn't miss a word. We understood that walls could not talk, but windows could hear and reveal anything if you were at the right place at the right time.

It was no surprise that the first voice we recognized belonged to Grandma.

"How old are you, son?"

In a nervous voice, the prisoner of love answered, "I'm twenty years old."

"Tell me, ain't you kind of young to be messing around with Doretha?"

Grandma wasn't fooling around; she was getting right down to business. She was trying to find any weak link in this new relationship.

Throughout the interrogation, our mama never once came to Stank's defense. Was this a test to see if Stank could stand up against the pressure—and, more importantly, to see if he really loved my mama?

Contrary to our belief, Grandma was only toying with this young romantic who she felt was too young to know what love was all about.

"What's your people's name?" This question was one of the big guns. The proverbial question of "Who's your mama and daddy?" had entered the conversation. If you knew somebody's parents, you knew something about that particular person's character. This was the question that would reveal almost everything.

There was a sudden silence, and for a moment we thought everybody had left the room. His voice began with a crackle that caused him to clear his throat.

"My daddy's name is Leo Avery," Stank began. "He works at Cub's Seafood, the fish market downtown."

"I know your daddy; he's the one who scales and cleans fish," Grandma said.

"Yes, he's the one," Stank answered, clearly wanting to move on from this area of questioning. "My mama's name is Hattie Wall Avery."

"Where do you live?" Grandma asked. It was another loaded question.

"One thing I can say about Grandma is that she knows what she's doing," I whispered to Curtis.

Grandma knew that if she knew who Stank's parents were and what side of the tracks he was from, she would know all she needed to know.

"We live on Dixon Street," Stank reluctantly answered.

Everybody in Newtown knew that Dixon Street was the place where you could find bootleggers on almost every corner. This was dangerous ground for Stank, and yet my mama still didn't come to his defense.

"What's wrong with her?" Curtis asked in astonishment.

"I hope Mama don't say nothing; then maybe that man will leave her alone," I answered. "I hope we never have to leave from Grandma's house."

"Well," Curtis whispered, "you won't have to worry about that. There is no way Grandma will let Mama keep seeing somebody from Dixon Street."

Grandma's next question seemed to let Stank off the hook. "How did you get a name like Stank?"

"I wonder why she let him off the hook about Dixon Street?" I asked Curtis.

Curtis reassured me. "I don't know, but you can bet Grandma has a plan."

One of the things we learned about Stank was that he was a very animated storyteller. He could tell a story so vividly that you could almost see it happening right before your eyes. Now he was in the conversation on familiar ground; this was his element.

With a sigh of relief, he began to recount the story of how he received such an unusual nickname—a name that had stuck with him into manhood.

"My real name is Franklin Delano Avery. My mama named me after the president," Stank said with pride. He spoke with such force now, as if he were reclaiming a name that had been buried so long it had lost its meaning.

"When they started running city water through Newtown, my daddy gave me and some friends of mine the job of tearing down the old outhouse," Stank continued. We already guessed how this story would end up, but we still sat glued to every word that filtered through the window. "After tearing down the building, we made a dare with each other about which one of us could jump over the open outhouse hole."

"Why would you make a foolish bet like that?" Grandma interrupted. "Why in the world would anybody in their right mind jump over a hole where God knows who all had used the bathroom?"

"Well, Mrs. Gladys, you know how boys can be," Stank justified.

"Would you jump?" I whispered to Curtis.

"You doggone I right I would," he said without hesitation. "I wouldn't let those other boys think I was chicken."

Personally, I knew I would have done the same thing if I had been faced with such a decision. Yes, I would have done the same thing I knew Stank was going to do. We began to see a different side to this strange man who had come to take us from paradise. Maybe there was more to him than met the eye. At least he was the kind of person who lived for the moment. He had a thirst for living, for meeting whatever challenges life placed before him.

"Mrs. Gladys," he continued, "they would have laughed at me if I didn't jump."

"So you jumped," Grandma said with a sound of laughter in her voice.

"Yes, Mrs. Gladys, I jumped," Stank answered, "but missed making it to the other side by just a few inches. They could have kept me from falling in, but my friends just looked at me, waiting for me to fall."

Stank groaned and shook his head as he remembered the event. But then he looked at Grandma and proudly said, "Ever since that day, I've always thought about my chances before jumping into anything else."

Grandma Gladys didn't know how to respond to such a strong determination. We knew that Grandma was in a fight.

It wouldn't be long before this man would end up taking us from Grandma's house.

"Did they laugh at you?" Grandma asked.

"Yeah, they laughed, and not one of them tried to help get me out," Stank answered. "I climbed out by myself while they stood there holding their noses and calling me Stank."

With no one willing to help him, Stank had to clean himself beneath the family's outdoor pump.

"I can understand why nobody wanted to get anywhere near him," Curtis whispered.

"Yeah, especially after he fell in that stinking hole," I added, holding my own nose as if the smell was seeping through the window ledge we sat beneath.

The name made sense. They called him "Stank" as a derogatory term, but it had become a badge of honor that showed determination and self-reliance.

Round one of the interrogation was over, and Stank had certainly won some major points with the story about his nickname. However, we knew Grandma would never give up that easily. Round two began with Grandma Gladys saving the best for last.

"Why you want to get tied up with a woman with all these children?" Grandma said, driving a nail deep into the coffin of this relationship. She finished it off by saying, "You are too young to get tied up like this. You don't know nothing about raising no children that ain't even yours."

We heard footsteps running from the room. We knew it was Mama.

The interrogation was over and it appeared Grandma had won.

But the words my grandma spoke ran like a bolt of lightning through my spirit. I never thought of myself as a liability, but now the die was cast that would cause me to question my self-worth.

I am certain Grandma never would have spoken such words if she knew we were listening, but nothing could change that now. What we had heard definitely would impact us.

Summer disappeared with the changing of leaves. Never had I seen such beautiful colors. Colors never mattered in New York. There had always been one color, and that color was the darkness of despair. But the trees at Grandma's house were alive with bright colors. The trees were putting on their best show as if to prove to us poor, deprived, slum dwellers that nature could be beautiful when it was allowed to live free, away from the concrete and high-rise tenement houses.

The beauty of autumn was short, and when the colors were gone, so was Stank.

It seemed things were safe. Grandma Gladys was not going to let us get away from her that easily.

But Grandma Gladys was wise; she seemed to know that Stank would be back. Therefore, she made her move and put agent Beulah on the case again.

"Beulah, I want you to find out as much as you can about that boy's family," Grandma instructed.

"Okay, Mama," Beulah accepted with joy.

With the changing seasons came new journeys. It was time for school. The May 17, 1954, court decision of *Brown v. Board of Education* had long been handed down, but for whatever reason, this southern city had not as yet implemented its mandate. Old ways die hard and long deaths in small towns like Laurinburg.

On a clear fall day, Curtis, Mama, and I walked in excited silence toward the segregated I. Ellis Johnson School. The community was officially called "Lincoln Heights" but was better known by its colloquial name of "Cross the Creek." There was indeed a creek that separated the two communities of Newtown and Lincoln Heights. Lincoln Heights was considered to be the mecca of Black living in Laurinburg. This distinction was mainly because of the fact that both I. Ellis Johnson School and The Laurinburg Institute were located in the community. The Laurinburg Institute was a Black-operated prep school known for producing such sports celebrities as Charlie Scott and Sam Jones. It had even been rumored that the jazz great Dizzy Gillespie was somehow connected to the school.

However, with all its glamour, we were warned to stay away from the institute.

"If the institute is so famous, why do we have to stay away from it?" I asked my mama in wide-eyed wonder.

"We left New York in New York," she answered.

"What do you mean?" I asked, not yet satisfied.

"Boy, haven't you noticed how those children from up north talk and dress?"

I had indeed noticed that they talked kind of funny. In fact, it was the only thing I admired about New York. From time to time, I would even try mastering the New York dialect. I especially liked the way they said "ball."

"Why can't I talk like that?" I asked. "I'm from New York."

"Guess it's because you weren't born there," Mama explained.

I could never figure out why you had to be born somewhere to talk a certain way.

"But I know people who were born right here in North Carolina who go to New York and come back with an accent."

"That's because they go up there and come back home trying to be more than what they are," my mama explained. "Boy, you full of questions this morning."

"I'm sorry, Mama, but I just got to know things before I go to school. Anyway, I hate people who go up north talking country and come home with that fake accent," I declared.

Maybe that was why the people from Cross the Creek thought they were better than the people who lived in Newtown. They had both schools and all the New York people. I could only feel sorry for the people in Laurinburg who thought New York was all that and a bag of chips. My mama didn't have to tell me to stay away from the New York kids. I knew all about the suffering of New York, and that was all I needed to keep me from the institute kids.

I. Ellis Johnson High School was a huge school that covered grades 1 through 12. The school sat right in the heart of the Lincoln Heights community. I. Ellis Johnson was an architectural carbon copy of the other two Black schools, Shaw and Carver.

"Why do all the schools look alike, Mama?" Curtis asked.

Before Mama could answer Curtis's question, I pitched in my two cents' worth. "Maybe they think all Black people like the same things."

"Boy, you don't know what you're talking about," Mama said. "I don't know why they build them in the same style."

"They remind me of the high-rise projects in New York," Curtis replied.

"Yeah, they make you feel like you in prison—everybody in the same kind of cell," I said.

"Now, y'all stop that kind of talk and remember why you coming here," Mama warned.

"Okay." We sighed. "But it still ain't fair. White folks' schools are different, but ours are all the same."

What started out as a silent walk had become a lesson on small-town racism.

"I've got to register y'all in the office," Mama reassured us as we approached the school on McGirt Bridges Road.

The office was neatly arranged with its many degrees and pictures lining the walls.

"I wonder who that man is?" I whispered to Curtis, pointing at the picture that stood alone. It hung there like an omnipotent and omnipresent God guarding all who attended this school.

My mama's finger suddenly found its way to the familiar position that meant "quiet, and I mean now." We could hear the "ssh" sound that accompanied the gesture.

"That's a picture of the first principal," an unfamiliar voice answered from behind the wooden counter that stretched from wall to wall. "The school was named after him. His name was Mr. I. Ellis Johnson."

Now the voice had a face as she came from behind the counter.

"Who's the principal now?" I asked, looking at Mama.

I knew that if her expression changed I was in trouble. I learned to recognize what each expression meant. Therefore, I was searching for the look on her face that said, "You're getting on my nerves and I'm going to whip your butt when you get home."

"His name is Mr. Speller," the lady reassuringly answered, bending down and looking into my curious face.

In spite of my curiosity to know more, my mama's face spoke loud and clear. She gave me a look that meant "That's enough. You're already in trouble."

The questions stopped.

But just then a man who had to be Mr. Speller himself walked through the office. My eyes watched every move of this dignified Black principal. I had never seen a Black man who wore a suit and necktie to work. I stood comparing his clothes to my hand-me-downs. *One day, I'm going to wear a suit like that*, I daydreamed.

The same voice that had given us the name of the principal was now speaking to my mama.

"Mrs. Fairley, I'll take the boys to their classroom now. You can pick them up after school today. Our buses don't transport children that live within walking distance."

"Walking distance!" my mama responded. Then her voice rose. "You mean to tell me these children have to walk more than a mile by themselves?"

"They won't be by themselves," the secretary answered, trying to calm my mama down. "There will be crossing guards at each intersection, and there will also be other kids walking home."

"Why do they have to walk?" my mama asked, still not satisfied.

"The Board of Education won't allow the busing," the secretary dejectedly answered.

"So that's it," my mama responded. "Those White folk don't want their children walking, but they don't care about our children."

Knowing that it would be a battle of futility to stand there trying to solve a problem that had become socially accepted in the community, my mama turned toward the door with tears in her eyes.

"Come on, boys. It will be all right," the secretary said, trying to reassure us.

We made our way down what appeared to be the longest hall in the world. There was complete silence with only the sound of the secretary's clicking patent-leather shoes.

We passed classroom after classroom. I peered into the doors that were left opened at the sea of Black faces that crowded each room. I listened to the voices of teachers and students as they went about their work.

As we got closer to the elementary section of the building, my curiosity turned into fear. While walking down the hall, I noticed that most of the kids were dressed better than I was and they were bigger, too.

I broke the silence. "Will my brother Curtis be in my class?"

"No, I'm sorry," the secretary said. "You will be in different rooms."

It was as if she had driven a dagger into my heart. *How will I survive?* I was devastated. Why are they separating us? I wanted to ask, but I was already on the verge of tears and to speak now would just open the floodgates.

The secretary tried in vain to calm me. "Come on. It will be all right. You'll like your new teacher."

"Curtis, don't let them do this," I began screaming. "I don't want to go to that ugly teacher's class. I want to go home."

"Go on, Leonard," Curtis said. "We'll ask mama about this when we get home."

Reluctantly, I went into Mrs. Smith's class. The children were all staring at me as if I were some kind of mad man.

"Boys and girls, here is a new student who will be joining our class," Mrs. Smith said. She had a pleasant enough voice, and it drew the other kids' attention away from me at least for the moment. "Can you tell the rest of the class your name?" she instructed me.

Out the door I dashed, running toward the principal's office.

Suddenly, I felt a familiar hand reach out and grab me.

"Leonard, boy, where do you think you're going!" Curtis yelled.

"Come on, Curtis! Let's get out of here right now," I begged. "I don't like this school."

"Boy, don't you know what Mama will do to us if we leave this school?"

"I don't care. I'll take a whipping before I go back in that classroom without you," I cried through the tears that had begun to drip down my face.

Mrs. Smith brought the principal's secretary to help with the situation.

"Leonard," she began in her reassuring tone. "We are going to let Curtis stay in the class today, but tomorrow you will have to stay in Mrs. Smith's room alone."

That's all I wanted to hear. The secretary gave Curtis a note and instructed him to make sure he gave it to our mama when we got home.

Whatever was in that note made Mama really mad.

"Boy, what in the world is wrong with you? What are you doing down at that school acting the pure fool?" she scolded. "What I ought to do is make you cut me a switch so I can skin you alive."

"But Mama, they separated us," I cried with red eyes.

"That ain't no reason to act the fool."

"Why did they have to split us up?" Curtis asked.

"I'll find that out later, but in the meantime y'all going right back down to that schoolhouse, and Leonard, you gonna stop that acting up. Do you hear me, boy?"

The next day's journey began as it had the day before. *Here we go again*, I thought.

During the night, my mama had decided she had better go with us to make sure I didn't make a fool of myself again.

"Hello, Mrs. Fairley," the secretary sang from behind her desk. "What can I do for you today?"

Mama had never been one to mince words; she got straight to the point.

"I'd like to know why they separated my boys yesterday," she said in a tone that demanded an answer. "They're both the same age."

"Mrs. Fairley, we know that," the secretary answered. "The only way they can be in the same grade is if they were twins."

"Mama, we ain't no twins," Curtis said, stating the obvious but with an expression of pain and anxiety.

"Mrs. Fairley, is there something wrong?" the secretary asked with genuine concern.

"No, I'll be fine," Mama answered after gaining her composure. "Is there somewhere we can talk in private?"

"Yes, Mrs. Fairley, we can talk in Mr. Jones's room," the secretary answered, pointing to the closed door of the counselor's office.

"Leonard, you and Curtis stay out here until we get back," Mama half-heartedly commanded.

"Did you see how Mama looked when that lady asked if we were twins?" I whispered to Curtis.

"Yeah, she looked like she just saw a ghost or something."

It took what seemed like forever for them to come out of the office.

"I wish I knew what they was talking 'bout," Curtis said, squirming in a chair that was too big for him.

Finally, both women reappeared with a blank stare on their faces.

"Mama, what's wrong?" I cried, as I walked toward her across the floor of the silent office of the principal.

Every sound in the office was now audible. The clock's ticking sounded loud, and the clicking sound of people walking down the halls pounded in my ears. Whatever happened in there must have been bad, I thought to myself. I could see traces of tearstains on my mama's face.

"Why you been crying, Mama?" I whispered, afraid that if I spoke too loud the whole world would hear me.

"Leonard, I'm sorry, but you and Curtis can't be in the same classroom," Mama said with a hint of sobbing in her voice.

"That's all right, Mama. What's wrong?" I asked again, but there was no answer—only silence.

I went through that day, and most of the first grade, in a daze. My only concern was to find out what had happened in the office.

Whatever it was, everybody began to treat me differently. The teacher no longer asked me to tell who I was or where I lived. The secretary always made it a point to smile and speak to me every day.

Curtis even picked up on this unusual turn of events. "Leonard, why they all the time smiling and speaking to you? They don't do that to me."

"I don't know, but I wish they'd stop it. It makes me feel funny," I answered.

Summer vacation arrived with the mystery still unsolved. However, another mystery would unravel during the dog days of summer.

With the madness that was school, we had all but forgotten about Stank. One knock on the door changed that.

As usual, Grandma answered the door.

"Hello, Mrs. Gladys," a much more mature voice politely spoke. "I come to talk to Doretha."

It was evident that Grandma noticed something had changed about Stank. Somehow, he was not the same unassured boy who had come calling earlier.

"Come on in," Grandma invited without hesitation. "I'll go get Doretha. She'll be glad to see you."

Grandma Gladys' change of demeanor was a shock to us. What happened to bring about such a drastic change? This sometimes overbearing, never compromising general was now changing her stripes.

We also noticed something different about Stank. There was a new confidence in his step. But we didn't have long to look the new Stank over. Grandma had not changed so much that she would allow us to stay in the presence of grown folks as they discussed business.

"Y'all go on back outside," she ordered.

We made our way to our spy headquarters beneath the window, the place that had revealed most of what we already knew, and discovered shocking news—Stank had gone out and found a job.

Grandma's voice filtered through the windowpanes. "Where you working at, son?"

"I'm working at the chicken plant over on Jackson Street."

"What do you do over there?" Grandma's question came almost without time for Stank to catch a breath.

Grandma Gladys was her old self again. She realized that a job meant that Stank was serious about my mama.

"I catch chickens."

"Catch chickens!" I whispered in disgust to Curtis.

"I know Grandma ain't gonna to let Mama get tied up with somebody who catches chickens for a living," Curtis replied.

Grandma began her next barrage of questions. "How much do you make catching chickens?"

"I make fifty cents for every one hundred chickens I catch," Stank proudly said.

I ain't no genius, I thought, but even I know you had to catch a whole lot of chickens to make any money like that.

Grandma Gladys already knew where this conversation was leading, so in order to stop playing around, she asked with all the tact of a python already wrapped around and squeezing its prey, "Boy, how you think you gonna feed a family on a job like that?"

But Stank was on his toes this time. "Mrs. Gladys," he answered, "didn't your husband raise thirteen children on less than that?"

The silence was deafening. It took all of ten minutes for Grandma to respond. Stank had scored the coup de grace. He had done what no other man had ever done. He had beaten Grandma Gladys at her own game.

"Okay, Stank, you can come to see Doretha, but don't think I'm gonna let her just waltz out of here with a man who can't take care of her and all these children. I'll let hell freeze over before that happens."

The shock of the now-finished epic battle left both of us sitting stunned and glued to the ground beneath the window. I doubt if vise grips could have closed our mouths gaping wide open in disbelief.

The bed mattress was the first thing to appear in the hallway.

"Where did that come from, Mama?" I asked.

"That ain't none of your business child. Now go somewhere else and play and stop sneaking around that hallway being nosy."

Why was Mama being so secretive all of a sudden? The answer came quicker than I expected or could handle. I knew the welfare system was on Grandma Gladys's back about so many people living in her house. My Uncle Frank had informed us when we first stepped off the train from New York that it was only a matter of time before we would have to move out. I just didn't think it would be so soon. The mattress, along with the other pieces of furniture that suddenly appeared in the hallway, should have warned me that the day was fast approaching for our departure.

Stank was not only working now, but he had also proven he could make do on what he was earning catching chickens. It was his money that bought the furniture. It was he who found the house on King Street.

Somehow, I knew Grandma would put up one last fight. It was not like her to give up so easily.

The day arrived when Stank found the last ounce of courage to ask Grandma if we could move in with him.

"Mrs. Gladys, I know the welfare people are giving you a hard time about all these people living in this house. Let me take Doretha and these children to the place I've found on Evans' Quarter."

"I ain't letting Doretha and these children go from me to shack up with you," Grandma replied, but they were words with no force or strength.

Grandma was backed in a corner—by a man who was determined to have my mama and a system that gave her no way out.

Within the next week, we were moving to Evans' Quarter. The heartache was unbearable, but "to everything there is a season," and this was a season we had learned to live with all too often—the season of being uprooted from the places where dignity's blooms were short-lived. Not only did the blooms die, but the roots were torn from their nurturing soil.

As we approached the house at 217 King Street, we soon discovered that Grandma had once again been prophetic. The house was a shack.

Yet Mama's face beamed with all the joy of a woman who was moving into a mansion. If love so completely blinded a person like that, I vowed never to fall in love.

We began the loathsome task of unloading the few pieces of furniture that once stood in Grandma Gladys's hall. That seemed so long ago and so far away. There was none of the excitement that existed when we first moved to North Carolina.

Noticing this, my mama put her arms around me.

"Leonard, you've got to look on the bright side. This house may not look like much, but if you search hard enough, you can find the silver lining."

"Mama, I'm going to have look real hard to find a silver lining in Evans' Quarter, but I'll try if it kills me."

Chapter 2

Deadman's Creek

The small community was appropriately called Evans' Quarter because the Evans family owned most of the property on the west side of town. The quaintly gabled Evans house, which stood just past the railroad tracks from our house on King Street, was a mansion with lattice woven banisters and a screened porch. I will always remember it as the house with the golden pear tree. Many days, I climbed over the hurricane fence for lunch. The pears were often all I had to eat.

But our pathetic house in Evans' Quarter was about as far from a mansion as you could get. The house was more like a barn with its tin exterior and three rooms. The three-room shanty that was home for us had been used as a storage house for a funeral home. In fact, some of the old caskets were still in the garage that was connected to the place where we lived.

Could it be true that silver linings existed in the midst of life's dark clouds? With much fear and trembling, I had left the love, safety, and certainty of my grandma's house to follow my mama as she chased her pipe dream. One failed marriage would have been enough for me. Hadn't my mama learned her lesson? What could have possessed her to follow yet another man on some uncertain destiny?

If silver linings really existed, our present living conditions would be a stern test of that truth. It would take a great deal of imagination to visualize the silver lining within the dark cloud of moving from Grandma Gladys's house into a place that had once been used as a funeral home garage.

The house had no furnace. I can vividly recall how winter's cold breath would seep through the holes in the walls and almost freeze your body. It wasn't uncommon to wake up breathing mist. It was so cold that we would make believe we were smoking cigarettes with our visible breath.

The bathroom was an outside toilet. You had to stand on the stool to flush it. After growing tired of standing on the toilet in the winter, we were always happy when spring and summer arrived. In those months, we abandoned that unpleasant chore, and our bathroom became the vacant field near our home. It became a game for us during the nighttime hours to see who could tell a ghost story that caused someone to abandon their squat and run home screaming.

Curtis would usually begin his story with, "Bloody Bone goin' to get you tonight." Even after we had been in Evans' Quarter a while and I had heard the story over and over again, it still had the power to send me streaking toward the house.

Curtis always added something new. "Yesterday, when I was looking into that garage, I saw one of those caskets open and there was a dead man in it," he would say. "Later on, I went back and he wasn't there."

"Please, Curtis, don't tell that story while we're out using the bathroom," I cried.

"No, go on and finish," Calvin said. "Tell us what that man's name was."

Curtis didn't need much prodding to continue.

"I heard a voice in the garage that said 'Bloody Bone goin' to get you tonight.'"

Before Curtis said another word, and without pulling up my underwear or pants, I was running toward the house—tripping over the clothing that hung around my ankles. In seconds, I was up again, and in a flash, I was in the house screaming, "Bloody Bone goin' to get me tonight!"

It was stories like those that gave me nightmares—which kept us up all night long. What was there to keep me from believing that "Bloody Bone" had not escaped from the dead or risen from one of the caskets in the garage that was attached to our tin shanty?

One thing we learned in Evans' Quarter was that the world can provide many playful adventures, especially when you have four brothers to share them with. That summer day back in 1967 was the beginning of an adventure that would inflict pain and joy on my brothers, Calvin, Curtis, Darryl, and Willie—and on me.

Calvin, the daredevil, always insisted on doing something dangerous that he knew Mama would never approve of. "Come on, Leonard, let's get the boys and go jump Deadman's Creek."

Curtis, the older brother, whose mama-hen complex always reminded us that Mama had left him in charge, would reply half jokingly, "What if one of us falls in that creek? Who's going to pull him out?"

Deadman's Creek meant just what the name implied. It was never a question that we would be in big trouble if one of us fell in. If the water didn't kill us, Mama would once she found out we had attempted to jump the forbidden creek.

Deadman's Creek was forbidden to us because some intellectually disabled boy had drowned in the creek the previous summer. The drowning made headlines, which was rare in a run-down area like Evans' Quarter. It was even rumored that the drowning victim's ghost still haunted the creek. I think the adults started the rumor to keep others from risking drowning.

On the other side of the creek, about a quarter of a mile away, stood our camp. We had gone through the labor-intensive process of building huts from sticks and pine straw, and we were determined that not even a haunted, forbidden creek was going to stand in the way of our enjoying the product of our hard work and hanging out in our camp.

If we didn't cross Deadman's Creek, we were left with no alternative but to take the long route to our campsite. We were not about to pass up the opportunity to cut down on some extra travel time if we could avoid it. So under Calvin's daredevil leadership, we decided to take the forbidden shortcut.

Surprisingly, we faced no obstacles as we started the journey, but with each eager step, I knew we would soon face Deadman's Creek. My brothers' footsteps behind me sounded so loud that I thought my heart was about to pound right through my throat.

Suddenly, Curtis broke my horror. "Calvin, you're crazy! Every last one of us will get it if Willie or Darryl falls into that creek! You know what Mama said. You know it ain't been that long since that boy went and got himself drowned down there."

"Curtis, why don't you be quiet? You make me sick. Every time we try to do something that's fun, you do something to spoil it for the rest of us," I responded, trying to keep my heart in my chest. "I wish Mama would leave somebody else in charge when she goes to work. Anyway, this is the shortest way to the huts and you know it. I don't know why you always whining. You sound like a baby."

In reality, my brave words only covered up my fear. I knew it was only a matter of time before Deadman's Creek would flow before us. *Was it really haunted? Would one of us fall in?* These questions cascaded through my mind. I would give anything to stop my legs from trembling and my heart from racing.

The wild grapevine that suddenly appeared before us did the trick, and for a while the fear of crossing Deadman's Creek was replaced by a new challenge. The grapevine ran down the trunk of a tall oak tree, but the purple ripe grapes swung from the canopy among the tall branches.

"Who's going to climb up there and ride the grapes down?" Calvin dared.

"I will," I replied without thinking.

Up the tree I climbed, and like Tarzan I rode the grapevine down to the ground where my brothers were already filling their pockets and their mouths with the grapes.

"Boy, y'all better not take all those grapes from me!" I yelled while trying to find a good place to land.

When I finally touched ground, there Willie stood holding what I thought were the best grapes.

"Boy, you better give me my grapes!" I shouted. "I done climbed up that tree, and did all that work. I deserve the best grapes. Give me my grapes or I'll beat your little narrow butt!"

Willie had no intention of letting go of those grapes.

"I'll ask you one more time," I said.

The next thing I knew, Willie was on the ground and grapes were spilled everywhere.

"Y'all stop that fighting! There's enough grapes for all of us!" Curtis screamed.

I felt the hand of my older brother jerk me from Willie's stomach where I sat as if I was riding a horse.

We gathered the grapes and were soon on our way again to Deadman's Creek.

In what seemed like no time at all, we were there—just a few feet in front of us flowed Deadman's Creek.

"It didn't take us long to get here," I said to Calvin in amazement.

Calvin ran toward the creek, and we all instinctively followed. It was time to jump; there was no turning back now.

Calvin jumped and, with little or no trouble, made it.

"Come on, Leonard!" he yelled, urging me on, happy he wouldn't get his butt whipped for getting wet. I guessed it was my turn, because if I didn't jump no one else would.

There I stood with the picture in my mind of the boy who drowned, and his haunted hands reaching from the bottom of the creek to pull me in as soon as I was over the water. But if Calvin could make it, surely I could.

I took a few steps back and yelled for Calvin to look out because I was coming.

"Move, Calvin! Here I come!" With closed eyes and pounding heart, I could feel myself sailing through the air over Deadman's Creek and then slowly descending to my destination on the other side next to Calvin.

Assured now that no haunted hands would reach out and grab them, Willie and Curtis made the jump without incident.

Darryl was the smallest of us; we called him "Pee Wee." It was a name Darryl was constantly trying to live down, and here was an opportunity.

But as soon as he jumped, I knew he wouldn't make it. And sure enough, Darryl dropped right into the center of Deadman's Creek with a splash. The water splattered on my face and ran down my cheeks like tears.

Darryl's blood-curdling screams echoed through the trees. "Help! Somebody get me out of here before I drown!"

With quick thinking, Curtis made each of us lie down on the ground to form a human chain. Hands and legs extended, Curtis reached over to Darryl and pulled him from his watery trap.

Wet and exhausted, Darryl began telling us of our impending doom. "You're going to get it now. Just wait until we get home."

Darryl's words chilled my bones like a prophet foretelling doomsday.

"I tried to tell y'all we shouldn't have come this way," Curtis said, brushing the mud from his shirt and pants. "That boy could have drowned," he added with tears welling up in his eyes.

While Curtis hysterically continued his ranting, I figured a way out of our peril.

"Wait a minute. Mama doesn't have to find out that Darryl fell in the creek. I know a way to keep her from finding out," I shouted over Curtis' hysteria.

"Well, tell us, Mr. Smarty Pants," Darryl spoke, still shivering as water dripped from his soaking wet clothes.

"It's only eleven o'clock. We can make it to the huts in time. We can stay inside and not go back home until Darryl dries off. Then Mama will never know the difference."

Our pine straw huts were magic. They were our pride and joy. When we built the huts, we made the decision to put them as deep in the forest as we could, even if that meant having to cross Deadman's Creek. With the care and imagination of master architects, we had taken tree limbs and pine straw to construct our own individual huts. We needed no reminders that there was a huge risk involved in building these huts this deep in the forest.

But the endless boredom we faced, along with the absence of conventional toys to play with, were the major reasons why in this case the joy outweighed the risk. Even if there was no money for toys or other forms of recreation, nature certainly supplied us with endless possibilities.

To build a good pine straw hut, you first had to find a wooded area with lots of pine trees. The more pine straw, the bigger and stronger the hut would be. It was unfortunate that the best place to find an abundance of the needed material happened to be located on the other side of Deadman's Creek.

Finding the ideal place, however, was only part of the process. The next step was to find a tree with the right height branch growing horizontally from its trunk. This was crucial in making the tent-shaped A frame. Old dead tree limbs long enough to reach the ground were placed on either side of the branch, and this technique formed the A frame. Smaller twigs were then collected and placed vertically across the tree limbs. It was important to place the twigs close together. These twigs would be the structure that kept the pine straw from falling inside the hut. Our tents would be like African huts with thatched roofs.

Yes, it must have been something to behold, five Black poverty-stricken boys building straw huts with all the seriousness of Thomas Jefferson planning and building Monticello. And we were building them on what must have surely been somebody else's property! We were depending on the magic of these huts to save us from getting into serious trouble back home.

So from Calvin's daredevil nature that gave us courage and my know-how in constructing straw huts, we created something that would keep us busy for the entire summer. At least that is what we thought.

"Who was the one who decided to build these things back here, anyway?" Curtis asked.

The question floated through the forest air as we worked frantically to replace some of the straw that had fallen off our huts.

"Leonard was the brain who started this mess about being pioneers. He's the one who showed us how to make these things in the first place," Darryl whined.

"Yeah, but I didn't pick this godforsaken place to build them in. Did I, Darryl?" I replied in self-defense. "Anyway, we wouldn't even be in this trouble if you had jumped a little further, now would we, Pee Wee?"

"It's too late to be fighting about that now," Willie answered as he walked between Darryl and me standing toe-to-toe, ready to fight.

"What y'all need to be doing is working as fast as you can to fix those holes in your tents," Curtis added. "We better get to work and stop fussing. We don't have all day. If we don't get back before Mama comes home from work, she'll know for sure that we've been up to no good."

Curtis's words rang true, and we began to work with surprising speed. We only needed to be reminded of what waited for us at home if we didn't take care of business.

We finished our repair work and there they stood, our five magic huts, waiting to be given the formula of five daredevils' adventures. On this adventure, our huts gave us a place to hide out while Darryl dried off from his fall in the creek. And Mama never knew we had crossed the creek—at least this time.

Many of my most treasured memories would take place in and around Deadman's Creek. We had nothing better to do than to play in God's big playroom. Was this what Mama meant by looking for the silver lining? We were one of the poorest families in the small town of Laurinburg, North Carolina. There was no other alternative but to take advantage of what God offered in the wide-open spaces near our rickety house. God had blessed us with imaginations that allowed us to appreciate simple beauty and recognize grand possibilities for adventure. It would have been easy to be envious and to dwell on what other more fortunate people had, but there was no time for self-pity. Evans' Quarter was our home now, and we were determined to live every minute to its absolute fullest. We may have been poverty-stricken outcasts, but we were not downcast.

Each morning, we came face to face with the decision of whether or not we would risk crossing Deadman's Creek again. Usually the decision came down to whether we dared to be brave or preferred the traditional safe route. But a frightening experience that we encountered taking the safe route one day gave us another reason to choose the dangerous crossing.

Mama's new boyfriend, Stank, had always been a prankster. He had obviously known about the rumors surrounding the death of the boy in Deadman's Creek. Stank also understood that we were told that anyone caught hanging around the area of Deadman's Creek would be haunted by the dead boy's spirit. I could never understand why he chose that particular place and time to frighten us, as we were nowhere near Deadman's Creek.

The safe way around Deadman's Creek was a dirt road running parallel to the CSX Railroad track. One day when we were walking along that road, the sun was setting, and it appeared as if God had used a masterstroke to paint the sky burnt red. Conversations about what we would be doing the next day kept us occupied as we walked along the railroad tracks.

Then I heard something strange.

"Did you hear that noise?" I asked Calvin.

"Leonard, you always hearing something," Calvin answered.

Suddenly, the howling sound of some strange animal became loud enough for all of us to hear.

"That's that ghost!" Darryl screamed.

"Y'all better come on here," Curtis yelled, looking back at us.

Curtis was already a good distance ahead. The distance between us didn't take long to make up. Running like the wind, I was soon beside Curtis.

"Why come y'all running in here all out of breath?" Mama asked with a mischievous grin on her face when we arrived at the house.

"Mama, y'all was telling the truth about that ghost. We heard him just a minute ago," Willie said after catching his breath.

"Yeah, we thought he would get us for sure," I confessed.

The back door suddenly flew open, and there in the doorway stood Stank with the same sly grin as Mama had. After scaring us to death, he had dashed through the woods and gotten back to the house before we did.

Well, I thought, *if that ghost is going to get us going the safe way, we might as well go across Deadman's Creek.*

Was it really the ghost or were we just looking for another reason to jump Deadman's Creek?

Whether to cross or not to cross the creek was a decision that kept us in all kinds of trouble during the summer.

Monday morning began with its usual routine. There was no smell of coffee. There was no aroma of bacon or toast. The only smell throughout the house was the odor of eight rank bodies sleeping in the same bed. No, there were no sounds of breakfast being made, not even the rattle of a pot or a dish. Breakfast was a rarity around our house.

But there was something different about this day. I could tell it was different as I stared through the torn blanket that served as a curtain for the window. I could feel the difference. The sun seemed to be brighter as it began to climb in the early morning sky. The breeze was cool as it blew against my face through the many broken windowpanes and cracks.

Yes, it was different, all right; there wasn't a cloud in the sky. It was the most beautiful morning I could ever remember. It was so lovely that the absence of breakfast and the emptiness of my stomach were engulfed in its beauty and, for the moment at least, I felt full.

Suddenly a deliberate whispering voice broke through my moment of peace.

"Psst . . . hey, Leonard," the voice said. "You up yet?"

As I turned, I saw it was Calvin standing over me.

"I might have known it was you. You get up before the chickens, don't you?" I remarked sarcastically. "Is Mama gone yet?" I asked, realizing that the morning spell was broken. Sure enough, the grumble of my stomach brought the reality of no breakfast.

"Yeah, she's gone to work already," Calvin answered.

I could tell by the sound of his voice that Calvin was ready to start the day with his usual thirst for adventure.

"What are we going to do today?" he anxiously asked.

"I don't know, but I know one thing; I'm hungry," I said.

"Well, you know it ain't nothing in the kitchen to eat."

Before Calvin could complete his answer, Curtis spoke up with his usual wisdom. "Why don't we sell some drink bottles at Mr. Nunny's store? I sure don't feel like eating no butter sandwich today."

One of the things I regretted most about living on Evans' Quarter was that we no longer had Grandma Gladys to cook for us. I could not find a silver lining in the absence of her cooking. I must have eaten every conceivable sandwich known to mankind—butter sandwiches, ketchup sandwiches, and mayonnaise sandwiches—trying not to starve to death. Therefore, Curtis's suggestion to sell bottles at Mr. Nunny's store was music to my ears.

Mr. Nunny's store was close to our straw huts, and therefore it was one of our favorite places to go. The store was a small, white, wood-frame building operated by a chubby white-haired man known to us as Mr. Nunny. He was one of the few people we trusted; his was a good soul. Mr. Nunny, unlike other storeowners in the community, let his concern for others outweigh his profit motive. It wasn't uncommon for other storeowners to exploit the already poverty-stricken people of Evans' Quarter. They would add all kinds of charges to customers' bills at the end of the month. Many people would end up owing their entire paychecks to oppressive storeowners. I am sure Mr. Nunny lost more money than he made.

Fortunately, our mama had a credit account with Mr. Nunny. Therefore, we were thrilled that our straw huts were close to his store. Oftentimes, we were the ones who were responsible for purchasing items for Mama. Domestic work kept her from always being able to personally purchase necessary items, and Mr. Nunny allowed her to send us shopping. Every chance we got, we took advantage of this arrangement by buying extra items, including candy. Mama soon put a stop to that by informing Mr. Nunny that none of us were allowed to purchase anything else unless we had a written list from her.

Unfortunately, none of us could write like Mama. Therefore, if we wanted anything from the store, we had two alternatives: get a note from Mama, which was next to impossible, or sell drink bottles.

I thought Curtis's idea to sell bottles was an excellent one, but the question remained as to how to get the bottles across Deadman's Creek. If that dilemma wasn't enough to discourage us, how in the world were we to get past all the dogs on Cleveland Avenue? Cleveland Avenue was the unpaved red clay street that began at the edge of the forest where we had constructed our straw huts. Mr. Nunny's store was located on Cleveland Avenue, and on this street lived some of the meanest dogs I had ever seen. I was not thrilled about trying to navigate through the dogs with drink bottles.

I could vividly remember my first dog bite, which occurred on Cleveland Avenue. It all happened one day as I walked with my mama toward Mr. Nunny's store. Just as we stepped out of the forest and onto Cleveland Avenue, the dogs came toward us.

"Now, don't you run, Leonard," my mama said. "If you run, that will make them bite you. So just be brave."

Be brave! I couldn't believe Mama said that. What planet was she from? What did she expect me to do, just stand there and let the dog bite me? I grabbed my mama's skirt so tight it was a wonder I didn't rip it off. The dog was much bigger than I was, and before my mama could finish speaking, I was running around her.

"Get him, Mama! He's going to bite! Don't let him get me!" I screamed.

Unfortunately, Mama could not save me, and the dog bit me on both ankles. I don't know what was worse, the dog bite or the shot I had to take at the county health department.

No, I wasn't too thrilled about this harebrained scheme of Calvin's. Although I was confident I could outrun the dogs now, trying to do it with bottles was a different story.

"Come on, Leonard," Calvin kept saying. "I know you're hungry. We won't let the dogs get you."

"Boy, you've lost your mind! If Mama couldn't stop those dogs, what makes you think you can?" I asked.

"All of us will be there. We'll protect you," Curtis added, trying to ease my worries.

"Well, okay," I hesitantly relented.

Curtis's words were the only thing that made me consider this crazy idea. I remembered how it was his wisdom that helped us get Darryl out of Deadman's Creek.

"Now tell me something. Where are we supposed to get enough bottles to sell so that we can get enough food for all of us?" I asked, hoping that logic would discourage my brothers from following through on this suicide mission.

"We'll find them like we always do," Curtis said.

Any treasure hunter worth his salt knows where to look for treasure. Motivation to get rich is his destiny, so he knows generally where to search for treasure. Hunger was our motivation, and like treasure hunters, we knew all the right places to search for drink bottles. We knew to search in the parks, near picnic areas, and especially on the roadside where passing motorists always threw their empty bottles. One person's trash is another person's food.

"Come on, Leonard. I promise we won't let the dogs get you."

"That's easy for you to say, Calvin. You've never been bitten, and you've never had to get those nasty shots," I said. "I already said I was going. I don't know why you keep talking. You better be quiet before you wake one of them girls up."

But my warning was too late.

"I'm going to tell it," a small voice spoke from beneath the mountain of coats that served as blankets.

"If you don't tell it, we'll bring you some candy back from the store," Willie said.

Candy was the magic word. The voice had come from Diane, one of our younger sisters, and she loved candy. Offering Diane candy was the lock that would hold our secret.

Confident that Diane would not tell, we gathered the old worn crates from beneath the house and headed out on our hunt for bottles of treasure.

"Come on, Leonard, with your slow butt!" Curtis shouted.

I was dragging because I was still not sure I wanted to do this.

The crates, which were designed to carry twenty-four bottles, swung between us. It took two of us to carry one. Bottles were a precious commodity. They were worth two cents each. Most stores would buy and resell them to the bottling company for cleaning and reuse.

"Watch this," Darryl called as he set up two bottles and began throwing rocks at them.

"What is wrong with you?" I yelled. "We've been out here all morning trying to find enough bottles to sell. You've got some nerve to be standing up there throwing rocks at money! You know we've got to buy some candy for Diane. We need all the money we can get."

With our knowledge of where to find bottles, it didn't take long for us to gather about three hundred of them. Time, it appeared, was on our side.

"Now comes the hard part," Curtis reminded us.

"How are we going to get this many bottles across that creek?" I asked Calvin. "We can't just wade. We ain't Jesus, you know."

I was still hoping someone would listen to a rational voice for a change.

Deadman's Creek was indeed a dangerous obstacle. The current was so strong that it could have easily swept our little bodies downstream. It was hard to believe that something as beautiful and refreshing could be so dangerous. The water was crystal clear as it rushed over the rocks. Plus, it was ice cold. Many times during the heat of the summer we would take our shoes off and dip our feet in the cold waters of our dangerous foe. However, we knew our limits. Pleasure could easily change to danger in the twinkling of an eye.

No, it would not be an easy task getting the bottles across, but we had come this far and were not about to change our minds now. It was our magic against the magic of Deadman's Creek—our best against its best.

"Well, it ain't doing us no good just standing around here staring at each other." My resolve to get to and then past this danger was now stronger than ever. All my attempts to discourage my brothers had fallen on deaf ears, and there was nothing left to say. It was time to take the big risk. "We don't have all day," I bravely said.

We borrowed a neighbor's wagon and started our journey through the woods. Once again, we would face Deadman's Creek. This time, jumping would not solve the problem—not with three hundred bottles. The current seemed stronger than ever, as if the creek itself was speaking to us: "Today, boys, it's my turn to win!" Never before had it frightened me so much. I know it might sound strange, but there we were, matching wits with a creek.

Just as it appeared that we would lose this battle, Curtis yelled, "What's that over there in the dirt?"

Curtis had spotted the front of an old locker door wedged beneath the sand. The creek had made its first mistake. The current had evidently uncovered just enough of the door, enabling us to see it.

"Someone must have used it before to cross the creek," I reasoned.

Maybe, just maybe, the boy who lost his life in that very creek had used it. Maybe he wasn't an evil ghost after all. Could it be that he was helping us against the creek?

"Well, what are we waiting on?" Willie asked. "Let's get that door and use it now!"

We dug the old locker door from its grave and placed it across the creek.

"Come on, let's go before the current washes the bridge away!" Calvin shouted.

Once again, we challenged the creek and won—or did we? For as soon as we safely reached the other side of the creek, in a last show of rage the creek washed away our bridge. We knew that on our return journey, we would be forced to jump; but for now, who was worrying about getting back? The anxiety of the moment melted from our faces.

Joy and triumph were the emotions that filled us.

"Boy, that was close," Darryl sighed.

"Yeah, too close. It was a good thing you saw that locker door, Curtis," Willie answered.

I was still not sure it was luck. Part of me believed it was the benevolent spirit of the drowned boy getting his revenge over the creek. Somehow, I pictured him standing over us having the time of his life, rejoicing over our victory.

But the journey was far from complete. In the excitement of getting over the creek, we had temporarily forgotten about Cleveland Avenue and the dogs. It only took the bark of one of them to make us realize we weren't exactly safe yet.

"Get in the wagon, Darryl!" I shouted. "We're going to have to run for it, and we don't want you to get left behind."

"I ain't running," Calvin vowed. "You just let one of those dogs try to bite me. I'll kill him with this stick."

Calvin picked up a large branch and began swinging it like a sword.

Calvin's bold words soon proved to be mere boasts, for as the dogs came closer, we all started running and screaming. The wagon jerked forward as Curtis pulled and I pushed without breaking stride.

"Hold on tight, Darryl! You better not fall out of this wagon. If you fall out, those dogs will get you for sure," Curtis commanded.

Nothing could stop us now. If Deadman's Creek couldn't stop us, we were not about to let some dogs get us.

Finally, we made it to the front of Mr. Nunny's store.

"What happened to you, Calvin?" we joked.

"I thought you weren't going to run," Willie said, laughing so hard that tears ran down his face.

"Well, I didn't see you standing around either, boy," Calvin answered, still out of breath.

We counted the bottles again to make certain none were lost in the dramatic confrontation. It was a stroke of luck that all three hundred of our hard-earned bottles had survived. Mr. Nunny came outside to find out what all the commotion was about, but gloating over our victory preoccupied our minds so completely that no one noticed him standing there at first.

"Mr. Nunny, you want to buy some bottles today?" I asked.

"How many do you boys have?" Mr. Nunny's response came with an expression of curiosity. He was still trying to figure out how we made it to the store with all those bottles.

"We have about three hundred," Curtis answered the amazed storeowner.

"If you boys were brave and resilient enough to get this many bottles across that creek, I can't very well refuse to reward your effort. Come on in the store and get your money."

My eyes grew wide as Mr. Nunny counted out six dollar bills into Curtis's eagerly waiting hands.

"What are we going to buy with all this money?" I asked as Mr. Nunny handed over the last bill.

After much debate and fighting, we decided to reward ourselves by purchasing food to fill our empty stomachs. Again, Mr. Nunny stood amazed. Why in the world would five boys think of buying "real" food first when there were all kinds of sweets surrounding them? Poverty taught us that this was a chance that didn't come very often, and our stomachs spoke first of food. But six dollars could buy a huge amount during that time, and soon fresh arguments erupted about what to do with the money left over after our food purchase.

"Y'all better not forget that Diane will tell Mama we jumped Deadman's Creek if we don't get her candy," Calvin said, reminding us of our deal with our sister.

So with some of the remaining money, we bought enough candy for Diane and ourselves. Once that was done, the arguments started again about what to do with what was left of the six dollars.

Suddenly, Willie came up with a rare idea. "Why don't we buy some slingshots?"

"What in the world do we need slingshots for?" Darryl asked.

"I'm thinking about all those dogs we've got to get past on Cleveland Avenue," Willie answered, knowing he had a good idea.

"Yeah, he's right for a change," I added. "I don't want to try and get back past those dogs without some kind of protection."

Finally, with renewed confidence and slingshots in hand, we began our journey back home. Cautiously, we approached Cleveland Avenue with our slingshots loaded.

Suddenly, from what seemed to be nowhere, a German shepherd came charging after us. We fired some rocks at him with our slingshots, but he just kept coming. The best plan was to scatter and head for the safety of our straw huts.

During the chase, my slingshot got tangled in a bush directly in the path of the huge German shepherd.

"Wait, I lost my slingshot! I've got to go back and get it!" I shouted.

"Come on here, Leonard! You might as well kiss that slingshot goodbye!" Curtis screamed back at me.

"I ain't leaving my slingshot here!" I said.

I reached back to retrieve my weapon, and the dog was right on me. I could feel his hot breath on my hand. I saw the familiar sight of snarling teeth and heard the vicious growling of an angry dog.

I don't know how I accomplished getting my slingshot without getting bitten, but I did. The dog chased us past our straw huts and in the direction of Deadman's Creek.

The locker door we had used as a bridge was gone, but who had time to look for it? We jumped out of instinct and fear. There was no need for prodding. It was do or die.

With our adrenaline pumping from fear of the dog, we all made it easily, even Darryl.

For once, Deadman's Creek became our ally. Safe on the other side, we knew the creek had given us the escape from the attack of the approaching German shepherd.

Safe and back home, we surveyed the damage to see if we lost or dropped anything.

"Boy, I'm glad we made it through that mess," Willie gave a sigh of relief.

"Me too, and I'm glad I saved my slingshot."

"If that would have been me, Leonard, I would have left that stupid slingshot where it was. You were crazy to go back there and get it!" Curtis said.

We had barely recovered from that day's adventure before we were searching for something else to ease our boredom. Deadman's Creek had given us more than enough excitement for one day, but we understood that our old friend and foe would be there waiting for us—waiting for us with our thirst for adventure to make it come alive again.

Imagination was never a problem for us. We always imagined a different life but also used our imaginations to make each day in our actual lives more bearable. Finding fun at Deadman's Creek was surely one example of what Mama meant when she said, "Always look for the silver lining, no matter how dark and cloudy the day might seem."

With our constant quest for excitement and the magic of the creek, the days would never be dull, and we wouldn't trade that for all the money in the world.

One thing was for certain, with imaginations like ours, our time in Evans' Quarter would prove interesting every step of the way.

Chapter 3

Lessons of Nature

It was an everyday occurrence. I would sit there on the school bus worrying myself almost into an anxiety attack. *Why does he have to come this way?* The questions would race through my anguished mind. *Wasn't there another route the driver could take besides the one that went right by my house?*

I never wanted anyone to see where I lived. Whenever anyone asked where I lived, I always found some way of avoiding answering the question. Riding by on a school bus was like living through hell. How would I respond if one of my neighbors yelled, "Hey, y'all that's where Leonard lives"? It was a heavy burden for a child my age to carry, but every day I was given no other choice.

People can be very cruel when it comes to their treatment of others who are less fortunate. Every day became a test of endurance, not only on the school bus but at other times. I could hear the whispers. "That boy smells bad." "Look at those clothes. They look like they haven't been washed in weeks." I could feel the disgusted looks burn through me everywhere I went. I heard the names other children called me. I understood there were parents who would not allow their children to play with me.

In many ways, I experienced silver linings, but only in nonhuman things. Without a doubt, Deadman's Creek had been one of those silver linings, but outside my immediate family, there were not many human silver linings in my life. I'm sure this was in large part because of the poor treatment I received from people I encountered outside my family.

The wonder of nature, though, had a strong positive influence on me. Animals did not discriminate against me. We shared the same world. Animals were colorblind. They did not call me names or make fun of my status in society. Animals seemed satisfied to share their world with their fellow creatures, including humans. They never attempted to take more than their share.

It was for those reasons that my trust in animals was far greater than my trust in people. Most of my early years were spent with an extraordinary attachment to animals. I must have tried taming every conceivable creature alive in the woods around Evans' Quarter. I drove my mama crazy with snakes, rats, lizards, and squirrels. I even had a baby turkey vulture. Rejection limited my expression and contact with other people, but animals were more than enough to fill the void.

Dreaming was another way I coped with difficulties. Dreaming was never a problem for me. Dreams were the only thing that helped me survive the shame of living in a tin shack with no bathroom and no furnace. Dreams were the only thing that helped me deal with having to sleep seven to a bed while using our winter coats for covers. What else could I do but dream of nights when we would not have to stuff the mattress holes with whatever clothing we could find so we would not get punctured by the exposed mattress springs? I dreamed during the day and awoke many mornings having dreamed of living under different circumstances.

I discovered quickly that being out alone in nature not only gave me the chance to be around the creatures that I loved, away from people I mistrusted, but also provided a perfect place to dream.

I called it the "Vision Tree" because it was the one place where I could dream without interruption. The large twisted roots of the huge oak tree rose above the ground far enough for me to sit in them. For hours, I would sit there and dream, hoping that at any minute God would change the circumstances of our lives. The Vision Tree became for me what the Oracle at Delphi was to Socrates. It was the place that gave me the greatest sense of personhood. Beneath the branches of this ancient tree, I was always somebody. I counted it a blessing to at least have somewhere that I could release all my pain, anger, and, strangely enough, loneliness. I viewed the Vision Tree as God's gift to me of peace and sanity in an otherwise unfair and violent world.

I never expected the tree to give me anything else besides its roots to think in and its shade for quiet dreams. I always thought the tree was special.

And proof of that came the day Moses dropped from its branches.

The featherless crow had evidently fallen from its nest. It was chirping helplessly and was so defenseless that I was immediately filled with compassion for the poor creature, so I had no choice but to pick up the bird and carry it home.

"Boy, what are you going to do with that baby bird?" Mama asked.

"I'm going to make him well," I confidently answered.

"Wild birds don't live well in captivity. You should have left it where it was at," Mama responded.

"But he would have been killed by a cat or something," I replied, stating what I thought should have been obvious.

The chirping soon brought out my other brothers and a sister, curious to see what was causing all the commotion.

"You know that bird ain't going to live," Calvin said. The same words had been said about my own life, but who was to say if, like me, this bird would not die? Hadn't Moses dropped from a special place? Wasn't this another gift to me from the Vision Tree?

"What are you going to feed that ugly bird, anyway?" Shelia asked.

On the verge of tears, I took my bird into the backyard and made it a nest inside an old dog food bowl.

"You're not going to die," I kept saying, wiping the tears from my eyes. "I'll find you something to eat. They'll see. I'll save you."

I could barely find enough food for myself, but somehow I felt God would make a way. I remembered hearing my Grandma Gladys pray and sing about God making a way somehow. If God were just and good, certainly he would do the same for a defenseless creature.

The next morning, I wasted no time checking on the tiny bird in the dog food bowl. God had answered my prayer; Moses was still alive! Armed now with renewed strength, I was certain God was on our side.

"First, I've got to find some worms," I whispered to myself.

With the smile of victory on my face, I struck out to dig earthworms for my new gift from the Vision Tree. Instinctively, I understood that worms would not be enough to sustain Moses's life, but there was little if any food from our table that I could share with him. Food was by far a precious commodity in our house. I was afraid my mama would give me the lecture about scarcity if I dared ask her for any food to feed a bird she didn't want me to keep in the first place. But at least I had to try; maybe I could catch her in a good mood.

"Mama, can I have some milk and a piece of that cornbread?" I begged.

"Boy, go on and get some," she called back.

After my initial shock at Mama's generosity, I mixed the milk, cornbread, and worms.

"They'll see. I will save you," I began to repeat again. "Come on, Black Moses."

You could barely see the tiny black feathers starting to develop on Moses's body. I named my bird Black Moses because Grandma Gladys never failed to share the story of Moses and the people of Israel every chance she got. I remembered how the Queen of Egypt found Moses floating in a basket on the Nile River.

The tiny black crow appeared to respond to its new name, as its yellow-edged beak stretched open to receive the special formula I had concocted for him. Black Moses looked so frail and helpless as he strained to keep his head up.

"Okay, I'm getting ready to feed you," I quietly said, almost afraid that if I spoke too loud I would kill the tiny creature.

The old medicine dropper served well as substitute for a mama bird's beak. I was overjoyed that Black Moses hurriedly gulped down the food I prepared.

"That's a good boy," I said as the hungry bird swallowed dropper after dropper of food.

Understandably, my overwhelming attachment to Black Moses appeared unhealthy. The daily chore of taking care of him consumed a great deal of time, but it was a labor of love. Helping Moses gave me a sense of worth. In the eyes of society, I was an invisible nobody, just another poverty-stricken person not worthy of being included in the census. I was just another out-of-sight, out-of-mind nobody. But Black Moses depended on me. I was never invisible to him.

As Black Moses grew stronger, my sense of self-worth also grew. I would walk around with a big triumphant smile on my face.

"He ain't so ugly now, is he, Shelia?" I deliberately teased my sister. "I told you I could do it, didn't I?" I ecstatically boasted.

One problem with silver linings is that they happen too far apart, and they don't seem to last for long. Black Moses grew so fast that before I knew it, he was a large and loud adult crow. His cawing kept us awake half the night and woke us early each morning. His constant need for attention, food, and care was becoming a concern for my mama. Therefore, I knew the day was fast approaching when I would eventually have to set Moses free. I hated to think about letting him go.

Obviously, Black Moses outgrew the dog food bowl. He began living in an old fish crate. Every day, I would free him from the crate in order to let him test his wings. Black Moses loved it even though his feet were tied with a rope attached to my hand.

"Boy, when you going to let that noisy bird go?" Curtis asked.

"I'll let him go when he can fly," I said.

"Leonard, you know that bird can fly, and you can't keep him forever," Mama warned.

I realized Mama could sense my reluctance to let Black Moses go. But she would have a fight on her hands if she expected me to give up the only thing that gave me joy. What could she say or do that would replace my newfound sense of being somebody?

I had grown distant from the neighborhood children and had no intention at this point of re-establishing any contact with them. I was doing just fine without their name-calling and constant cruelty. I realized that without Black Moses I would have to return to what I saw as willful attacks on my presence.

Despite my determination to keep Black Moses, I knew in my heart he needed to be free. Why punish him just so I might feel like somebody?

I noticed how he reacted when other birds flew over his cage. I again remembered the biblical story of why Moses had gone to Egypt. I remembered my Grandma Gladys placing emphasis on the words when she said, "God told Moses to go tell Pharaoh to 'let my people go.'"

Was I being a pharaoh when it came to Black Moses's freedom?

The day was almost an exact duplicate of the day when I first found Black Moses lying helpless on the ground beneath my feet. The sun was shining bright and strong. The only apparent difference was my feelings. It was the happiest day in my life when had I found the baby crow, and this day I didn't know what I was feeling. I was proud of my achievement of having raised a baby bird, but because I'd succeeded, I was losing my best friend. I was hard pressed to find a silver lining in all of this, although I knew it was best for Black Moses.

"Let him go," my mama's voice sounded behind me. She spoke loud enough for me to hear, but her voice was barely audible.

With one or two swoops of his now-powerful wings, Black Moses was skyward, and my love affair with him was soundly rooted in my heart.

Much to my dislike, after setting Black Moses free, I hesitantly started mingling once again with the neighborhood kids. The kids soon picked up where they'd left off—calling me all kinds of names.

"Look at crow boy," they yelled. "Leonard, you kept that crow so long until you look like a crow," they jeered. "Hey, you even smell like one."

These attacks caused me to miss Black Moses more than ever. I quickly learned to cope with their jokes, but privately I prayed for a new pet to help ease the pain.

My prayers were soon answered.

I could see the wire chicken coop through the maze of shrubbery that acted as a natural fence between our house and Nathaniel's house. As usual, I had to investigate this strange structure, and upon closer inspection saw twenty or thirty pigeons flying around the coop.

The pigeons, I soon learned, belonged to "Neckbone"—which was what everybody called Nathaniel. I just had to learn how Neckbone caught all those pigeons.

"Neckbone," I asked, "Where did you get all those pigeons?"

"You really want to know?" he laughed.

"Yeah, I want to know," I begged.

"Boy, you too little to be trying to catch pigeons," Neckbone joked.

"Please, Neckbone, just tell me what to do to catch pigeons," I replied with a swallow as the tears began to well up in my eyes.

"Okay, boy, I'll tell you how to catch some pigeons, but if you get hurt, don't blame me," Neckbone warned.

How dangerous can it be? I told myself. If somebody as sickly as Neckbone could do it, so could I. Neckbone suffered from asthma that he developed while in New York. His words were always spoken with a wheezing sound that made him sound like a snake. But it didn't matter to me what he sounded like—all I wanted was his secret.

I wasn't about to leave without gleaning from him all I needed to know about his trade in pigeons. Neckbone often sold his pigeons for twenty-five cents each. I would discover that many times people bought them for food. So I understood why he was reluctant to share his secret. He must have thought I would move in on his territory. After assuring him that all I wanted was one pigeon for a pet, Neckbone finally relented.

"Okay, boy, I'll tell you."

My eyes became glued to Neckbone as I watched every movement of his mouth.

"First," he began, "you get the strongest flashlight you can find and wait till night."

"Wait till night!?" I asked, growing worried.

"What's the matter—your mama won't let you out at night?" Neckbone teased.

"Keep going; tell me the rest," I asked as the adrenaline rushed through my veins.

"Well, after you get the flashlight, you climb to the top of the feed mill in Laurinburg."

"But that building is too tall. How do you expect me to get up there?" I asked.

Neckbone laughed and said, "That's your problem."

I could see why he was telling me everything now. I guess he reasoned that there was no way I could pull off such a task. Therefore, he continued his instructions, trying to frighten me with each detail.

"Now once you get to the top, there is a narrow board that reaches across the grain silos that you have to walk across to get to where the pigeons roost. If you make it that far, you lean over the roof of the grain silo, shining the light directly into the eyes of the pigeon you want."

"Why do you shine the light in their eyes?" I asked.

"The light blinds them and you can easily catch one."

"Will he get away when I take the light off him?" I curiously asked.

"Not if you lock his wings like this." Neckbone demonstrated grabbing one his pigeons from the coop.

"But that's so mean. It looks like it might hurt the pigeon. Ain't there another way you can keep them from flying?" I questioned.

"Listen," an annoyed Neckbone sighed. "If you want a pigeon, you'll do like I say. It won't kill the bird if you lock its wings."

I paid close attention to Neckbone's every action, and I was sure I could duplicate his pigeon-catching method. The only hurdle left to cross was how to get outside the house at night without getting caught, but as old folks say, "Where there's a will, there's a way." I certainly had a will; my will was so strong that I didn't hardly think about the danger I was putting myself in. This was a dangerous mission; I was facing bodily injury.

When the time came for me to put my plan into action, I slowly lifted the window and quietly climbed down one of the Vision Tree's branches that hung outside my window. Under the cover of darkness, I went in search of a new friend.

The Laurinburg Milling Company was owned and operated by the McNairs, a major corporate farming family in Laurinburg. It was rumored that they owned the town. One could easily see why this might certainly be the case. The Laurinburg Milling Company on Railroad Street produced all the seed, livestock food, and fertilizer that small farmers needed in Scotland County. The McNairs' monopoly didn't stop there. The local freight train depot and train line, Laurinburg and Southern Freight Line, ran right through the company's property. The McNairs even donated the land on which the high school was built. Maybe it was not a rumor; they probably did own the town.

The Laurinburg Milling Company was my destination on this summer night. The grain silos rose into the night sky. They must have been more than two stories high. Looking into the darkness, the apex of each grain silo stood in the glow of the moon's light. For the first time, I realized how dangerous this might be, but I had come too far to turn back now.

I suddenly remembered that Neckbone had failed to tell me where the ladder was that would get me to the top where the pigeons roosted. I walked around each silo, searching for the ladder. The grain silos had fences around them that were supposed to keep people from getting to the ladders, but once I spotted the ladder, I made it over the fence easily and raced to the ladder.

I climbed into the night. The higher I went, the clearer the sound became. It was the unmistakable sound of pigeons cooing, and it was here that my trembling legs ceased to shake. I knew I was in the right place. The cooing of the pigeons peacefully broke the silence and my fear of darkness.

I didn't know what they were saying to each other. Maybe they were telling each other about another crazy human being risking life and limb. Maybe they were saying, "If God wanted people to fly, God would have given them wings."

The cooing was the most beautiful sound I had ever heard. Although its message was unclear, the constant cooing warmed my heart.

I lifted the flashlight from my back pocket and aimed its bright beam toward the cooing pigeons. Just like Neckbone had said, there were many pigeons. I wasted no time shining the light up and down the edge of the silo roof. My large eyes stared in wonder at all the different colors of pigeons. No two pigeons were the same.

"Now which one will I catch?" I wondered.

My first impulse was to choose one that looked like Black Moses, but that impulse disappeared with one incidental flick of the flashlight. My little body was shaking so violently that it took all my remaining strength to hold the flashlight in one place. My hands were shaking so much that I almost dropped the flashlight, and as I grasped it tighter, it nervously moved and its light fell on a snow-white pigeon.

Immediately, I knew he was the one.

I cautiously made my way up the narrow board that Neckbone had told me about, trying not to fall off or disturb the pigeons.

"Please don't fly," I whispered under my breath, afraid that if I spoke all my plans would fly away.

I was not about to risk life and limb to go home empty-handed.

My knees were knocking together so hard it's a wonder the noise didn't disturb the pigeons. Sweat, born of anxiety and the exhausting work of walking the plank over a sea of grain, rolled down my face. I could feel the sting of the salty sweat as it rolled into my eyes. The journey across the roof was interrupted by frequent stops to wipe my face so my vision would not be impaired. I needed to be sure my focus remained on the white pigeon I had chosen.

The determination to catch the pigeon was stronger than all my fears. I wasn't even aware of how high above the ground I truly was, nor of the very real possibility of falling down and breaking my neck.

If this is what it took to feel the sense of self-worth I experienced with Black Moses, I was willing to take the risk.

Now how did Neckbone tell me to do this? I asked myself. The emotions of fear and excitement began to cause me to lose concentration. Neckbone's instructions were disappearing like a puff of smoke. *I've got to remember this part or I'll fall off this building for sure,* I reminded myself.

Instinctively, I laid down on my stomach, army-style, and at this point I began to remember Neckbone's directions. It's funny how much you can remember when you get your head out of the clouds. Quickly, I placed the bright light's beam directly into the white pigeon's face, blinding him, and then with my free hand I grabbed him.

The pigeon made little or no attempt to break free and seemed to calm down inside my hands. There was no need to lock its wings. It appeared to accept its fate. What seemed like an eternity was in reality only fifteen minutes.

With the pigeon safely in my hands, the stars above us, and the ground two stories below us, there was nothing to stand between my victory and me. But it would be a hollow victory if I didn't make it back to the ground without injury.

"I'll take care of you now," I said, repeating the words I had used to calm Black Moses. The calmness of the pigeon led me to believe that it understood. "You won't have to worry about finding food anymore," I rambled on in excitement. "I'll feed you every day."

The conversation with the pigeon made my descent much easier and the journey home faster. Before going to bed, I put my pigeon in a shoebox that was previously prepared as a temporary home.

Sleep was the last thing on my mind. I lay awake trying to think of a name for my pigeon.

The morning brought with it a ton of questions.

"Boy, don't tell me you found another bird," Mama said the next morning with a look that said, "Here we go again." "Where did you get that pigeon, anyway?"

Unexpected questions sometimes have the ability to make you think quickly on your feet. They can bring out the best of your creative imagination. My mind was working hard trying to figure out some way to protect myself from certain trouble for being out at night and risking my life.

"Neckbone gave him to me," I lied.

"Leonard, you know Neckbone ain't never give away anything. Now, where did you get money to pay for that bird?" she demanded.

Parents often make it hard for to use your imagination.

"He told me this pigeon wasn't eating, and because he knew how I saved the crow, he thought I might be able to save this one," I said.

Having accepted my explanation, my mama asked, "Where you going to keep this one?"

"I'm going to the fish market today and get him a fish crate, just like I kept Moses in," I answered.

"You're to keep that bird on the back porch. I'm not putting up with all that noise like I did with that crow," Mama scolded.

I was glad the interrogation was over, and now my creative energy could be used for something else besides thinking up lies.

Cub's Seafood Market was my next order of business. It was there that I would find a home for my new pet. Every month the fish market would order new stocks of fish that were delivered in wicker wood crates. Although the crates smelled like dead fish, they were the ideal things to keep pigeons in, or at least that is what I thought.

I had the inside track on securing a crate. Mr. Leo Avery, Stank's father, worked at Cub's Seafood.

I remembered peering through the window to get a glimpse of how they scaled the fish of various sizes. Once Mr. Leo was certain there were no more scales to be found on each fish, he took a huge knife and cut off the heads. The newly detached heads were placed onto a mountain of fish heads already stacked in the sink. Mr. Leo expertly used another shaper knife to slit the fish from gill to tail and pulled out all the entrails. Mr. Leo, at the age of almost eighty, should have been enjoying his retirement someplace where he was not covered with fish scales and had entrails of fish captured beneath his fingernails. But there he stood with the white hair of wisdom and covered in fish scales, too.

"Mr. Leo, can I get one of those empty fish crates?" I asked.

"Boy, what are you going to do with a fish crate? Those things ain't good for nothing," he stated.

"But I just want one. I got something I want to put in it," I responded.

Mr. Leo laughed and said, "I don't know what you going to put in it unless you've gone into the fish business."

"No, I ain't going into the fish business. I just want to put a pigeon in it," I said with all the seriousness I could muster. "I had a pet crow that I raised in a crate until he could fly and I let him go."

Realizing for the first time that I was serious about my strange request, Mr. Leo consented.

"Just make sure you don't get but one," Mr. Leo called behind me as I ran from the store.

I was sure the fish crate would protect Snowflake on our back porch. Cats are very resourceful when it comes to getting an easy meal. While securing Snowflake in the fish crate, I saw two cats eyeing him with great interest. I walked into the house searching for paper to put in the bottom of the fish crate, and before I knew what was happening, I heard what sounded like somebody dragging old boards behind them. The marmalade tabby's paws were inside the crate trying to get a grip on Snowflake. Reaching for the closest object I could find to defend Snowflake, I grabbed the broom and with all my might swung it at the cat's head. I swung with enough force to send the cat limping away, but not before he had done damage to Snowflake's wing and tail.

Again my imagination started running wild.

"I guess I'll just have to doctor you back to health," I whispered. My only medicine was a few aspirin and what I thought was cough medicine. "Drink all of this," I told my patient. Snowflake swallowed the mixture of aspirin and cough medicine.

I was confident that my prescription would cure Snowflake.

"Mama, can Snowflake sleep in the house tonight? I won't let him make noise," I begged.

"Yeah, just for the night," my mama agreed.

The next morning when I checked on Snowflake, his feathers were glistening like ivory, and his cage was covered with pigeon droppings.

My mama screamed with laughter. "You gave that bird a laxative!"

"Whatever it was, it made him well," I proudly spoke.

My mama's laughter turned into stern commands. "You get that fish crate out of this house right now. I don't want that filthy thing in my house another minute."

I had nursed Snowflake back to health; once again, I was needed. Snowflake, like Black Moses before him, became my preoccupation, and once again, every spare minute of my time was spent with an animal.

The more time I spent with Snowflake, the more I became convinced that he could not spend the rest of his life in a fish crate. Snowflake's life had been almost lost by being bound to a crate, but how else could I keep him?

Neckbone was my only hope. Neckbone would certainly know what to do.

"Neckbone, I don't want to keep Snowflake in that smelly fish crate anymore," I began when I went to see Neckbone. "Is there any way I can let him out and still keep him from flying away?"

"Boy, you're crazy!" Neckbone laughed. "It ain't hurting that pigeon none to stay in that fish crate."

"Please, Neckbone," I begged. "I don't want Snowflake to spend the rest of his life in that stinking crate."

"Well, you can do one of two things. You can clip his wings with scissors or feed him sugar water," Neckbone instructed.

Cutting Snowflake's wings was the last thing I dreamed of doing. If it were a choice between cutting his wings and leaving him in the fish crate, the fish crate would be my choice.

"If you give sugar water to a pigeon, he'll come back," Neckbone stated.

"You mean if I feed Snowflake sugar water he might fly away, but will always come back?" I anxiously asked Neckbone.

"Yeah," Neckbone answered, now seeming eager to teach me his trade. "But you have to feed it to him for about a week to make sure he gets the taste."

For the next week, I fed Snowflake sugar water just as Neckbone instructed. The dreaded day finally arrived. The same feeling of apprehension that gripped me on the day of Black Moses's freedom was present as again I stood ready to set a friend free.

"What if Neckbone was wrong," I murmured to myself. "Snowflake, I'm letting you go, and if you come back home I'll have some good sugar water waiting for you," I spoke into Snowflake's face.

Against the blue sky, Snowflake's wings glistened like silver as he flew instinctively in the direction of The Laurinburg Milling Company. *Would his homing skills and the taste of sugar bring him back home?* I wondered.

Three days passed with no sign of Snowflake.

"Neckbone lied to me," I cried into my pillow. "He just wanted me to lose my pigeon."

Two more days passed; the feeling of rejection clouded my mind.

"Don't nobody like me," I said as tears welled up in my eyes. I came to the conclusion that I would never see Snowflake again.

A few days later, though, as I started the long walk from the milling company toward home, I looked up to notice that the sky was filled with pigeons. I had spent almost every day at the milling company praying that Snowflake would come back. Now there were so many pigeons that their flight almost blotted out the sun. I rubbed my eyes to make sure I wasn't dreaming.

My face was now wet with tears as I looked skyward. I could spot Snowflake even in a group of a million pigeons.

"Snowflake, you came back!" I yelled. My heart pounded as I shouted, "They must be heading to my house!"

The pigeons made their classic soaring turn, then made a beeline in the direction of my house.

I dashed down the hill as fast as my legs would take me. My heart raced a million times a minute. Down the hill I tumbled, not taking time to remove the grass from my hair.

"Boy, look at what that stupid pigeon of yours did!" Curtis blurted. "He brought all those other pigeons to this house."

"Where is Snowflake?" I asked.

"Boy, what do you mean? All those pigeons look alike to me."

And then I saw my pigeon. "Snowflake, you did come back. Neckbone was right, and you brought back some of your friends," I rejoiced. "Here's your sugar water," I declared as I reached for the treat to keep my promise to Snowflake.

If there was one thing I could count on, it was that Snowflake would never abandon me. Yes, he would fly off and stay awhile, but just like Neckbone said, he always came back.

Neckbone's willingness to be honest with me became one of those simple moments that taught me I could trust people. Snowflake's and Neckbone's loyalty taught me my first lesson of faith. There are things in this world that you could count on after all. People might let you down, but love will always bring them back home.

Snowflake's loyalty taught me always to be true because someone back home is waiting, even if home is a shack. Snowflake had come home, even though all I could offer him was sugar water. Home is the place where silver linings are always present, if we just open our eyes and look for them.

Chapter 4

The Pine Street Patriots

We had lived in the Evans' Quarter community about five years, but on one strange day, without notice, we were told to load the black 1968 pickup truck backed up to the front door of our tin shanty.

It was an all-too-familiar scene. Our nomadic lives had already consisted of three moves. Now, here we were moving across town.

We felt all sorts of apprehension about moving. Each experience of moving became worse than the last. Why couldn't we just stay in one place?

We had lived in Evans' Quarter longer than we had lived anywhere else and had grown close to our little community. In those five years, Evans' Quarter had become the closest thing to a homeplace for us. Naturally, my brothers and I knew every inch of Evans' Quarter like the backs of our hands. We knew all the places to get the best grapes, apples, and pears. We knew the location of every tree we could climb for the fruit without getting shot at with rock salt. We knew the neighbors who were generous and who would often give us small amounts of food. Mrs. Bernice was certainly one of those angels. We would borrow everything from her—a cup of sugar or a stick of butter for rice or grits. She never turned us away.

Although we hated to move, it was time to go. We had outlived our typical stay as a family, anyway. We only lived in one place for an average of two years before being evicted or before the house fell in, whichever came first.

"Boy, I hate to move," Curtis mumbled under his breath so Mama wouldn't hear.

"Come back here, Curtis, and take some stuff to the truck," Mama shouted in a familiar tone of voice.

Our mama's high-pitched, stern tone was one we had all grown to learn. As she yelled, I remembered all the trouble we had gotten into in Evans' Quarter over the years that had caused her to raise her voice with us. I remembered the first time she found out we had jumped Deadman's Creek and the time I set the field beside the house on fire. But also, of course, there were so many times we had heard that voice providing comfort, guidance, and compassion.

There were other voices that had become etched in my memory. One was Mrs. Almeta, an avid Seventh-Day Adventist who gave me my first introduction to religion. I can still see and smell the musty old upright piano on which she taught us verses of Christian music. I can still taste the candy she would reward us with for memorizing Bible verses. But more than anything, I can see the pictures of Solomon, Moses, David, and Jesus that Mrs. Almeta would unroll from the quarterly Bible Picture Lesson Charts. It never mattered to Mrs. Almeta that we were inadequately dressed for church, which was what her house was for us. She always welcomed us in our ragged clothes and our bare feet. We loved her house; it was the greatest church.

The more good times I remembered, the more I hated to move. If you could have seen the house we were moving from, and especially if you had lived in it for a while, you might think it strange for me to be unhappy to be leaving our home. As I have described before, it was not much of a house. But despite the flaws in the condition of the house, the cold winter nights, the privy outside, and the caskets in the garage, we still hated to move. The shack had been our home for five years, and it seemed as we were preparing to move that the good memories far outweighed the bad.

A voice woke me from my fond remembrances of the past.

"Come on here, Leonard," Calvin said, grunting. "Help me get this thing on the truck."

It did not take very long for us to load our possessions on the pickup. We had never owned that much, just the bare necessities: one bunk bed, a small black and white Zenith television, clothes, and cooking utensils. The most treasured item was the battery-operated radio. It was our only source of entertainment when the electric company would cut off our power. Every month, there were weeks when we would go to sleep to the sound of that radio.

"Is that everything?" Willie called.

"Yes," I answered dejectedly.

"Go back and check to make sure," Mama said.

In the quiet solitude of our empty shanty, I said my last goodbyes to my old friends— Deadman's Creek, Mr. Nunny's store, and all the others.

"Come on everybody. It's time to go," a voice echoed through the house.

It was indeed time to go, and vainly, within my heart, I wished that the truck would not start. For a minute, I thought my wish would come true. The truck started to stall as it sputtered and strained, but suddenly, it found strength from somewhere, and we were on our way.

The truck clanked and squeaked its way down the familiar dirt road that we had walked a million times to get across town to my grandma's house. The dirt road of Covington Street was the road my mama would walk on her way to work or downtown to buy food. Every day, we took turns watching the road for signs of Mama's return. We could tell if she was returning by the expression on the face of each watcher who returned, without him or her even having to say if Mama was coming or not.

I took a final sniff of the dust of Evans' Quarter, not by choice but because the truck kicked up so much dirt. In fact, it threw up so much dust that my last vision of Evans' Quarter was clouded. However, there would be nothing this new location could do to cloud out the memories of our neighborhood. Somehow, through all the trials and tribulations of poverty, we had discovered silver linings that were now difficult to leave behind.

There we were—five boys sitting on the back of that '68 pickup—trying to make some kind of sense of our feelings. We didn't know what to think. On one hand, we were sort of glad to move from the tin shanty. The place we were moving to surely must be a little better than this old place. But on the other hand, we knew it would be hard to find another playmate, friend, and foe to take the place of Deadman's Creek.

"What did they say the name of that place we're moving to is?" Calvin asked.

"I think Mama said it's called Newtown," I answered.

"Newtown . . . it must be a sick place to live in with a name like that," Willie blurted, still unhappy about moving.

Willie said what we all were thinking—that our new home must have no personality and couldn't possibly be an exciting place to live, considering our spirit of adventure. We were all making jokes about our new home when the truck suddenly began to slow down.

According to the street sign, we were on Pine Street. The street had a very steep hill and a house at the very foot of the hill. This particular house would later become one of our favorite targets for fun. We would learn that a cranky old bachelor named Mr. Ernest lived in this house. Mr. Ernest always took advantage of the children in Newtown by persuading them to do chores with the promise of payment. However, long after the chores were completed, the money from Mr. Ernest hadn't appeared. Our revenge came by way of rolling car tires from the top of Pine Street onto his front porch.

The truck soon stopped.

"Get out of the truck!" Mama yelled with excitement in her voice. "Here we are!"

"You mean this is where we're going to live?" I said with apparent disappointment.

The house did in fact appear to be in better shape than the one on Evans' Quarter, but at the time we didn't care. We were still not quite ready to accept our separation from Deadman's Creek and other memories surrounding our struggle to survive.

"Yes, this is our new home," Mama said.

The house was an apartment house, which in reality should have been one dwelling, with a large tin roof and outside toilets that stood side by side out back. The house was located just behind the old Laurinburg Milling Company, the two-story abandoned mill where I had braved serious injury to get my beloved pigeon Snowflake and that would later become affectionately known to us as "The Barn."

Before we took one piece of furniture off the truck, we had already begun spying out possible adventures.

Newtown was a lot closer to Main Street Laurinburg than Evans' Quarter. As a result, we had more neighbors. I was certain there were more boys, and lots of boys meant lots of fun. As we unloaded the truck, I daydreamed about all the endless possibilities of mischief. Newtown was our new home, so we had to make do with what it offered us.

We discovered that the old woman, Miss Mary, who lived in the other apartment, had two dogs, Weasel and Spot. Spot was obviously old as dirt. He had gone blind in one eye and we always teased him on that side. What Spot lacked because of health problems and old age, Weasel easily made up. When we'd tease old Spot, Weasel would ferociously attack and chase us. We loved every minute of it until Miss Mary made us stop.

Miss Mary had never married, and the possibility was slipping away because she was already ancient. Like many older unmarried Black women in Newtown, Miss Mary was a scavenger. It was not uncommon to see her out in the early morning searching the streets for bottles and metals to sell. There she would appear, pushing her cart with Spot and Weasel running along in front of her.

Our new home was beginning to look better all the time. At least there were dogs around, which reminded us of Mr. Nunny's, and there was certainly something mysterious that surrounded Miss Mary. We would learn that she believed in "roots" and American-type voodoo.

She wore many of the vestments of her trade around her neck and ankles. Miss Mary always appeared to be talking to herself—maybe she was chanting voodoo spells. There were always jars with unidentified objects in them around her house. We made up our minds to investigate the jars and the spells.

However, our first excitement was in Spot and Weasel.

"Boy, Weasel is some mean dog," Darryl said.

"Ah, I ain't scared," Calvin spoke bravely. "I've seen meaner dogs in Evans' Quarter."

I could feel that old adventurous spirit welling up in my soul again as I looked at "The Barn" and the mystery woman, Miss Mary, as replacements for Deadman's Creek. Surely there was some hope in Newtown. We were sure there had to be something to keep boys busy.

It was early Saturday morning when the fun started. There was a sudden knock on the door.

"Who is it?" Calvin asked.

"It's Fred," a voice called back.

"Fred who?" Calvin answered.

"Fred, your next-door neighbor," Fred answered with a certain urgency in his voice.

Fred had made himself known to us on the day we moved into Newtown. I remembered him as the boy who wouldn't lift a finger to help. It was easy to detect Fred's laziness; his body language gave him away. With arms crossed and leaning against the truck, all he did was stand there, watching. Maybe Fred was hard at work sizing up our family, trying to determine who we were—these new invaders crazy enough to move into Newtown. Fred looked amused, as if he were saying, "Don't they have any idea where they're moving to? Don't they know Newtown's reputation? Newtown was a ghetto, a haven for Laurinburg's Black, poverty-stricken underclass."

Fred was a short boy with big protruding front teeth. His nickname suited him very well; everybody called him "Bosnack." Fred's father had given him the nickname, and it stuck. It's funny how sometimes our nicknames grow on us and we begin to look like whatever people call us. Fred certainly looked like a Bosnack. I didn't know what a Bosnack was, but if it had anything to do with teeth, Fred had the perfect name. His teeth were the first thing you noticed. I could tell just by looking at him that Fred knew all the good things to do in town. It is always good to have a friend like Fred, especially in a new part of town that you don't know anything about.

With a friend like Fred, we didn't have to waste any time trying to find something to do.

The next day, a familiar voice came knocking on our door. "Hi, Leonard."

"Get up. It's Fred," Calvin said.

"So what, I'm tired. Why don't you go back to sleep," I said, still half asleep.

"But it's Fred. Don't you want to see what he wants?" Calvin asked.

Calvin finally succeeded at waking me up.

"Well, I might as well get up now," I said. "I don't know why Fred is coming around here waking everybody up, especially after he didn't help us unload the truck."

But on the other hand, I thought, *why complain when opportunity comes knocking?*

Soon we were all awake and ready to go—where we were going did not matter as long as it spelled fun and adventure.

"Do y'all want to know what's inside that old feed mill?" Fred asked.

Those were magic words—words that spoke of a mystery—words that made our imaginations run wild with anticipation.

"But won't we get in some trouble for going in there?" Darryl asked.

Darryl's flashback to his almost fatal encounter at Deadman's Creek caused him always to be cautious about adventures that were potentially dangerous.

"No, it ain't no alarms or watchmen, if that is what you mean, scaredy-cat," Fred joked.

With the mention of alarms, I remembered my own ordeal at the Scotland County Courthouse, but I couldn't let that ruin my chance of discovery. We had lived next door to a garage full of caskets and funeral home equipment for five years and never attempted to investigate. If I could help it, I wasn't about to let another opportunity slip through my fingers.

"I've been in there a thousand times and nothing has happened to me," Fred assured us.

That was all we needed to hear. We never stopped to take the time and think about danger when something new and risky presented itself to us. When you are young, you do not take time to think. Anyway, if you think about stuff too long, you will never do it. That was our motto: Do first, think later. We never suffered from paralysis of analysis. We really followed our impulse for adventure wherever it led us. It is a wonder that we all were not dead by now—I mean, with all the crazy stuff we found to do. As I think about it now, I can't help believing that God must have been a very good mother to us. He certainly took good care of us.

"Come on! Let's go!" I said bravely. "I'm ready to go and see what's in there."

After walking through a path that led us to the rear of the barn, we started to climb up the big wooden steps that would eventually take us to the secret entrance. On the porch of the barn we found all sorts of old outdated milling machinery. The machinery obviously was used to produce, grind, and bag the livestock feed sold to farmers. The huge machinery of mass production became our playground. The old grinding tools with big wheels were enough to break our bones or crush our fingers. We had no idea what the technical names for the machines were, but whatever they were, we saw them as something for play.

We immediately began to enjoy our newly found playground of old discarded rusted machinery. We played everything—army, pirates—and we even tried our hand at playing Tarzan as we swung on the old exposed sprinkler system pipes.

Suddenly, Willie reminded us why we had come. "Come on, let's see what's inside before it's too late," he anxiously shouted.

One by one, we slipped through a narrow hole that had been made by the town drunks. The hole was ingeniously concealed. Besides the drunks, we were the only people in town who knew its location. Both groups seemed to tolerate one another and share the space, as long as no one betrayed our mutual trust. The drunks knew that if they told anybody about the place, they would lose a safe haven to drink and make their own moonshine—that stuff we called "mule." Mule was a mixture of cheap chemical ingredients that slowly consumed your vital organs beginning with the liver. Many of the community alcoholics lost their lives to this slow death.

Inside the barn, you couldn't walk without stumbling over the empty methanol cans left behind by our mutual tenants. We knew if we told anybody about the illegal operation of the alcoholics, we would lose one of our most favorite places to play. The benefits of the barn were important to both groups, and as a result, we looked out for each other. We often cleaned up the evidence of their occupation as amateur distillers.

Soon, all six of us had gotten inside. We climbed up a ladder that led to a loft full of hay where the drunks usually slept off their binges.

"Come on, I'll show you how to flip over in the hay from up here," Fred said.

Fred took a running start and did a diving flip right over into the hay.

"Come on! It's easy," Fred boasted.

"Boy, you must be crazy! I ain't jumping from way up here. I might break my neck!" I yelled back down to him.

"It's only about ten feet," Calvin said.

"I don't care. It's still far enough for me to break my neck, and I ain't jumping," I cried.

"Go on, boy! You ain't going to get hurt," Calvin said.

I began to argue with Calvin. "Since you're so brave, why don't you jump, Mr. Hero," I said sarcastically.

"If you move out of the way and give me some room, I will," Calvin said.

I moved, and Calvin ran right by me. He flipped awkwardly but unharmed into the hay.

"Boy, this is fun," Calvin said with hay dangling from his hair.

"I'm going to jump. I'm going to jump," I kept saying to myself, building up my courage.

The thought of jumping from such a height frightened me, but I didn't want to be the only one not to do it—everybody else had jumped at least once. I didn't want to look stupid or scared.

"Well, go on!" I heard a voice call from the floor.

They were all sitting on the ground looking up at me.

"Come on," they kept saying.

"You won't get hurt."

Finally, without thinking, I was airborne. It felt so good to be flying through the air, and I thought to myself, *Why in the world was I scared?* Maybe I had forgotten our motto and was thinking too much. It really felt good and was so much fun that I was fighting and shoving to get back up the ladder to jump again.

We finally grew so tired that we could hardly move to get back up the ladder. There we sat, out of breath, too tired to jump again. Right there on the floor of the barn, we decided we needed something to call ourselves.

"Why don't we start a club and start saving money?" I suggested. "We can sell bottles like we used to on Evans' Quarter. Fred ought to know somebody that will buy them."

"What are we going to call the club?" Curtis asked.

Everybody began to think—at least this time—because this was serious. Our name would be important. Our group needed a name worthy of our adventurous spirit.

"Let's call ourselves 'The Pine Street Patriots,'" Willie answered.

"What kind of name is that for a club?" I asked.

Willie began to explain. "That's the name of the street we live on, and we are like patriots."

Fred spoke up. "And that's also the name of the football team at Laurinburg Junior High School. That team never loses a game. They are one tough team."

"And we're tough!" Willie yelled.

Everybody agreed, and The Pine Street Patriots were born. The club eventually grew larger as we made new friends. The more friends we made, the more mischief we discovered.

We had apprehensively moved from Evans' Quarter, leaving Deadman's Creek and Mr. Nunny's store—things that we thought could never be replaced. Although we had left our friends behind, we brought with us to Newtown that same spirit of adventure that had sustained us through good times and bad—that same spirit that had made us look past our poverty and see the richness of life. Yes, we brought this spirit with us to our new home, and this made the move at least tolerable for us.

Newtown, as the name implies, became our new adventure field. There was so much to do, and as The Pine Street Patriots, we were determined to try our best to do it all.

Chapter 5

Family Circle

Poverty has a way of turning the old cliché, "Birds of a feather flock together," into stark reality.

I never had to go to school or read a book to learn what poverty was. Poverty always peered back at me when I looked into the mirror or out the window. I needed no sociologist to tell me I lived in a rural ghetto. I felt it with each grumble of my empty stomach. Poverty was forever present when I looked into the faces of the only friends society allowed me to have. Our community was like a monastery of shacks occupied by half-clothed ragamuffin monks living from hand to mouth. The wood-framed, tin-roofed houses were truly arranged in geographic clusters in the shape of a monastery. Our house sat in the shadow of the old Laurinburg Milling Company warehouse. This building was at the top of Pine Street and could easily, with a little imagination, be seen as the abbey of our cloister. Yet our community was actually a ghetto in all its appalling realism.

But not even a southern ghetto with its invisible oppressive hands could choke out friendship and community. Even in oppression there is a sense of community, a family circle. We supported one another with all the fellowship and hospitality of a monastery. The lessons of sharing were not just talked about—they were lived out as a necessity for survival.

My mama could make a meal from anything. She would go into the kitchen where there appeared to be nothing to eat, and the next thing we knew there was food on the table. I shall never forget the mountain of biscuits my mama could make appear with just flour, water, and leftover cooking oil. I can still smell that wonderful aroma blowing though my memory.

It often appeared that my mama cooked more than the eight of us could eat at one sitting. But Lord knows we always tried to eat it all. What child in his right mind wouldn't attempt such a feat, particularly after going hungry for hours and sometimes days? Therefore, as selfish as it sounds, we did our best to eat everything before us. I even came up with the ingenious solution of stuffing my pockets with extra biscuits to eat at night before going to sleep. Yes, I did my part at devouring all my stomach could hold. Who knew when and where the next meal might come?

In spite of our attempts at trying to eat more than we could, Mama's words that "your eyes are bigger than your stomach" always proved prophetic.

Although Mama would create her mountain of biscuits and chicken when the food was available, that wasn't always the case. In fact it often wasn't. Plus, her work kept her away from home for many hours most days, and she didn't always have the time to prepare a meal for her hungry children. My mama did domestic work, and she would sometimes bring home leftovers—which we gladly devoured—from her boss's house.

Our biggest meals were on Sundays. During the week we would sometimes go a whole day without eating. Mama would get paid on Friday, and she would stop by the grocery store on the way home and buy enough food to feed a small army.

I could not understand why Mama seemed so joyful while she cooked. It didn't seem to matter to her that she often used her last measure of flour. A song of happiness, hope, and vision flowed from her mouth and filled the kitchen on 217 Pine Street. The mysterious sound of joy came from deep within her soul as she realized this meal would feed not only her children, but also others who were enticed by this little slice of heaven in the midst of the hellish poverty where we dwelled. It was my mama's willingness to share that helped our circle of friends to grow.

Yes, Sunday was the day my mama would end up with more than her share of children.

"Lord, I have so many children I can't keep up with them all," she would say.

During the summer months, we would often have our supper with the back door open and the rickety electric fan humming to keep us cool during the heat of the "dog days." These times provided some of the most tender and humane experiences in my life. One of the children who often joined us for Sunday dinner was Fred. I can still see the hunger in Fred's eyes as the heavenly aroma of Mama's biscuits and fried chicken drew him to our opened back door.

"Mrs. Doretha," he would say, "you cook the best chicken and biscuits in the world."

Those were the only words my mama needed to hear for her to say, "Come on in and sit down and have some supper."

On one particular Sunday, before us sat two large trays of homemade biscuits plus a platter of fried chicken and steaming collard greens seasoned with salt pork. The old electric fan hummed as it blew out the heat that had built up from baking biscuits and frying chicken. The fan not only pushed out some of the heat but also blew out the odor of the freshly cooked meal.

Mama must have planned it that way, because almost on cue, Fred showed up, pressing his nose against the screen door.

"What do you want?" Calvin asked.

"Can I have one of those biscuits?" Fred responded.

"Wait a minute. I'll get you one," Calvin quickly answered.

Shelia would have none of that. Shelia was one of the eight brothers and sisters who sat at the table.

"No, Fred ain't getting none of these biscuits," she whimpered. "Mama!" she yelled, but the noise of the rickety fan drowned out her weak voice.

Despite Shelia's unwillingness, Calvin reached over to the pile of biscuits and grabbed one for Fred.

"I'm going to tell it, Calvin!" Shelia hissed as she got up from the table. "You just wait till I go tell Mama that you're in here giving away our food."

"I don't care what you tell," he snapped back. "Fred can have one of these biscuits. There's enough for all of us. Why you want to be so greedy anyway?"

"You ain't nothing but a big tell-it-all," I followed, defending Calvin.

There's one in every family, and Shelia was ours. Shelia was the one who always complained about everything. She was the one who always got everybody into trouble. Shelia was the supreme tattletale. There was nothing that escaped her owl eyes. At the dinner table, her eyes worked overtime scanning to see who was trying to eat more than their share.

Shelia was already on her way toward the door, stomping with a stern uncompromising look on her face.

"I'm going to tell it. I'm going to tell it," she repeated, not paying any attention to where she was going.

The old electric fan was sitting in a chair with its taped cord stretched across the doorway. Shelia walked straight ahead, occasionally looking back at Calvin to see if he was taking any more biscuits from the tray.

Before she knew what had happened, she tripped over the cord, sending the fan tumbling to the floor. In her determination to make sure Fred would not get a biscuit, Shelia apparently had forgotten the fan.

All at once, the chorus of "You're going to get a whoopin'!" rose from the table.

Everybody was pointing at Shelia crying in unison, "I'm going to tell it and you're going to get a whoopin'!"

Shelia was on the verge of tears as she turned and marched back to the table.

"I'm going to eat. I'm going to eat," she rhythmically chanted, and each time she said those words her head bobbed up and down.

Before Shelia reached her chair again, my mama's booming voice yelled over our ever-present chorus predicting a whoopin' for Shelia.

"What are y'all doing in there?" her voice thundered.

"Uh, oh, Shelia you're going to get it now," Calvin said.

With all the commotion, Fred darted out of sight underneath the porch.

My mama's footsteps grew closer and closer as she made her way from the front of the house. With each step, we grew quieter.

"Who knocked this over?" my mama asked.

The fan lay on the floor where Shelia had left it, the blades still turning.

"Shelia did it!" everybody yelled with joy.

The time had come. The tables were turned. The tattletale was now being told on. We could not resist. Shelia had tattled so many things on us, and this was sweet revenge.

"It ain't my fault, Mama," Shelia said in a squeaky voice. "Calvin was getting ready to give Fred a biscuit and I was just coming to tell you," she finished.

Shelia's scanning owl eyes were now reduced to pleading pools of sorrow. How quickly accusing eyes can turn to fear. Shelia knew she was on the verge of trouble.

"I was just gonna give him one," Calvin spoke in defense.

"Yes, there is still enough for all of us," I said on Calvin's behalf.

"Shelia just wants to be greedy, that's all," Calvin added, more confident now that I was on his side.

"Well, where is Fred now?" Mama said as she lifted the fan from the floor.

By now, Fred had hidden himself underneath the back porch.

"Calvin, you know where that boy is because you gave him the biscuit," Shelia said.

Shelia's hopes of not getting a whoopin' depended on finding Fred to prove that Calvin had indeed already given him a biscuit.

"Come on out, Fred," Calvin called.

Fred slowly crawled from beneath the porch with biscuit crumbs around his mouth. He had apparently tried to eat the whole biscuit at once, and his cheeks were pushed to their absolute limits. He looked even more like a chipmunk than usual as his biscuit-filled mouth caused his protruding teeth to stick out further. Fred, however, was unsuccessful at trying to conceal the evidence, which appeared not only in his stuffed cheeks and the crumbs around his mouth but also in his pockets, which were crammed tight with the remnants of what he could not force into his mouth.

"Fred, what's that you got in your pocket?" my mama asked.

"It's just some rocks I picked up to throw at the train," Fred muttered meekly.

Mama had to bite her lip to keep from laughing. She of course already knew that Calvin had given Fred a biscuit, and she found Fred's attempts to hide it hilarious.

"How did those bread crumbs get around your mouth?" Mama continued.

As Fred was trying to think of his next lie, Shelia blurted out, "That's the biscuit Calvin gave him!"

"Be quiet, Shelia," Mama scolded. "You're already in enough trouble for knocking that fan down."

A big grin came across Calvin's face as he realized he was out of danger at least for the moment.

"You like my biscuits that much, Fred?" Mama asked.

"Yes, ma'am," Fred answered, giving himself away. As soon as Fred opened his mouth, the remaining biscuit tumbled out.

Mama laughed. "Sit down, boy, and let me fix you a plate."

Fred's eyes grew big as saucers as the screen door rapidly swung open. Fred wasted no time finding himself a place at the table.

"Yes, Mrs. Doretha, you sho' can cook," Fred said between mouthfuls.

My memories of Mama's wonderful biscuits, fried chicken, and collards may be so strong because such complete meals happened once a week at most. Food was hard to come by in Newtown. Without sharing among families, many people would have gone hungry. There was a Social Services Department, but all the rules and regulations kept most people from applying. The rules were really strict. According to the department, you couldn't have a television set or any spare money. You were not allowed to make over a nickel above the established poverty line. Those who did manage to get assistance were always subjected to the degrading visits of "the welfare lady."

Without notice, the Social Services Department would send out their field representatives to see if clients were following the strict rules and regulations. In order to counter the efforts of the department, most families had children whose job it was to look out for "the welfare lady," and when they spotted her they ran calling, "The welfare lady is coming! The welfare lady is coming!" This was the cry that sent the family scrambling to hide the few secondhand gifts given through the charity of guilt-ridden employers for domestic work.

If this weren't enough to make you feel like dirt and trash, the questions the welfare lady asked made you feel that way. The Social Services Department had a way of making you feel less than human. Being Black and from Newtown wasn't enough for them; they had to show you and tell you to your face that you were nobody.

"How many more babies you think you're gonna have?" they would ask, as if mothers wanted to go through the hell of watching even more children begging to be fed.

Many people in Newtown subjected themselves to this subhuman treatment, which was blanketed under the title of "humane government aid." There was nothing humane about it. It was like tossing scraps to animals, and that is exactly what those receiving assistance got. They were degraded for a few cans of army surplus luncheon meat, cheese, peanut butter, and a few bags of dry beans. Being treated like a dog for the sake of receiving powdered milk, powdered eggs, and yellow grits was a hard pill for many families to swallow.

Providing such food items was the government's chief practical means of waging the "war on poverty." It was food, and it did keep many families from starving to death. And these were the items that sustained us in the late 1950s and into the 1960s. Grandma Gladys used this food to feed the "army" that invaded her house when we moved from New York to North Carolina.

Every month, my Uncle Frank would carry Grandma Gladys to the welfare distribution center with her welfare vouchers. When they got there, they waited in long lines with other people to verify their vouchers. The Chevrolet station wagon returned to 226 Center Street loaded with rectangular boxes of welfare cheese, which functioned not only as cheese but as chewing gum. The cheese came wrapped in thick wax paper that became chewing gum if chewed thoroughly. The vouchers also purchased huge five pound cans of peanut butter, boxes of butter, bags of dried kidney beans, black-eyed peas, and the thing I hated the most, split peas. And no trip to the welfare office would be complete without those dreaded yellow hominy grits.

All these items came in the standard packages of the USDA, but there was no doubt that they had also been used for the U.S. Army. With a few exceptions, most families in our community were expected to live a month on their rations.

Fred's grandma was one of those who did not qualify for assistance because she owned a house, even though, like all the other houses in Newtown, her home was just a shack with a tin roof. Mrs. Lucy did whatever it took to make ends meet.

Every morning, she would call to Fred and his cousin Robert, "Fred, you and Robert get up so you can get to the A&P early."

One would think she was giving them the grocery list and money to buy food. However, this was not the case.

Every evening at closing time, the A&P grocery store would throw out those items that they felt were unfit for human consumption. They tossed into the garbage things like old chicken, old bread, vegetables of every description, and other day-old or week-old items that decent folks wouldn't eat. It was these things that Fred and his family depended on for food when there was no money.

"Come on, Robert! Let's go before the garbage man takes that stuff to the dump," Fred cried.

"Okay, I'm coming. Let me put on my shoes," Robert whined.

In the early hours of the morning, Fred and Robert did their grocery shopping in the dump of the A&P before it opened so that they wouldn't get caught. It wasn't very hard to understand why Fred would stand at our back door looking for a meal.

Yes, there were many days when all we had to eat was a pot of buttered rice shared between eight people. I remember the times when I would spread my rice around my plate to make it appear that I had more than the two spoonfuls Curtis would serve us. There was never enough to go around.

Curtis was the brother my mama left in charge when she went to work. His job included cooking what grits or rice my mama had laid out for us to eat for the day. I hated to see my mama leave Curtis in charge. He always used his status to serve himself more, and as a result, arguments broke out.

"Curtis, look at your plate! You know that ain't fair," I protested.

"I know what I'm doing. Mama left me in charge, anyway," Curtis retaliated.

"She didn't tell you to eat everything."

"If you don't like what I gave you, Leonard, give it back, and I'll give it to somebody else," Curtis ordered.

Curtis knew that would settle the argument. The last thing anybody wanted to do was skip this opportunity for what might be the only meal of the day.

However, even those meager times had their flashes of hope. Sometimes we would take magazines and play "This Side Is Yours."

The Sears catalog became our personal wish list. Our hearts would long for the riches that unfolded before us in its pages.

"Come on y'all, let's play 'This Side is Yours,'" Curtis would say. "Okay, Leonard. Whatever is on this page belongs to me, and whatever is on the other page belongs to you," Curtis said, explaining the usual rules of the game.

"Look at my new car," I screamed as Curtis flipped the page to a brand new station wagon.

Curtis laughed and said, "That ain't nothing, look at what I got." His page was an advertisement for a new refrigerator filled with all kinds of food. "Look at all my food. I got ham, cake, and ice cream."

Curtis called out the items as if someone had just given him a million dollars. In many ways, that is what it was.

"It's our turn!" Calvin and Darryl yelled—anxious to see what dreams would unfold before them in the magazine.

"What would you do, Leonard, if you had a million dollars?" Curtis asked as we watched Calvin and Darryl play.

"A million dollars!" I shouted in disbelief. "I don't even know what I'd do with one hundred dollars."

"I know what I'd do," Willie answered. Willie's answer came in the form of a song. Everybody listened as he began to sing.

> If I had a million dollars,
> I tell you what I'd do,
> I would go to the store and
> I would buy everybody some clothes.

Immediately, we all joined in and started singing Willie's song, and for a while the pain of hunger died and the vision of riches took its place.

Our whole circle of friends would meet at my house on Sundays. There, in front of a color television set my mama's boyfriend, Stank, had bought her, we would watch *Lost in Space* while savoring the smell of food coming from the kitchen. After watching *Lost in Space*, we would make our way to the front porch, and there we would play a game we called "That's Your Car." We would sit on the porch, and each of us would take turns claiming the cars that came down the street.

"Okay, Sylvester, it's your turn. The next car that comes by belongs to you," I said.

Suddenly an old truck rolled by, smoking as it came.

Everybody started laughing.

"Ah, look at Sylvester's truck," we all said, laughing hysterically.

"It's your turn now, Leonard," Sylvester quickly said.

We heard the clippity-clop of horse's hooves. Down the road came Mr. Jake with his mule and wagon.

Mr. Jake was one of the few persons who still traveled the streets of Laurinburg in a horse and wagon, and he would always have a bunch of dogs and children chasing behind him. The wagon swayed from side to side.

"Giddy-up, Smokey," said Mr. Jake, his familiar voice blending in with the clanking sound of wood and loose metal.

A mule named Smokey pulled the wagon. Smokey never seemed to be bothered by all the commotion that followed him. He always kept moving at the same slow deliberate pace.

"That's worse than my old truck," Sylvester said, laughing as the tears rolled from the sides of his eyes.

"Well, y'all can laugh all you want to, but I'm going to catch a ride on the back of that wagon," I responded.

Mr. Jake looked at us as we made our way to the street, and in his deep husky voice he warned us, "Don't y'all boys jump on my wagon."

Catching a ride on Mr. Jake's wagon was a ritual that every child in the community took part in.

We walked slowly behind the wagon as it moved down the road, and one at a time, we took turns jumping on the wagon, only to hear

Mr. Jake shout, "Get off my wagon or I'm going to tell your mama!"

It sometimes seemed like Mr. Jake had eyes in the back of his head. Many times, before we could jump, he was shouting. But the more he shouted, the more we tried to jump on his wagon.

The only thing that made us stop was the voice of Mama calling us to eat. It was nothing short of a miracle that all of us were able to gather around the table. But the greater miracle was our willingness to share our food, even though we weren't sure where the next meal might come from. There we sat, condemned to poverty, but sharing a meal. We were outcasts among outcasts, sharing not only food but something that society could never dictate or take away.

Regardless of what the world said we were, there was always friendship and love. We had to be family to each other, for we had no one else.

Yes, poverty might breed poverty, but sometimes it also creates bonds that are never destroyed—bonds that can't be broken by rejection, degradation, or subhuman treatment. These were the bonds of hope and of always reaching for the silver lining, no matter how dark the clouds got, hoping that one day God would grab your hand and lead you to that silver-lined cloud.

Chapter 6

Rummie

Almost everybody knew him by his nickname "Rummie." Fate, it appeared, had dealt Rummie a bad hand. He was considered to be the community fool, a title that was unjustly given. It was totally beyond his control that Rummie was born intellectually disabled.

Rummie's mother was a chronic alcoholic, and during her pregnancy she fed her disease excessively. Despite her constant state of drunkenness, one could still see some remnant of former beauty in her eyes. It was hard to believe that she had once been her family's pride and joy. It was not that they had stopped loving her, but only that their hopes and dreams for her had vanished.

Rummie's mama had been groomed to be a debutante, and from her old photographs one could easily see why. She was beautiful, and no one could understand what caused her to change. If anyone had a chance to make it big from Newtown, it was Rummie's mama. But being born in Newtown was a stigma that neither beauty nor intellect could overcome.

It was an implied fact that all the Black people in Newtown accepted: You could only go so far before the name and place brought you down. If you were from Newtown, that alone determined your place, the premise being that if you were from Newtown, you were nobody, and nothing could change that.

The local community had rejected Rummie's mama in the citywide beauty contest. With little trouble, she had won all the contests among the Black schools, and it was understood that she would also have little trouble winning the citywide contest. The letter from the contest committee arrived with much hope and anticipation. However, the words written on the paper were like a knife being driven through her heart: "No colored girls can participate."

No one really knew what a traumatic experience rejection had been for Rummie's mama. She had now become what the power structure fated her to be, just one more piece of Black trash from Newtown with no future. It was shortly after this experience that Rummie's mama became a frequent customer of every bootlegger in town. Bootleggers practiced the illegal trade of selling alcohol from their homes, offering credit to anyone who had a job. They ran long tabs on customers and at the end of the month did whatever it took to collect their money. Rummie's mama was a credit customer. As soon as she ran out of credit at one bootlegger, she would move on to the next.

It was a general rule in Newtown that since the "White man" wasn't giving away anything, you had to get ahead any way you could, even if it was illegal. Black people were regarded as trash anyway, so most of the people in Newtown lived like it. It was an attitude of "rip off or get ripped off."

Many people opened their homes to all the winos and alcoholics who would gladly spend their last fifty cents on a shot of "creek liquor" or "mule." Rummie's mama was a welcomed sight to bootleggers when she had money or anything of value, including food. Sometimes she would steal food from her parents and trade it for something to drink. Thus, the family often went without food. It seemed as if there were bootleggers at every other house; thus, getting drunk was never a problem for Rummie's mama.

The bootleggers, it seemed, had no idea or concept about morality. Why should they? They were only trash; plus, no one had been moral in their treatment of them. The effort to survive in Newtown overshadowed all morality.

Rummie's mama's pregnancy didn't stop the bootleggers from making "an honest dollar," as they would often say in order to justify themselves. Unknowingly, they were preparing an unborn customer for his place in society.

Rummie's place was clearly marked. It was common knowledge that his mama was drunk when she went into labor. When the first labor pains struck, his mama crawled under her bed. Rummie's first cry into the world was what alerted his granddaddy to call the rescue squad. Rummie's birth took place underneath a bed, and that was indeed symbolic of his ultimate place in the society of Laurinburg.

Rummie's grandparents were very protective of him. Although it usually meant going through twice the problems and headaches of raising a "normal" child, Rummie's grandparents took it upon themselves to try to raise Rummie—something his mama was incapable of doing because of her addiction.

Several times, the Department of Social Services suggested that Rummie be placed in a group home for the intellectually disabled, but each time his grandparents refused. Finally, they gained legal control as Rummie's guardians. It was hard for people in the community to understand why Rummie's grandparents took on such a burden. No matter how hard they tried, they could never give Rummie the kind of supervision he needed.

He was always behind because of his intellectual disability, but that didn't stop him from being active in our circle of friends, "The Pine Street Patriots." We were all social outcasts, and it really didn't hurt to have another in our group. Adding Rummie to the group was a choice we would never regret. What he lacked in brains, he more than made up for in the spontaneity of his actions.

Rummie was a master at sneaking away from home without anyone knowing where he was. Rummie utterly hated being kept inside behind four walls. Therefore, he was always trying to find new ways to escape. Nothing short of a jail cell could contain Rummie. The lure of unsupervised freedom constantly beckoned him to our group.

Threats to that freedom, real or perceived, were hurdles Rummie crossed by any means necessary, including bodily injury to anything living standing in his way. Every time he would run away from home, Rummie's grandparents would send his cousin to find him.

I remember one day they sent her to find him where we were playing baseball.

"Come on here, Rummie," his cousin commanded.

"I ain't going home. I want to play," Rummie screamed back.

As she came closer, Rummie picked up a baseball bat, and when his cousin got close enough, he hit her in the ribs as hard as he could. There was a horrifying scream as she folded, clutching her ribs. She fell to the ground still screaming, and Rummie threw down the bat and ran in the opposite direction away from his grandparents' house.

Rummie would do anything to play outside, away from the watchful eyes of his grandparents, including breaking three ribs in his cousin's body. Rummie's mind was devoid of any rational sense or order, and that is the way he played and lived, with no constraints.

Ours was the age of the western, and Rummie especially liked the television series *The Wild, Wild West*. Everything that James West, the star of the show, did, Rummie tried to do.

Everybody in our friendship circle loved to play cowboys. I always dreamed of owning the cowboy outfit on display at Wood's Five and Dime Discount Store. The outfit came complete with silver cap guns, a holster, and a white cowboy hat. The reality of never owning such a prize didn't diminish my desire to play cowboys. Imagination would have to suffice. No, we didn't have any store-bought equipment. Our horses were cut from a tree we called a "milk tree" because when you cut it, the sap looked like milk. We always left some leaves on the end of our stick horses for a tail. Therefore, when we rode through there was always a cloud of dust, and one could tell the hero was on the way. The reins used to guide our horses were strips of bark we'd tie around the head of our stick horses. Our guns were sticks as well.

There were occasions when Indians were a part of our games.

Again, the milk tree provided us with excellent props. Wooden bows bent and strung with clothesline wire made strong weapons. The tips of our arrows were made with the caps of soda pop bottles hammered until they enfolded around the tip of the shaft, and pigeons' feathers graced the end of each shaft to ensure accurate flight.

Although Rummie was intellectually disabled, he could be very ingenious when it came to playing cowboys. There is one episode of cowboys that will forever stick out in my mind specifically because Rummie was involved.

"Come on! Let's go," he kept prodding us.

We were in the middle of trying to determine what to do with the fresh new day that was ours to dispose of. Our group had grown to include about ten, and this number made for good arguments.

"We don't want to play no cowboys," Fred screamed.

"Well, I do," Rummie yelled back.

"We can use the barn as a jailhouse," Sylvester said.

"Yeah," Rummie replied with a sinister grin. "I can show you what James West did last night on TV."

Every time Rummie mentioned James West, he would mimic the theme song with uncanny accuracy.

One thing you could count on while playing cowboys with Rummie was the almost frightening realism with which he played. Once something became locked into his mind, there was no stopping Rummie. He stored every detail of that week's TV episode inside his head, to be replayed when we made the decision to play cowboys.

On this day we finally decided to play after much debate. Before we could finish picking teams, Rummie had already jumped on his stick horse and was heading for the barn in a cloud of dust.

"Giddy up," Rummie commanded, still humming the theme song of *The Wild, Wild West*.

"Let's go get him," Fred yelled.

Soon all of us were gone in a trail of dust.

But despite how hard we looked, there was no sign of Rummie anywhere.

"I know how we can find him," Darryl suggested.

"What do you mean, you know?" Sylvester asked. "We already looked everywhere."

"Why don't we split up?" Darryl answered.

"That sounds like a good idea to me," Calvin said.

We split up into two groups. Darryl, Sylvester, and Willie went one way. Curtis, Calvin, Fred, and I went the other way. Unfortunately, there was still no sign of Rummie.

"We ain't going to find him," Calvin said.

"Whatever he saw on *The Wild, Wild West* must have been good," I responded, obviously tired from looking for Rummie for so long.

"Didn't Sylvester say we could use the barn as a jailhouse?" Curtis asked.

"Yeah, that is what he said, ain't it?" Calvin answered.

"Hey, I bet that is where Rummie is hiding," I said.

Soon, we were on our way to the barn.

"Yeah, that must be where he is," I repeated. "I bet he's waiting to do some damage, and he's hiding up there in the barn."

Before we reached the barn, we heard some mumbling like somebody trying to say help.

"Come on! Let's hurry up and see who that is," Curtis said.

The scene we saw is one I will never forget. There, lying in the path that led to the barn, were Darryl, Willie, and Sylvester. They had obviously figured out where Rummie was hiding before we did. There they were lying—face down, hands tied behind their backs, and gags in their mouths. It was one of the funniest scenes I have ever witnessed.

In spite of our attempts to withhold our laughter, the howls automatically flowed from our gaping mouths.

"Boy, what happened to y'all?" Curtis asked through the tears of laughter rolling down his face.

"It won't be so funny when Rummie jumps down off the top of the barn and finishes tying all of you up," Darryl said, as I pulled the gag out of his mouth.

"How did he manage to tie all y'all up?" Calvin asked. "There is no way one person should have been able to tie up all of y'all like this."

He stated what should have been obvious.

"He got us one at a time," Sylvester answered. "Every time one of us stopped to untie the others, Rummie jumped us from behind."

Suddenly, we spotted Rummie, lying down on the top of the barn, crawling toward us on his stomach. He was still humming the theme song of *The Wild, Wild West*. From where we stood, we could see Rummie's eyes dancing with excitement as he looked down on his prey, his next captives.

"We see you, Rummie," I yelled, to stop him from jumping down on us. When Rummie reached the ground, the same sinister grin was on his face. We knew that look. It was the look that thirsted for more.

"Man, how you like that?" he said. "I told you I was James West, didn't I? Come on, let's play some more."

"No, Rummie, we ain't going to play no more cowboys today," Sylvester screamed.

"You play too rough," Willie added.

"I ought to knock your head off right now, boy, for tying me up," Darryl said.

"Well, you said you wanted to play cowboys," Rummie dejectedly answered. "I was just doing what James West did. I thought y'all wanted to play some cowboys."

"We didn't mean for real," Willie replied, obviously embarrassed.

If we had not decided to check the barn, Darryl, Willie, and Sylvester would have remained tied up the whole day.

Although Rummie was oftentimes destructive, there were times when we felt sorry for him. We did not pity him because of his condition. "Pity" is the wrong word to be used for someone whose imagination knew no limits. Even the word "sorrow" had to be qualified when talking about Rummie. We felt sorry because of the physical injury he often suffered. Because of his almost reckless abandon at portraying his favorite television stars, Rummie subjected himself to more than his share of bumps and bruises. Almost all his favorite characters were action heroes.

Besides cowboys, Rummie liked nothing more than playing Tarzan. He liked Tarzan so much that he would rip his pants to make them look like the animal skin outfit that Tarzan wore. As usual, Rummie went all out in his portrayals of the "Ape Man." Once while playing Tarzan, Rummie jumped from the top of a peach tree and landed on a broken soda pop bottle. The broken glass penetrated his bare foot, causing a deep puncture wound that would have easily slowed the average person. I don't know how Rummie made it home with such a deep wound, but there he was, hopping home with blood staining the dirt and grass.

Rummie's grandparents didn't believe in going to the doctor. It was a waste of money that they didn't have. Alcohol was the remedy of choice for every cut, regardless of how bad it was. It was mainly out of necessity that they practiced this painful remedy. They couldn't afford to run to the doctor every time Rummie got hurt, which was quite often.

I don't know if we felt sorry because Rummie had gotten hurt or because he was forced to stay in bed, which during the day was foreign territory for him.

"How you feeling, Rummie?" Curtis asked.

"Man, I'm all right. I just wish I could go outside," Rummie answered.

"Well, you'll be out there again pretty soon," I said, trying to comfort Rummie.

Nothing we said could make Rummie feel better. His face and body language were clear indications that he was not the kind that spent all his time in bed. Rummie just didn't look right lying there; it made him look sick. Most of the time, Rummie wouldn't wait until he was completely healed before he was back outside again.

Once while swinging in his favorite oak tree, Rummie got tangled up in its branches and he accidentally cut himself around the groin.

"Get the alcohol!" his grandma shouted. "This boy done got hurt again."

His cousin suddenly appeared with the cure-all remedy.

"Grandma, don't pour that stuff on me!" Rummie yelled as she tipped the alcohol bottle forward.

Rummie's pleading screams fell on deaf ears. His grandma began to pour, and as soon as the alcohol made contact with the delicate wound, Rummie knocked her down. He started running through the house, like a wild man from the jungle, knocking everything down. Rummie's screams could be heard a block away as the alcohol burned its way into the wound.

It was next to impossible, however, to keep Rummie from playing Tarzan. Despite the painful experience, he was soon back at it again, swinging in the same tree with his torn and ripped pants.

Rummie's grandparents' lives were a constant nightmare, but it was their love that kept them trying, no matter how frustrating, to care for Rummie. They had lost hope in Rummie's mama, and the energy they had once spent on grooming her as a debutante was now redirected toward Rummie.

Rummie required almost all of their attention, even when he was under their watchful eyes around the house. Often times, they would have to wake in the early morning hours to keep him from running away from home. But most of the time, Rummie would rise with the crack of dawn and was God-knows-where before anyone ever realized he was gone.

It was hard for us to understand why they wanted to keep Rummie inside. It was a dangerous thing. When he was home, he subjected his grandparents to headaches on top of headaches. One incident began one morning when they caught him trying to run away.

"Where you going, boy?" a husky old voice called as Rummie

was beginning to make his escape through the back window of the kitchen.

"Nowhere, Granddaddy," Rummie answered.

"Then what you doing up there in that window like that?" his granddaddy asked.

"Shoot, Granddaddy, y'all won't let me go nowhere," Rummie said. "All I want to do is go outside and play. I won't get in no trouble."

"Come up here and look at TV with us," his granddaddy commanded.

Rummie walked slowly through the big house with its high ceilings. The house that Rummie called home was built in the late 1920s or early 1930s. It had very high ceilings with long-corded single-bulb fixtures swinging down from them.

The house by outward appearances looked decent enough, but inside you quickly became aware of the harsh reality of Rummie's home life. The house had the peculiar odor of rank urine, which wasn't surprising. Rummie's grandparents were no spring chickens. They were at least in their seventies, and with no inside bathroom, the house was filled with toilet pots. It was Rummie's job to make sure the pots were empty. However, the smell made it quite clear that the pots went for weeks at a time without his attention.

The house was fairly large, and most of the antique furniture looked as if it hadn't been polished in years. On the old potbelly wood stove that occupied the center of the main room, there was snuff spit and tobacco juice—signs of that great southern pastime of dipping snuff or chewing tobacco. As if this wasn't enough, there was also the smell of old whiskey, thanks to Rummie's mama. It wasn't really hard to see why Rummie liked the outdoors; at least there was plenty of fresh air.

But this was one of those rare occasions when Rummie had been caught before he made it outside.

"Come on, Granddaddy, let me go outside. I won't get into anything," Rummie cried.

Rummie had on his Tarzan pants. Therefore, it was safe to assume he wanted to play Tarzan. If his clothes didn't give this away, what he did next made it very clear.

"Where you going now, Rummie?" his grandma asked, as Rummie slowly moved from in front of the television.

"I ain't going nowhere but in the hall," he grunted back.

Once out in the hall, Rummie jumped up and grabbed the hanging light cord. Sparks began to fly everywhere, and soon all the electrical power in the house was out.

"What happened?" his granddaddy asked.

"Rummie's out there in the hall swinging on that cord," his cousin answered.

"Get in here, Rummie," his granddaddy yelled.

When Rummie reached his grandfather, his granddaddy took off his belt and proceeded to try to discipline Rummie. On the first strike of the belt, Rummie went crazy. Nothing that was standing was safe. Rummie ran through the house screaming and breaking everything in sight.

After this experience, Rummie's grandparents decided that he was better off outside. With his new freedom, Rummie became more active in whatever the Pine Street Patriots did.

But no one wanted to let Rummie just waltz back into our group. Rummie had to somehow pay for tying up Darryl, Willie, and Sylvester.

Every summer, watermelons were shipped from Florida by the truckload. The "watermelon men" would park their trucks near the Laurinburg Southern Railroad dock. The temptation was too great for Rummie, and there he sat eating a whole watermelon when we suddenly approached him.

"Rummie, I'm going to call the police!" Curtis screamed, startling Rummie.

"Come on, y'all, don't call the police," Rummie cried. "I'll let y'all have some, if y'all don't get me in trouble."

Rummie had no idea that it wasn't the police he needed to be worried about. Here was our chance for revenge, and we knew it by the look on Curtis' face.

"Darryl, go get one of those watermelon crates," Curtis ordered. With glee on his face, Darryl retrieved the crate and we immediately began to assemble it.

"What y'all doing with that crate?" Rummie asked.

"We'll call the police if you don't do what we say," Curtis responded to a frightened Rummie.

"All right, what do you want me to do?" Rummie submitted.

"Take off all of your clothes and get in this crate."

"I ain't getting in that crate naked!" Rummie shouted.

"Well, I guess we'll just call the police," Darryl said.

"Okay, but y'all better not leave me in here," Rummie continued pleading.

The crate was turned upside down over Rummie's naked body.

"How long you going to leave him in there?" Sylvester asked.

"Just long enough to let him know he better not ever think about tying nobody up no more," Curtis replied. "We'll let him out in a couple of hours."

Rummie never tried a trick like his James West stunt on us again. He was now back in the group.

Although we didn't have many so-called social privileges, there were times when people were very generous to us. The Laurinburg and Southern Railroad Company gave us permission to use their vacant lot to play baseball. They let us play there to keep us from playing on the boxcars that were parked on the tracks at the depot. We would have a field day playing army in the empty boxcars. Like little hobos, we would even eat what snacks we had in the boxcars. When the train would pull out from the depot, we would hop a ride on the boxcars. No matter how hard the railroad officials tried to stop us, we kept right on doing it. Their giving us the space to play baseball was an attempt to keep us off the trains, and for a while this new space kept us busy.

"Want to play some ball, Leonard?" Fred asked.

"Yeah, if we can get the rest of the group together," I answered. Living in town was something I learned to love. It didn't take very long to gather people together because we lived so close to each other. We were soon at the field and began picking teams.

"I don't want to play no baseball," Rummie grumbled.

"Well, I know you don't think we are going to play cowboys," Willie said.

Once Rummie set his mind to do something, there was no changing it.

"Well, I'll play by myself then," Rummie snapped.

Our minds had become occupied with the baseball game, when all of a sudden we heard someone scream.

"Look at Rummie!" Darryl screamed.

Rummie had made his way up the side of a boxcar and onto the top of a steep building. He was sitting straddling the building with a heavy chain tied to one leg. The weight of the chain was slowly pulling him down to almost certain death.

"Come on, we got to get up there and get him down!" I shouted.

All of us dropped our gloves and started climbing the boxcar to save Rummie.

When we did finally get him down, Rummie seemed to have no idea of the trouble he was in.

"Why did y'all come bothering me?" he said. "I was doing like James West."

I tried reasoning with Rummie. "Boy, don't you know you could have got killed?"

"No, I wouldn't have got killed. James West don't never get killed," Rummie replied with confidence.

Rummie's grandparents had, so to speak, turned Rummie over to us. They could no longer do anything with him, so we took it upon ourselves to watch and protect him. We were almost as bad as Rummie when it came down to getting in trouble. But there was always something restless about Rummie's manner.

It was bound to happen sooner or later despite our efforts. Rummie was born to follow in his mother's footsteps. He grew bored with the things we did and started spending his time at drink houses. The crazy things Rummie had done in the past were minor compared to what would happen next, now that he had started drinking.

It was usually during the weekend that Rummie's mama would get so drunk that she would just fall out, becoming unaware of anything around her. She drank every day, but the weekend was her time to see just how much she could drink.

One was always aware of what this was doing to her outward appearance. If drinking could do this to her face, eyes, and complexion, what in God's name was the toll on her soul, her spirit, and not to mention her inner organs? We had already learned firsthand the outcome of such a life in the death of our father.

Rummie's mama was stretched out across her rickety bed that Saturday evening, unaware of the events that were about to take place. In fact, she was unaware of anything conscious. She could not hear Rummie standing by her bedside asking for money to get a drink of liquor.

"Give me fifty cents!" he kept crying.

After several attempts at trying to get his mother's attention, Rummie tiptoed to his grandfather's shaving equipment and pulled out the razor. He made his way back to his mother's bedside and began calling again.

"Come on! Give me fifty cents!"

Rummie's mama could only respond with a snore as she turned over on her back, sleeping off the alcohol.

No one knows what went through Rummie's mind, but it is certain to say that he wanted that drink. There was no rational way for Rummie to wake his mother up. He did not think rationally when he wanted something.

The razor struck Rummie's mama across the thigh, laying open her flesh to the point where the bone was exposed. For a second, neither she nor Rummie moved. He stood motionless as the blood rushed from the open wound.

Rummie's mama screamed as the warm blood or its smell woke her up.

Everybody rushed in the room.

"Go call the ambulance!" Rummie's granddaddy yelled at Rummie's cousin.

"Call the police, too," his grandma shouted as his cousin made her way to the neighbor's house.

Everyone was afraid to approach Rummie as he stood there staring into space with the razor still in his hand.

"Well, I told her to give me the money," he kept saying. "All I wanted was some liquor. She had some. Why couldn't I have some of it?" he asked, still seemingly unaware of what had happened.

The ambulance and the police arrived at almost the same time. The policeman carefully took the razor from Rummie as the ambulance attendant placed Rummie's mama on a stretcher. It took twenty-two stitches and ten clamps to close the gash in her leg.

The police questioned Rummie and asked his grandparents if they wished to have him sent away. As usual, his grandparents said no. In their hearts, they felt Rummie had suffered enough because of the way he was born. The guilt of what they considered their failure with Rummie's mama would not allow them to let Rummie go.

Slowly, Rummie began to recognize and accept his grandparents' love. He gradually became involved with our group again, having learned a lesson on love. He was still spontaneous in all his actions, but there was a different look on his face.

Rummie now had a look of compassion in his eyes. Although we continued our string of mischievous deeds, we all had learned a valuable lesson. We had learned that even the community fool deserves a silver lining at least once.

Chapter 7

The Kenny Pool

Summer is just not summer unless you have a place to swim. Although the city operated a public swimming pool, we were never in the position of being able to pay the fee. Plus, with all the creeks and ponds around us, who needed to take a chlorine bath anyway?

Our summers were spent trying to find the nearest and deepest body of water we could come across. We had many swimming holes, but our favorite had to be the Kenny Pool.

I don't even remember how or why we named it the Kenny Pool. The name was simple enough and easy to say. There were none of the restrictions of the public pool. The public pool required swim trunks, and once you paid the three-dollar fee, you had to take a shower before getting into the water. It didn't make sense. Why get wet to get in the water? At the Kenny Pool, there was no dress code. Why, you could even swim naked if you wanted to.

During the heat of summer days, we often made our way to the Kenny Pool. What we called a pool was really a creek about five-and-a-half feet deep that was located about five hundred yards from the busiest highway in town. The creek divided Gill Street and North Main Street. North Main Street was the beginning of the Black community and Gill Street was the White folks' side of town.

The Kenny Pool was right down our line. Many days we would start fishing and end up taking all our clothes off and joining the fish for a swim. The water of the Kenny Pool was as black as coal, which was typical of the creeks in Scotland County. The water must have been black because the floor of the creek bed was covered with the black dirt of the Carolina Sandhills. Our Black bodies blended in well with the charcoal water as the sunlight reflected its rays off the surface. The water was so black that it was almost impossible to tell if we were wearing clothes or not, unless we stood up.

The middle of dog days in Laurinburg was no picnic. It was usually hot before the noontime sun had a chance to make its daily climb to the top of the sky.

"We better get started with what we going to do today," Curtis said.

"Yeah, because if we wait too long, we're going to get baked by the sun," Willie answered. "We don't want to get no blacker."

"Yeah, you already Black enough, Willie," Darryl joked. "You look like somebody put you in an oven and forgot to take you out. You look like a Black crispy critter."

"Who you calling Black?" Willie retaliated. "You're blacker than this asphalt we're standing on."

While Darryl and Willie continued to fight it out, the rest of the Pine Street Patriots arrived at our usual meeting place. We would wake up with the chickens, before anybody else woke up. Most of the time, we would sneak out the window to avoid waking anybody up.

It had become a ritual of summer. Every day, we would meet on the porch of the barn and make plans where the only witnesses to our sometimes-dangerous deeds were the old rusting milling machines. There they stood, guardians of so many secrets, not only our secrets, but those of the Black hands that toiled over them in days gone by—Black hands that wiped away tears and sweat, Black hands that were worn and callused. Rummie's grandfather would often tell us about the days when working in this mill was all many Black people had to look forward to.

Despite the difficulties of the work, somehow these old machines had been the hope of many families looking for a silver lining. These rusting guardians had now become our hope and our playground. We would meet there despite our empty stomachs and ragged clothes. This was the one place where probing and judgmental eyes could not dictate what we could or could not do with our day. Here, we could leave behind the worry over food at least for a while. Our minds were preoccupied with the thoughts of living for that moment in time when we would discover something new.

"What are we going to do today?" Curtis asked.

It was obvious by his expression and the tone of his voice that he wanted to go swimming. There were other motivating factors behind Curtis's desire. The Kenny Pool was also a source of food. Often times, we would stop by a pear tree or an apple tree on the way, despite the danger of being shot by angry owners with shotguns loaded with rock salt.

Once we got to the water, there was the possibility of catching not only fish but also crayfish and boiling them until they turned red, breaking them open, and feasting on their delicious meat. Maybe it is true that crayfish are a poor man's lobster. We couldn't tell you. It's a wonder that we even knew the word lobster. We certainly didn't know what one tasted like.

"I think we ought to go swimming at the Kenny Pool," Curtis anxiously said.

"Boy, you must be crazy," I answered.

"Why come you don't want to go?" Curtis fired back. "Ain't you hot standing out here in the sun?"

"Yeah, I'm hot, but I don't feel like fighting with those redneck White boys," I said.

These boys were our White counterparts and were just as poor as we were. However, their skin color made them feel justified in their attitude of superiority over us. They would call you a "nigger" in a minute.

I remember going through their neighborhood one morning. I was trying to make my way to Jackson's Grocery Store when suddenly a little boy no more than four or five years old walked out of his yard with a stick.

He stuck out his tongue, and as I felt the impact of the stick on my back, I heard him say, "Nigger, go home!"

It was that kind of experience that made me have second thoughts about going to the Kenny Pool. We heard stories of people who were attacked walking down Gill Street after dark. It didn't take much to provoke the people on Gill Street to come after you, day or night.

The Kenny Pool was directly in the path of Gill Street, better known as "Redneck Alley." This is where the "White trash" lived. They were trapped just like us but would not take out their frustrations on the system that held them in economic bondage. I guess it is true that oppressive systems of injustice make sure that the oppressed turn on each other. That certainly was the case for the two economically oppressed groups from Gill Street and Newtown.

All the anger over their plight of rejection and poverty seemed to flow aggressively when they met us. Neither group had, as the old folks say, "a pot to piss in," but that didn't seem to matter when we dared go into each other's neighborhood. Whenever we went to the Kenny Pool, we had to fight our way in and back out again.

"Come on, Leonard. You know we can take them," Fred said.

"Yeah, Leonard, you know they never stopped us before," Darryl replied.

"I know that, but it's too hot to be fighting," I said, trying to rationalize.

Why did we have to fight for the privilege of swimming in a creek that none of us owned? Why did we have to fight to swim in something that was probably polluted anyway?

The eagerness to swim won out, but I wasn't so sure that it was not the eagerness to fight that made us decide to go. The confrontation was bound to happen, regardless of the heat.

When we arrived at our swimming hole, hot and tired and ready to cool off, we found some other kids already there.

"Hey, look at those White girls swimming in the Kenny Pool,"

Fred shouted.

"Let's run 'em out," Willie responded.

There was no other place the girls could have come from. It didn't take a genius to realize that they were from Gill Street. What self-respecting upper-class White girl would be caught swimming in a dirty creek? The fight had come to us. It never took more than a glance from us at these White girls in swimsuits to send the rednecks of Gill Street on the warpath.

"We done walked this far, and I ain't about to turn around," Sylvester added.

Sylvester knew that there was really no sense in turning back now. We might as well pay for our swim, knowing we would have to fight anyway.

Before we knew what had happened, Fred had thrown a rock and hit one of the girls on the breast.

"I'm going to tell my big brother!" the girl squealed. "You niggers are going to get it now, just wait until we get back!"

They all jumped out of the water and ran toward their homes.

"I ain't going nowhere," Calvin boasted. "I came here to swim and that is what I'm going to do."

"Come on, y'all. Let's get out of here," Fred whined.

"How come you ready to go now, Fred?" I asked. "You were the one who threw the rock."

Fred was always like that. He'd be the first to instigate trouble and the first to run when it came. He was the one who would watch you fall and almost break your neck, and then he would laugh.

"Here they come!" Curtis screamed.

"They don't look like boys to me," I quickly said.

The girls had brought not only their big brothers but their fathers, too. For a Black boy to watch a White girl in a swimsuit in the Deep South was serious business in those days; it was certain they wanted to teach us a lesson we would not forget.

"Y'all can stay round here all you want to, but I'm getting out of here," Fred said, his voice giving way to his obvious fear.

Following Fred's lead, we all started running back toward Newtown. If we could just make it back to our side of town, we would be all right. They wouldn't dare follow us back to the "Black side," where the odds would be in our favor.

"Wait a minute!" I yelled. "I lost my shoes."

"You can kiss those shoes goodbye," Sylvester said.

"I just got those Hush Puppies, boy, and Mama will kill me if I lose them," I said.

It was a choice between getting beat up by the rednecks or getting a whooping from Mama. I decided to try my luck with the rednecks— at least I could fight back against them. If Mama got a hold of me, all I would be able to do was stand there and take it.

I had learned the hard way how precious anything new was to my mama. I had learned the price you paid when anything hard to earn like new clothes were lost, torn, or soiled.

My mama bought school clothes once a year, just before school started. One year, the morning of the first day of school, I stood proud and excited in a new pair of pants—pants that had spent the summer on layaway at the Laurinburg department store. Mama gave me the standard lecture: "Don't you go to school and get those clothes dirty, and if you do, you know what's waiting for you when you get back to the house." I realized that if anything happened to those pants, I wouldn't be able to sit down for a week.

The bus rolled to a stop, and children started pushing to get off.

"Move out my way," I heard a voice behind me shout. Evidently, I wasn't moving fast enough, and Buckwheat pushed me down to the ground.

Tears welled up in my eyes as I stared in disbelief at my muddied pants. Without a second thought, I lowered my head and went at Buckwheat with both hands flying.

Somehow, I ended up on the ground again, getting more mud on my new school pants. Well, if I am going to get a whipping, I might as well make it worth it, I reasoned. Buckwheat sat with both knees across my stomach in victory. He made one fatal mistake. He lowered his face near my mouth to gloat over his apparent victory. I lifted my head far enough to grab his ear with my teeth. Buckwheat howled in pain, but I refused to let go until I drew blood. If I had to pay for getting my clothes dirty, Buckwheat was going to pay, too. I knew my mama wouldn't care about an explanation. She would only see her hard-earned money destroyed.

That was one day where the whipping didn't seem to hurt quite as bad. I wasn't the only one who paid.

Now, faced with the possibility of another whooping from Mama, this time for lost shoes, I was ready to stand up even to the redneck men from Gill Street.

We'd finally made it back on the Black side of town, after what seemed to be an eternity with the devil breathing down our necks.

"I ain't running no more," I said. "I got to get my shoes."

When I stopped, everybody stopped.

The rednecks, without realizing it, had crossed over to our side of town.

"Now what's this my daughter tells me?" said the daddy of the girl Fred had hit. "One of you Black niggers hit her with a rock. Now which one of you was it?"

"We just wanted to swim," Willie answered.

"Ain't you got no nigger creeks to swim in on your side of town?" he snapped.

I looked at those huge arms and noticed he held my brand new pair of Hush Puppies. I began to cry with anger as tears welled up in my frightened eyes. It was Buckwheat all over again, only this time my foe was a man, not a boy.

"What's wrong with you, nigger?" He laughed. "Are you cryin' because you scared we going to beat you?"

"Give me my shoes!" I shouted.

"We going to give 'em back as soon as we teach you niggers a lesson," he replied, paying no attention to my giant teardrops falling into my mouth.

"I'll ask you one more time," I said, trying to fight back the tears.

We had stopped running underneath a grove of pecan trees, and there on the ground in front of me was a large pecan tree branch that had fallen from one of the trees.

"Please, mister," I said. "Give me my shoes."

My tears were now tears of anger. I slowly lifted the branch off the ground and then began swinging it in every direction. My one intention was to get my shoes back by any means necessary. I never gave a thought as to who was in the line of fire. I was trying to save my butt from Mama.

By now, everybody had followed my lead and had picked up branches and begun swinging them threateningly.

We must have scared those rednecks pretty good, because they were soon all running back toward their part of town, even the grown men, and we were chasing them back toward Gill Street.

"Look at them run," Calvin victoriously screamed.

Upon our return, we found my Hush Puppies lying in the pecan grove where the man had dropped them. The fear of punishment from Mama gave me the strength to fight for what was mine. That fear saved us from what was certain to become a street brawl.

"Boy, I sho' am glad I won't get a whooping from Mama," I sighed after everything was over.

After that incident we had no more trouble from the rednecks of Gill Street, and the Kenny Pool became our private swimming hole.

We loved going to the Kenny Pool, especially once we didn't have to worry about the rednecks anymore. The Kenny Pool was a prize worth fighting for—it provided not only reprise for the heart but food for the stomach.

Homemade fishing poles were our stock and trade. Fred was always responsible for stealing some fishing line, hooks, and lead from his father's tackle box. His father, Mr. James, was a shadetree fisherman when he wasn't drunk. The rest of us were responsible for cutting our own poles, which were usually the same sticks we used for horses.

"Come on, y'all. I got the hooks and everything," Fred yelled from his yard.

"Okay," Calvin answered. "Let me get the hoe so we can dig some worms for bait."

Standing on the banks of the Kenny Pool, we'd take turns looking for spots where earthworms might be. As quick as the worms were out of the ground, we placed them on fishhooks dangling on lines tied around the end of milk tree poles.

"Can I go?" Rummie begged.

"Me, too?" an unfamiliar voice said.

It was the voice of Thomas, Fred's cousin from Macintosh housing projects.

"Rummie, you can go, as long as your granddaddy knows where you are at," I said. "Thomas, you can come too, if Fred says it's all right."

We stood there with our makeshift fishing poles before the final thing that blocked our path to the Kenny Pool. The highway was much traveled, and many of the passing motorists would slow down and stare at us.

It was interesting to try reading their faces as they would slow up and stare in disbelief at our little ragtag army. Most of them looked upon us in disgust with a self-righteous turning up of their noses, but some looked at us almost wistfully, as if they were remembering something from their younger days. These people seemed as if they themselves wanted to stop and join us.

This busy highway with its curious onlookers was not enough to keep us from the Kenny Pool. We were never concerned about how they felt. It was a game to us, standing there trying to read their faces until we got the first break to run across the highway and on over to the Kenny Pool.

"I'll be glad when this traffic stops," Darryl sighed.

"Me, too. I'm ready to fish while the fish are biting," Fred said.

"Boy, how do you know when the fish are biting?" Curtis asked.

"Because my daddy is a fisherman," Fred proudly answered.

"No, you mean part-time fisherman and full-time drunkard," Willie replied jokingly.

"Just wait till we get over there," Fred fired back defensively. "You'll see what I mean."

Soon our homemade fishing poles were dangling out into the water, and surprisingly, the fish were biting pretty well.

"See, I told you that the fish would be biting," Fred triumphantly stated.

"You were just lucky, that's all," Curtis said.

Within hours, each of us had caught at least two fish and were fighting over whose fish was biggest.

Rummie was the first to suggest we stop fishing. "Man, I'm getting tired of fishing now," he grumbled. "Why don't we go swimming so I can show you how Tarzan dives?"

"It is kind of hot," Sylvester said.

Almost before he could get the words out of his mouth, we were putting our fish in a bucket of water and peeling off our clothes.

Splash! Rummie was the first to hit the water.

"Did you see that dive?" he shouted, naked as a jaybird.

"Yeah, Rummie, do that dive again," Calvin said excitedly.

Rummie took a running start and did a belly buster.

"Man, Rummie, that's just the way Tarzan does it," Calvin laughed, falling backward into the water.

"Do it again," we all shouted.

It didn't take much encouragement before Rummie was again counting off paces so that he could get his dive just right. The paces counted, Rummie was now ready to attempt his third dive. He stood there like an Olympic diver.

Willie's words broke Rummie's confident concentration.

"Rummie, here comes your granddaddy."

"I thought you said he knew where you were?" I asked.

Rummie didn't answer. He turned around and made a quick dash across the highway. There was no time for him to put on his clothes or to look both ways before crossing the street. Rummie knew he was in trouble.

The next thing we heard was the squealing of automobile tires as a car tried to avoid hitting Rummie.

When we realized he hadn't been run over, we laughed ourselves silly. I will never forget the looks on people's faces as they swerved in amazement, barely avoiding that naked boy running across a busy street in broad daylight.

Soon, the excitement of the moment ended, and we were again trying to figure out what to do next.

"How many fish we got?" I asked.

"We have about twenty freshwater perch," Fred, the fishing expert, answered.

"Well, I'll tell you what we ought to do," I said. "We ought to camp out tonight and have fish for supper."

"But where are we going to get all the stuff we need to cook all these fish?" Darryl asked.

"I can get the cooking oil," Thomas eagerly spoke up.

"I'll get the cornmeal and the frying pan," Sylvester said.

We were still making plans as we walked home. Everybody was to bring their own blankets, covers, and equipment to make tents. We decided to camp out in the vacant lot where the old Methodist Church once stood. The church parsonage was all that remained. The demolition of the church left an open field. We were sure our parents would let us camp there since it was close to our houses.

When the Pine Street Patriots camped out, there were no Coleman lanterns or gas cooking stoves. There was no Boy Scout equipment—no tents or sleeping bags. When the Pine Street Patriots camped out, it was bare bones. Sleeping quarters were made with old bed sheets braced by tree limbs and driven into the ground at the corners. We prayed it wouldn't rain. Cooking space was arranged by having someone steal the oven rack from their mama's stove. A hole was dug for the fire, and the oven rack was placed above the hole on two bricks.

Of course, somebody had to steal pots and pans as well as cooking grease.

It didn't take long for everybody to reach the campsite with the necessary items, but putting up the tents was another story. Arguments naturally broke out, and sabotage was the rule when you thought somebody's tent was going up faster than yours.

"Who's going to clean these fish?" an exhausted Curtis asked.

It was the chore no one wanted to do. No one wanted to spend the night smelling like fish and having fish scales clinging in their hair.

"Fred, why don't you clean them since you know so much about fishing," I said.

"No, Leonard, you do it," Fred quickly retorted.

It was getting dark, and so I took the job while everybody sat around and watched.

"Is the fire ready?" I shouted as I cut open the last fish and scraped its entrails out.

"Yeah, the grease is hot and everything is ready," Sylvester answered.

We put cornmeal on the fish and put them in the pan. It was hard to believe that we had caught these fish from the black water of the Kenny Pool as I watched them crackling in the hot grease.

Once we had cooked all the fish we began to devour them. It seemed like only seconds ago that I had taken these fish from the pan, and now they were all gone.

"Boy, y'all are greedy," I said.

"Who you calling greedy?" Darryl shot back. "Look at all those fish bones on the ground around you!"

"What we going to do now?" Calvin asked.

I'd always heard people say that after a big meal you went to sleep. That old adage had no truth or validity with us. The meal only gave us more energy.

"Ain't it some tires in the back of the tents?" Willie asked.

"Let's roll them up the hill and let them roll down," Fred said.

When you stood at the top of Pine Street, there in plain view sat

Mr. Ticky's house. His house just happened to be in the path of our tires.

We soon got a few tires up to the top of the hill and rolled them down.

"Look at my tire," Calvin yelled. "It's rolling up on Mr. Ticky's porch!"

We all scattered into the nearby bushes as the tire hit the front door of Mr. Ticky's house. The other tires missed, but Calvin's was a direct hit.

"Who is it?" a voice called from inside.

We silently waited until we were sure that Mr. Ticky had decided that no one was really at his door.

"Go on, Calvin, and get your tire," Darryl whispered.

After Calvin finally got up the nerve and retrieved his tire, we made our way back to the top of the hill.

"Let's do it again," Calvin said.

"Okay, but this is the last time," I said.

The tire rapidly descended from the top of the hill. We ran back behind the bushes. This time the tire bounced up on the porch.

When he heard the first noise, Mr. Ticky opened his door—and the tire rolled right into his house. We could see things falling as the tire went though Mr. Ticky's living room.

"Who did that?" Mr. Ticky angrily said.

Of course, we did not answer, and he slammed his door shut again.

"I ain't doing it no more," Calvin whispered.

The door to Mr. Tickys house flew open once more.

Darryl flinched and said, "Oh no, he's coming to get us."

We could hear Mr. Ticky mumbling something as he pushed the tire out of his living room.

We slid from beneath the bushes and, without being seen, sneaked back to our campsite.

Morning came early with a blanket of dew covering the ground and the tops of our tents, causing them to sag.

"It can't be morning yet. We just went to sleep," I sleepily said.

"Yes, it is, and I'm going to get me something to eat," Fred said.

"Yeah, I'm going home and getting back in the bed," Sylvester said, yawning.

"Boy, you sho' do look ugly when you wake up," I teased Sylvester.

"Who said I was woke yet?" he snapped back. "I couldn't sleep with y'all over there keeping all the noise. I don't know what was worse, y'all or them dogs barking all night."

"Just go on home, boy, and go back to sleep," Darryl said. "We'll come and get you later on so that we can finish cleaning up this mess."

Our spirits were restless, but thanks be to God that he created a world that can tame the restless soul. God, it appeared, had given us all we needed to make us feel like somebodies. We had no money to go the public swimming pool. However, God in his goodness opened our eyes and let us see his treasures unfold in our lives.

We were poor, yet rich, and that was a paradox we could live with.

Chapter 8

First Love

Grandma Gladys died a few months after I met Mable. I was fifteen years old, and one of the true silver linings in my life was about to be taken away.

Grandma Gladys suffered a brain hemorrhage that started to bleed behind her eyes. She died in February, in the cold of winter, and it tore my world apart. This was the woman who had given me the ability to hope against hope. This was the woman who, with God's help, saved my life. Where was the silver lining behind this dark cloud?

I heard the whispers of my mama and her sisters and brothers—the silent talk of how it had all happened and the funeral arrangements. My Grandma Gladys's death was such a traumatic experience for me. There was talk of not allowing me to attend her funeral.

In the solitude of my heart, I yelled at God. I questioned God's motives behind her death. Someone was going to let me know why. If my family refused to talk to me, I reasoned that I had only one other alternative. I would walk down to Morris Funeral Home, where my grandma's body was prepared for viewing, and talk to her directly.

And that's what I did. Feeling no fear, I walked up to Grandma Gladys's open casket, leaned over, and whispered into her ear.

"Mama, where's the silver lining?" It had been years since I had called Grandma "Mama." It was what I'd called her until I understood she was not my mother.

When there was no answer from Grandma, everything went black.

I felt the arms of the funeral director lifting me from the floor. Sitting in Mrs. Ella's funeral home office, I had no idea what had happened to me. She dialed my Uncle Frank's telephone, and within ten minutes he was there to take me home.

I didn't attend my Grandma Gladys's funeral. All my life I had believed her when she said, "Behind every dark cloud there is a silver lining." But now, no one could answer my question, "Where is the silver lining behind the dark cloud of Grandma's death, that silver lining that she had always talked about?"

I lived silver linings. Although poverty was real, I knew joy in my circles of friends. I lived silver linings in spite of circumstances. It was because of Grandma Gladys's words that I was able to live life with joy, regardless of the dark clouds brewing over the horizon.

But the question remained lodged in my heart like an evil stone: Where is the silver lining in the death of my first love? For Grandma Gladys was truly my first love.

It took some time for me to realize that Grandma Gladys had not lied to me. No matter how cloudy it gets, the sun is shining above the dark clouds. The silver lining had been present throughout all of my questioning, all of my pain.

Mable was that silver lining. Mable was my first love outside the Pine Street Patriots. The silver lining was always there. I just needed to clear my mind and by faith know that Grandma Gladys, even in death, did not lie to me. I just needed to cleanse my soul with tears. I needed clear eyes and an open heart to recognize Mable as the silver lining that would open all the other doors of love yet to be discovered.

I remember my first step on this new journey. It was that time of the year again, time for another rite of passage into adulthood. I had never been particularly fazed by social events; being labeled a social outcast took care of that. Even if I weren't an outcast, the high school prom would never faze me. I really had no reason to be interested; I was only in the ninth grade at the local junior high school.

The prom was two days away, and everybody in town was talking about it as if the world were coming to an end. There was so much talk that nobody even noticed that a new family had just moved into the neighborhood. I was so frustrated by all this talk that I didn't notice, either; I was usually the first to know about such things.

It was the evening of the Scotland High School prom when I finally realized that the formerly vacant house was now occupied. The neighborhood was buzzing with questions about the new occupants. I think the excitement was centered on what family could afford to rent the only brick house on Pine Street.

Despite all the commotion, the Pine Street Patriots were still looking for adventure.

"Why don't we roll some tires down the hill," Fred remarked, suggesting one of our favorite pastimes.

"That sounds good to me," I gladly answered. "Maybe it will help get our minds off all this crazy talk about the prom."

"Okay, then, let's get goin'," Curtis said.

"Where can we get some good tires?" Willie quickly asked.

Fred answered, "We can go to Bub's Service Station."

His real name was James, but we knew him as "Bub." Bub was one of the few Black persons who owned a business. His Gulf Station was where most Black people took their cars to be serviced. Bub was a tall dark-skinned man who had attended Hampton University on a scholarship provided by the McNairs, the same McNairs who owned most if not all of Laurinburg. "Mr. Bub's" replaced Mr. Nunny's as the location where we sold our soda pop bottles.

Mr. Bub's was also the place where people often picked up used motor oil to pour over the leathery skin of dogs afflicted with the hideous disease known as the mange. The mange to a dog must have been like leprosy to human beings. It was sickening to watch dogs walk around with their fur falling out and their skin wrinkled. But I loved to chase them down and pour the oil over their backs and watch them roll in the grass trying to rub the oil off, only to stand with grass stuck all over them.

Bub's little Gulf Station was the hot spot for Black people. So it was there that we went to get old tires. Bub would even let us get inner tubes to use whenever we went swimming at the Kenny Pool.

We had passed that house a hundred times or more but had never noticed someone living in it. Everybody in town knew it to be the old parsonage of the local Black Methodist church. No one had lived in it since the church was torn down and rebuilt across town. We dared not go near it since it was always under the watchful eyes of the city police department. It was obvious that someone was watching the house, because it was in very good condition. There was none of the usual spray can graffiti on the walls, no broken windows, and no beer or wine bottles around the house, which is more than I can say about the other vacant buildings in the community. This particular house even looked a lot better than some of the houses that people were living in.

"Come on, Leonard," Curtis shouted. "I'll race you down the hill."

"Okay, but you know who is goin' to win," I bragged.

I knew Curtis would probably win. Both tires were larger than the two of us, but that was part of the fun. Trying to guide the tires was a constant struggle that racing intensified. I knew Curtis could handle his tire.

Therefore, in order to make sure that I at least had a chance, I asked Fred to stand at the foot of the hill to judge who won.

"Fred, go down there and make sure that Curtis don't cheat," I said.

"Wait a minute," Fred replied. "I want to get in on this race, too. I bet I'll whip both of you."

"Aw, boy, stop crying and get on down there by Mr. Ticky's house. You can race the winner," Curtis shouted.

After mumbling a few words under his breath, Fred finally reached the foot of the hill.

"Okay, Willie, you tell us when to go," Curtis said, as we lined our tires up behind a line drawn in the street.

"On your mark! Get set! Go!" Willie yelled.

We started out at full speed, and much to my surprise, I was winning. My tire was racing down the hill well in front of me, but I was gaining ground. I had to reach my tire in order to guide it away from Mr. Ernest's house.

I was on my way to an upset win when all of a sudden my eyes caught sight of someone standing on the front porch of the vacant house. Immediately, I stopped to see who it was.

Fred started yelling, "Come on, Leonard! Come on! Keep going! You're winning! What's wrong with you, boy? You've finally got a chance to win! Come on or you're going to let Curtis beat you!"

I was frozen. I could not move. I wanted to move. Boy, how I wanted to beat Curtis. It was as if my legs were saying, "Move, you fool," but my eyes were saying, "Stay here and look."

Curtis soon crossed the finish line without my having moved another muscle.

"Boy, what are you staring at so hard?" Willie asked.

"You let Curtis beat you! What happened?"

"Wait a minute," I said. "Someone has moved into that house."

"That ain't no reason to let Curtis win the race," Fred replied, frustrated with me.

"But it's a girl, and she's pretty," I sputtered.

"You mean you lost the race just to look at a girl?" Fred scolded.

Why was I standing there like a fool staring as if I had lost my mind? What was so different about this girl?

There she stood, wearing a blue prom gown waiting for that all-important step into womanhood, unaware that she was to be the first door I would walk through on my way to manhood. By now, I had forgotten all about the tire race; everybody was screaming to get my attention, but nothing seemed to be able to tear me away from what I saw.

Mable was a beautiful girl, and I couldn't understand why nobody else noticed it. Everybody kept reminding me of the race I had just lost, and they couldn't understand why it didn't bother me.

What was wrong with me? I had never before noticed much about girls, but there I stood studying every detail about Mable. It was like I had never seen a girl before. She had a kind, gentle face with a creamy complexion.

From that day on my life with the Pine Street Patriots would be drastically altered. I went through all the stages of that unstable but joyous disease known as first love. I couldn't sleep. I couldn't eat. It appeared that I would never get that picture of Mable standing on her porch out of my mind.

I had to find some way of rationalizing her beauty. I had to understand how one girl could affect me so completely. How could one girl make me forget the Pine Street Patriots? I was no longer interested in rolling tires, catching pigeons, or any of the things that had previously captivated me. The only thing I was interested in was trying to get Mable to notice me. *Was God playing a cruel trick on me? Why wasn't I warned in advance that something like this would happen? What was I to do now?*

My heart just would not let go.

Mama was the first to know something was wrong. Once she knew, Mama didn't waste time naming it.

"Leonard, what little girl is got your nose wide open?" she asked.

"What do you mean my nose wide open?" I replied, trying to figure out what she meant.

"I've been noticing how you been acting. Nobody acts like that at fifteen unless some little girl got them cutting flips."

I was not cutting flips, but I was going crazy trying to figure out a way to get Mable to notice me. What I did next proved what a fool I had become. I wrote what I thought was Mable's name on the asphalt of Pine Street in big letters for the whole world to see:

LEONARD LOVES MAYBELL.

The Pine Street Patriots never let me live that one down.

"Leonard's in love with a girl, and he can't even spell her name," Curtis teased.

But that was not the end of the embarrassment. Before I had the opportunity to change the spelling, Mable and her sister walked by and read the message. Not even embarrassment could keep me from making a fool of myself.

No one seemed to be able to break the spell I was under. I couldn't talk to anybody in the Pine Street Patriots about it; they would only laugh. My mind was a thousand miles away, filled with thoughts I had never had before. That night, I made plans about how to approach this new experience.

I decided to do something about all those crazy feelings the following day.

By now, the news was all over town about the new family, mainly because of the efforts of our resident nosy box, Mrs. Lucy, Fred's grandma. Mrs. Lucy was a short silver-haired widow, and her dark complexion made her gray hair look like snow. Being a lifelong resident of Newtown, Mrs. Lucy knew practically everyone. If she didn't know you personally, she knew some distant relative of yours.

Mrs. Lucy had a rather notorious reputation for getting into people's personal business. She was the local FBI. No one moved up and down Pine Street without Mrs. Lucy discovering something about them.

There was more to this silver-haired gossip box than could be perceived without really getting to know her. She was the ultimate inquisitor and stored all gathered information in her brain to be used at a later date. Often times, Mrs. Lucy reminded me of a great vulture, and at other times she was like a great con man. When we first moved to Newtown, she made sure she found out everything about us. Mrs. Lucy knew every detail of our move from New York. She knew all about my mama's family. It was amazing what she knew.

Mrs. Lucy could have very easily been the kingpin in any sting operation. She had it down to a science. In order to find out about our family, she would invite us over one by one and give us candy, cookies, and whatever else she thought we wanted. After drugging us with the truth serum of sugar, Mrs. Lucy would question us for hours about where we moved from and everything else she wanted to know.

When she found out that we were really a softhearted family willing to do whatever it took to get along with people, she began to borrow everything from us. One day it was a cup of sugar; the next day, a cup of salt. Mrs. Lucy even borrowed dirt from our backyard to fill in a pothole in her yard.

She became a human parasite because she knew we would help. Maybe that is why she was so nosy, always trying to seek out and devour her next prey. Despite all her negative traits, I saw Mrs. Lucy as a survivor; she did whatever it took to get by.

I remember vividly how Mrs. Lucy would sit on her front porch every day watching people come and go downtown. If you lived "across the creek," another Black ghetto in Laurinburg, your path crossed right by Mrs. Lucy's house. It was the only route walkers could take to get downtown. Mrs. Lucy took advantage of her strategic location.

I got my first sight of Mrs. Lucy in action one day as all of us were playing in the big sycamore tree in front of her house. Unlike Zacchaeus, Mrs. Lucy never climbed the sycamore tree for information. She simply wove her web with words that drew from you what she wanted to learn.

No one knew his name or where he came from.

"Do you know that boy coming this way?" Mrs. Lucy asked, directing questions at us through the branches of the tree where we sat.

Everybody answered, "No."

"Ain't that Mrs. Ethel's boy?" she asked Fred.

"Grandma, I don't know who that is," Fred whined.

"Boy, you mean to tell me you don't know who that is, as much trouble as you get in," she halfheartedly scolded.

Before Fred could answer, the man was in front of the house and

Mrs. Lucy started doing what she did best. The poor man never had a chance.

"Sho' is warm this morning, ain't it?" she asked.

"Yes, ma'am," a husky voice answered.

"Are there many people uptown?" Mrs. Lucy asked, slowly trapping her victim.

"Not many; it's gettin' kind of hot," the man answered.

He came to a complete stop and seemed to be enjoying the shade of the big sycamore tree. He never realized he had been trapped and was about to be picked clean of information by the queen of nosiness. Before he left, we knew who he was, where he lived, who his parents were, and even what he had eaten for lunch.

When news got around about the new family, everybody knew without a doubt that the kingpin of nosiness was on the job. Mrs. Lucy was a master; if anyone could find out about Mable's family, she could. She had already warned us about that "nappy-headed, foul-mouthed young'un Essie."

Essie was Mable's baby brother. I saw this as an opportunity and was determined to make sure he would get to know me first. Everybody else in our group either ignored or made fun of Essie, and if you could have seen him you would know why. Essie was a sickly looking child who had been babied by his older sisters. It was obvious he was the only boy and the youngest child.

Mable's mother was dead. Her father left the children in Laurinburg to live with two older sisters, Alta Marie and Fern. Alta Marie was married with a family of her own. Being the oldest child, it was her task to keep the family together. Essie, being the youngest, was lavished with protection.

Mrs. Lucy had been unusually accurate about him. Essie's hair looked like it hadn't seen a comb in ages. He had what we called "police car hair"—it rolled up and parked anywhere. My hair wasn't in the best shape, but Essie's was outrageously nappy.

Mrs. Lucy was also right about his foul mouth.

What Essie lacked in physical size he made up in the size of the curse words he used. Ole Essie could say some curse words that I had never heard of before. But I was still determined to be his friend, because he was part of my plan. I guess you could say the motive was right; Mable was the sole intention for my starting a friendship with Essie.

The day began bright and early, but I could not remember ever being more frightened. I just could not understand it. I had jumped Deadman's Creek without fear, but now, I was afraid. I had jumped from great heights into a haystack without fear, but now, I was afraid. I had been shot at with rock salt and thought it was fun, but now, I was afraid.

I just couldn't understand why I was so scared now.

I started my plan by introducing myself to Essie, who was pulling a model car behind him.

"Hi, Essie, that sho' is a nice car," I said.

Looking stunned, Essie said, "Who are you, and how do you know my name?"

"I saw you moving in, and Mrs. Lucy, the lady who lives in front of you, told me your name," I answered.

"So, you like my car?" Essie said.

"Yes, it's nice all right. What kind is it?" I asked.

What came next was a complete description of the car.

"It's a 1970 Plymouth Road Runner," Essie began. "It's got dual overhead cams and dual exhaust."

"Man, you sure know a lot about cars," I said.

"Yeah, I got a lot more in the house. You want to go see 'em?" he asked. "Oh, yeah, what did you say your name was?" he continued, rather nonchalantly.

"My name is Leonard. I live in that house behind Mrs. Lucy," I answered.

I noticed that Essie wasn't really listening so I stopped talking. He was paying more attention to his car than he was to me.

"If you think this one is something, just wait till you see the rest of 'em," he said. "Come on. Let's go inside and see the rest of the cars."

I couldn't believe things were going so smoothly. Here I had just met Essie and he was inviting me inside his house. I really didn't take time to try to figure out why he was so eager, and to tell you the truth, it didn't matter. I was glad that I was getting an opportunity to finally see Mable, and that was all that mattered to me. Maybe Essie was glad that he was finally getting away from all the girls in his family, but for whatever reason, here was my chance.

There she was, sitting inside the living room watching television. How can you be descriptive of a feeling? Is it possible to put into words what your eyes see in your first love? Maybe that is what they mean when they say that love is blind.

When I walked into Mable's house it was like being in a zone. I blocked out everything else. Nothing else mattered. There was absolutely no way I could put these emotions into words. It all made no sense. *What was happening to me?* If this was what love was about, I was more than happy to oblige being a prisoner.

"Who is that you got with you, Essie?" Mable asked.

Why did she have to speak?

I was already reduced to a rubber-kneed weakling. Mable's voice simply compounded my state of foolishness.

I wanted to answer so badly, but no words would come forth. I must have looked like a complete idiot. Fifteen years old, and now I couldn't talk.

Seeing that I was unable to speak, Essie quickly answered, "His name is Leonard. He lives across the street in that red house."

For once I was happy Essie was around. He became my Aaron. I am not sure how badly Moses stuttered, but I am certain he had nothing on me—especially if I had to talk now.

My eyes were glued on Mable. Apparently, my eyes had deceived me the first time I saw her standing on the porch. She was much prettier up close and personal. Suddenly, all the clichés used to describe beauty came to mind. Being new at this love thing limited my vocabulary on the subject. All I knew was that Mable was "happening."

She had my attention, that was for sure. I had never been in love before, but in her eyes I saw love, or should I say I felt it. Her voice made me shake all over. Mable's words ran all through me. When she spoke, I should have responded, but I couldn't say a word. An attempt to describe her would go beyond the range of clichés, beyond the range of words. I couldn't describe Mable if you paid me a million dollars.

Beauty has a way of humbling the proudest creature and making bold the most wretched. I had no other way of knowing how I would get Mable to notice me. That's why I was here now inside her house with nappy-headed, foul-mouthed, car-loving Essie. No girl had ever given me the time of day, and I had never before wanted one to. Yet, here I was, wooing the prettiest girl on the block, and an older woman at that.

I doubted my ability to win over someone like Mable. My status in life never caused me to doubt my worthiness before, but with these new feelings, I felt inadequate. We were one of the poorest, if not the poorest, families in Newtown, a fact Mable could have figured out by just looking at my clothes.

When you are trying to court a girl, there must be some voice in your head telling you to make sure to do all the right things, such as wearing all the right clothes and making yourself presentable. "Fix yourself up if you want to win that girl," the voice seemed to say.

It was telling me I'd have to do a lot more to win over a girl like Mable.

But I was captured, and for the moment, at least, it did not matter how I looked or what people said I was. My only concern now was to share the love welling up inside me. I had no idea how it would turn out. My feelings were trampled by society. I could not help but think Mable would do the same. Would she just laugh at me? Would she see me as a nobody?

I was determined, despite my fear, to trust my heart. I was willing to take a chance, even if it meant the pain of rejection. I could not turn back now.

Once inside Essie's room, I could see that he was a real car buff. There were cars of every conceivable model. Cars, however, were the last thing on my mind, as my conversation switched to questions about Mable.

"How old is Mable?" I asked.

"Seventeen," Essie answered hesitantly. "Now tell me, Leonard, ain't this a bad Camaro?" he asked, attempting to change the subject, but to no avail.

"Does she have a boyfriend?" I responded.

Essie was beginning to get impatient with all the questions.

"I don't know," he snapped. "And I don't care either. Come on! Get that car and let's go back outside."

Essie must have thought that if he could get me back outside, I would stop talking about Mable.

Once outside, I continued my assault on Essie with more questions about Mable.

Finally, poor Essie couldn't take it anymore. "Why don't you ask Mable yourself, if you want to know so much about her," he grunted.

"I am only asking you these things because one day, I might be your brother-in-law," I answered.

I finally had Essie's attention.

"You just wait till I tell Mable what you said! Just wait till I tell her you are in love with her!" Essie screamed.

The foundation was laid; now all I could do was wait.

The following day would be one I will never forget. That early spring Saturday in May would be the end of what appeared to be an eternity.

The Pine Street Patriots were all together getting ready to go fishing. I had already assumed that Mable would never speak to me.

I saw Mable walk out of her door, and immediately I forgot all about fishing. If Mable said no, I would simply forget this thing called love and never trust my heart to anybody else. If she said yes, everything about me would change. Something in my heart told me today was the day.

She opened her brother-in-law's car door and sat inside. Mable watched us as we gathered all our fishing equipment.

What will I do if she rejects me? I asked myself.

I had been rejected before, and it hadn't bothered me, but this was different. I had rightly or wrongly placed all my emotions into the hope that Mable would accept me.

Suddenly, she motioned for me to come to her. She had noticed me! That was a start.

Proudly, I stood there in my rags. The wait was over.

"So, you're the one who's been asking about me. You're the one who wrote that note on the street," she said with a smile.

"Yes, I'm the one," I answered, surprised at my boldness.

"How old are you?" she asked.

"I'm fifteen," I said.

Well, that's it, I thought to myself. *I might as well go fishin.'*

"Don't you think you're kind of young to be talking about love?" Mable asked.

I don't know what possessed me to say what came next. Maybe I knew subconsciously that this was it—here was my chance to finally be loved for who I was. For what seemed like the first time, I viewed myself as special. If I saw myself that way, maybe Mable would also. Grandma Gladys always told me I was special, and talking with Mable made me realize that I was. They made sense now, my grandma's words. All the things I had gone through prepared me for this moment.

"Give me a chance to show you if I am too young or not," I boldly said.

At first Mable didn't say a word. Then she got out, closed the car door, and turned to me and asked, "Leonard, will you walk me to the store?"

There I stood, standing next to the prettiest girl in town who had just asked me to take a walk with her, and for a moment I was speechless.

I finally got the nerve to say "yes." I never knew how just one word could change a person's life.

My life certainly changed once Mable became a part of it.

I even started looking for a job, the first of which included picking cucumbers for a local farmer. During cucumber harvesting season, a farmer would ride through the streets of Newtown searching for eager teenagers looking for work.

Mable and I sat in our usual place of conversation as summer made its first turn toward fall. We always sat on the front porch of her house. I loved sitting there in full view of everybody that walked by. I wanted everybody to know that Mable was my girl.

"What are those people doing around that truck?" Mable asked.

"I don't know, but people are all around it like somebody is giving out money or something."

"Let's go see what's going on," Mable suggested.

We didn't know what we were getting into as we walked toward the farmer's truck to see what the deal was. As we met both boys and girls coming from the truck, we noticed the smiles on their faces.

"Do y'all want a job?" asked the pot-bellied farmer. You could tell he was a farmer by the field dirt underneath his fingernails and covering his clothes.

"What kind of work?" I replied, trying to impress Mable.

"Picking cucumbers," was the answer that rolled from the man's lips in the long southern drawl typical of the region.

"How much do you get paid?" I asked in the manliest voice I could muster.

"Y'all get paid fifty cents for every quart bucket of cucumbers you pick," he answered, looking at both of us.

I really felt like a man, standing there with the love of my life negotiating for a job.

"How do we get to the cucumber field if we say we wanted to work?" I asked.

"A truck will come and pick you up at the corner if your parents say it's all right."

The farmer's words reminded me that I wasn't an adult yet.

"Okay, I'll be there," I said, reclaiming my manhood.

The truck appeared bright and early the next day, just as the farmer said it would. I stood at the corner, and when Mable showed up in work clothes and a signed permission slip, I was speechless. Fred and Curtis also stood, amazed and disappointed.

Fred whispered under his breath, "Why she always got to follow him everywhere?"

"Well, I know you won't get any work done today," Curtis spoke in my direction.

Curtis and Fred were still upset over the fact that I allowed a girl to come between the Pine Street Patriots and me. Both he and Fred tried ignoring me during the entire ride to the cucumber field, but I could see and feel the anger in their eyes.

Before us ran rows and rows of cucumbers; there must have been miles of them. All the workers gathered beneath the farm shed to be given instructions.

"Y'all must make sure you pick the right size cucumbers," the foreman shouted, as he held up an example. "Make sure you fill your bucket, or you'll be sent back without your money."

The foreman showed us the window where we were to take our buckets of cucumbers once they were filled.

"When your bucket is checked, and everything is all right, the person behind the window will give you four quarters for both your buckets. Any questions?" he finished.

"This is going to be easy," Fred grinned. "Let's see who can make the most money," he challenged us.

The majority of teenagers in the field that day were Black. I thought, This is the way it must have looked on slave plantations. I was embarrassed to be there with Mable.

Fred and Curtis had already been to the pay window at least four times before I filled one bucket. Mable and I spent the time talking and passing love looks. It was in a cucumber field that we stole our first kiss. So what if Fred and Curtis made more money than we did? I had received something money couldn't buy.

But now I wanted a real job so I could take Mable on a real date. I wanted to make enough money to take her out to one of those Black movies like *Shaft* that was playing at the Gibson Theater on Main Street. All the Black exploitation movies were shown at the Gibson Theater: *Shaft, Super Fly, Foxy Brown,* and *Trouble Man,* just to name a few.

I had been to the theater all of three times—each time with at least some of the Pine Street Patriots. If we couldn't sneak in, we used free matinee coupons clipped from the Laurinburg Exchange newspaper. The first movie I ever saw was *Pufnstuf*. But now that I was a man with a girl, I needed money to go see a real movie.

Washing windows for five dollars a day was the ticket. "The Glamour Shop" job came courtesy of Fred's aunt, Barbara Ann. She worked at the downtown dress shop for women. Both the Gibson Theater and The Glamour Shop were well within walking distance of Newtown.

Mable and I spent many weekends walking to the theater hand in hand. Cars would stop and men would whistle and make catcalls at Mable. "Hi, baby, what's your name?" "Is that your little brother?"

Those words always stung. Mable always assured me that there was no reason to be angry or jealous.

"Leonard, I've made my choice and nothing can change that. I love you and don't you forget that." Mable reached over and with a passionate kiss made sure I understood loud and clear.

But I was still jealous. I remember the time Alrechio, the boy I assumed was my replacement in the Pine Street Patriots, called Mable a "red-bone fox." "Red bone" was the term used to describe light-skinned Black girls.

"I'd like to try my luck with the red-bone fox Mable," he teased.

We rolled down the hill together with my fist giving him a good going over.

"What did you say about Mable?" I screamed the question with each blow.

"Leonard, you must be crazy," Curtis said. "Rechio didn't mean nothing. He was only teasing."

"Well, he had no business talking about Mable like that," I said between deep breaths of exhaustion.

My days as a Pine Street Patriot were indeed numbered. All my time was spent with Mable. She was a gift from God, especially after Grandma Gladys died. There was no way I could have made it through that experience without another love to bear me up.

I did not understand how Mable did it. I was only fifteen. Maybe it was because she understood lost love, having lost her mother. Whatever it was and however she did it, I could see my grandma's promise of a silver lining in every minute spent with Mable. I tried to love her with what little understanding I had about love, but she always found a way to give more.

Mable was truly a silver lining in my life. She taught me that love doesn't consist of material or conditioned limitations. Mable could have chosen anybody. Why did she choose a skinny underage poverty-stricken boy like me? Mable taught me that love opens all doors and breaks down all barriers. She taught me that love is the greatest silver lining of all. Through Mable, I realized that every moment of life has its silver lining if we but trust in love.

I trusted the love of my Grandma Gladys. I trusted the love of a family circle. I trusted love through animals. I trusted love in the Pine Street Patriots. I trusted love in the hardest of times.

Now I knew the true source of all silver linings. Therefore, I understood that if I trusted love, it would always reveal, in all life's circumstances, the next silver lining.

It was through my love for Mable that I gathered the courage to seek my birth certificate. Surely, I thought, a driver's license would impress her. My trust in her love for me had indirectly opened the door of discovery. It led to the discovery of my birth. It led to the discovery of God's desire to teach me that I was somebody. It led to the discovery that I was born to love and to be loved in spite of poverty, the struggles for status, and the world's desire to say I didn't count because of the color of my skin and my social location.

I was a person with a history shaped by each and every silver lining. Now with a courage born of love, I could walk into any courthouse and ask for a delayed birth certificate. It crushed my heart that Grandma Gladys never lived to witness me holding that certificate stamped with a government seal proving I was not invisible. In my heart, I knew Grandma was rejoicing as I gave my birth certificate to the driver's education teacher.

But the greater certainty was that Grandma Gladys knew long before this thin piece of material validation that I was somebody and much more. Her words of spiritual validation still echo through my soul when I feel like giving up: "Remember, Leonard, behind every dark cloud there is a silver lining."

Chapter 9

Fields of Dreams

I had always dreamed of attending Laurinburg Junior High School. The classical Greek architectural structure had two huge columns towering skyward. These columns supported the roof like Atlas holding the weight of the world on his shoulders. I always got the impression that I was ascending to the very top of Mount Olympus every time I climbed up the countless stairs that led into the building.

Laurinburg Junior High School was constructed in 1922 and was used as the segregated Laurinburg High School until Scotland High School was occupied in 1968.

My fascination with Laurinburg Junior High was largely a result of previously attending a segregated school that was a carbon copy of the other African-American schools in the county. I knew that I was going to school to learn, not to admire the building, but I was tired of walking the halls of a bland, one-level structure. Why did I have to attend a school with no architectural style?

Laurinburg Junior High School was different. This building had personality! Its walls seemed to hold countless secrets. I wanted to know what power this building gave the generations of White students who separated themselves from us behind its massive walls. Segregation with its Jim Crow laws had indeed made Laurinburg Junior High School a haven for the White children of God.

Summer was a time that we usually wanted to last forever, but the summer of 1972 brought with it new dreams—dreams of finally getting the opportunity to attend Laurinburg Junior High in the fall. The heat of that summer brought with it a preoccupation with Laurinburg Junior High, and this was one summer that I wished would end quickly. Everything we did that summer was somehow connected to that school.

We had already taken the audacious liberty of naming our group of friends after its football team. And it wasn't long before we decided to cut the bottoms off our T-shirts to create football jerseys.

"Leonard, have you lost your mind!" my mama would scream. "You're already walking 'round here half-naked!"

She spoke the truth.

"What in the world are you going to wear when winter comes and all your T-shirts are useless?"

"But Mama, you don't understand. All the boys on the football teams wear their jersey cut like this. It shows off their stomach muscles."

"Yeah, but I bet those boys ain't foolish enough to cut up all their clothes. I bet they will have T-shirts for the winter," Mama said, still not understanding. "I'm around here raking and scraping to keep y'all in decent clothes, and as soon as my back is turned, you cutting them up!"

My mama ranted on like a mad woman. "I'll tell you what—I don't care what the style is. I better not find another T-shirt with the bottom cut off it!"

But I was a fool for Laurinburg Junior High School, and my T-shirt jersey had to be perfect, even if the consequences meant one of my mama's infamous whippings. A teenager had to do what a teenager had to do.

The Pine Street Patriots followed my lead, and we played all of our sandlot football games during the summer in T-shirts with the bottoms cut off. The damage to our T-shirts extended beyond just cutting the bottoms off them. We went a step further and dared to write our favorite player's number on the back with green magic marker.

"Leonard, what number you going to choose?" Fred asked before clawing for the magic marker.

"I'm gonna be number twelve, and nobody else better take it either!" I answered Fred before releasing the marker.

"I don't want that number anyway," Fred shot back in my direction. "I want a wide receiver's number, because I'm the best pass catcher around here."

"Fred, you know you're dreaming," Glenn countered. "You know good and well that Kish Johnson is the best wide receiver at Laurinburg Junior High."

Fred refused to let the argument go. "Uh, Glenn, you need to have your ears checked." he retaliated. "Sylvester, you heard me. Tell that moron what I said. I said I was the best pass catcher around here. I didn't say nothing about Laurinburg Junior High School."

"I wasn't paying you no attention," Sylvester responded, much to Fred's dismay.

"Y'all just jealous," Fred huffed. "We'll see who's the best once we get to The Field."

Our sandlot football field stood in the shadow of two slum landmarks, the Laurinburg Milling Company and the Laurinburg and Southern Railroad Shop. "The Field," as we affectionately called it, was a multipurpose sports venue. The mostly dirt playing surface area doubled as a football field and a baseball diamond. It was the ideal setting for ragamuffin want-to-be superstars like the Pine Street Patriots.

"Come on! Let's go!" Robert screamed from Mrs. Lucy's back porch.

In lightning speed, everyone was standing in Mrs. Lucy's backyard dressed in white cut-off T-shirts.

"Leonard, where's your T-shirt?" Fred said, grinning.

"Yeah, Leonard, you were the one fighting over the number twelve. Now let's see it," Sylvester said.

"Don't worry. I got my shirt and you'll see when I get ready to show it to y'all," I answered.

"He ain't going to show us that T-shirt until we get to the field 'cause he's scared his mama might see him!" Fred knowingly replied.

Fred was right. After my mama's warning, I had taken the precaution of hiding my T-shirt underneath my bed mattress. On football game days, I would slip it underneath the shirt I was wearing until I was out of her eyesight.

"Just wait 'til we get to the field, Fred. You better hope you don't catch one pass near me, because if you catch the ball where I can reach you, I'm going to hit you so hard your grandma's going to feel it!" I yelled in Fred's direction.

"I ain't worried about you, Leonard. You got to catch me first," Fred replied.

"That won't be so hard because you limp-legged and pigeon-toed on top of it," I said, laughing.

We used the time on the field during the summer to hone our skills in hopes of making the junior high football team in the fall. It went without saying that Coach McCracken was a tough disciplinarian and a no-nonsense person when it came to his football team. You could not just walk on the field during tryouts and expect to make the team. Therefore, we played that summer so hard and intensely that we ended up with injuries that would have surely sent the average person to the hospital.

On the first play, Fred got the football, and he tauntingly decided to run right in my direction. Like a hunter looking at his prey down the scope of a hunting rifle, I eyed Fred as he ran toward the two oak trees that served as the end zone.

I heard the voices from the sidelines, "Run, Fred! Run!"

As Fred got closer to the end zone, I could see a big grin plastered across his face. He was licking his chops in great anticipation of scoring.

"He's going to run right over you!" Sylvester cried—at least I think it was Sylvester's voice. I could not tell who it was.

I had tuned out everybody and was focused on the speeding body heading in my direction. My only concern at the moment was how I was going to stop this rumbling ball of momentum. Fred outweighed me by at least fifteen pounds, but I did not care.

I was determined to pay him back for causing everybody to laugh at me in Mrs. Lucy's backyard. Instinctively, I lowered my head like a charging bull and rushed straight for Fred's stomach. On impact, I buried my head into his midsection, wrapped my arms around his legs, lifted him off the ground, and forced him backward flat on his back.

"Man, Leonard, that was some kind of hit!" Glenn cried as he rushed towards me, his eyes wide with amazement. "If you do that in front of Coach McCracken, you won't have any trouble making the team."

"He just made a lucky hit," Fred embarrassingly cried, wiping dust from his clothes.

Eventually, we grew tired of punishing one another and decided that maybe some cross-town rivalry might be in order. Sandlot games with other community football teams were ferocious competition. Carolina Park, Cross the Creek, Muda Grass Hill, and Washington Park all sported teams that fought for summer bragging rights on the playing fields of their respective communities.

No one wanted to lose in front of their home crowds. The most feared football team was from Washington Park. They had been the team to beat among the Black community for as long as anybody could remember. Theirs was a hard-earned reputation, but almost everybody knew it had been won mainly because of one particular player.

Every community had at least one secret weapon, and Kish Johnson was Washington Park's. Kish was a born athlete who excelled not only at football but basketball and baseball. If we could defeat Washington Park, surely Coach McCracken would have to take notice. Whipping Washington Park would be the talk of Laurinburg; nobody had been able to beat them for two straight years.

Kish was the star athlete on the Laurinburg Junior High School football team. It seemed like he played without effort. Kish was the major reason why Laurinburg Junior High had defeated all the county junior high schools. They had beaten I. Ellis Johnson, Shaw, Carver, and Rockingham. Kish was a two-way starter on the team; he played wide receiver on offense and defensive back on defense.

It was with both excitement and anxiety that we all agreed with Fred that we should play Washington Park.

"Yeah, that's a good idea, Fred. We can see if you're as good as what you claim to be," Curtis said.

"That's right. We'll see where all your bragging will go when Kish gets through with you," I added.

The game would take place on enemy territory. We were the only team that played all of our games "away," and the Washington Park event would be no different. Our godforsaken home field was a hand-me-down, with the Laurinburg and Southern Shop as a backdrop and the train tracks running parallel to our makeshift gridiron. It was a miracle that we did not suffer more noncontact injuries from all of the rocks and holes that littered our field.

Washington Park, on the other hand, played their sandlot pickup games on the well-manicured county parks and recreation field. This field had chalk-marked yard lines and the luxury of all luxuries—goal posts. Washington Park was the only Black neighborhood with a county park right in the community.

The closest park to those of us unfortunate enough to be born on the wrong side of the tracks was in redneck territory at Jaycees Park on Gill Street. So if we wanted to play Kish Johnson and the Washington Park team, we had the choice of either risking getting our butts kicked on a ragged field like ours or walking to Washington Park. It would be bad enough if we lost. When it could be easily avoided, we did not want to risk becoming the laughing stock of Laurinburg on two accounts—losing the game, and losing on our rundown, ragged field. But if we could win the game on their field and against their number one weapon, we felt we would be assured some spots on the junior high team. The news would certainly get spread all over town, and Coach McCracken would surely get word of our victory.

"We better stop trying to kill each other and save ourselves for the game against Washington Park," Fred said.

"But we still got to hit hard or else those boys over there will kill us, and we can forget about playing for Laurinburg Junior High School," Robert responded.

"Yeah, you know we got to get ready for Kish," I reminded them.

"I'm getting tired of y'all talking about Kish like he's some kind of God. He ain't all that good," Sylvester replied scornfully.

"Okay, let's start drawing up our plays," Curtis said, claiming our attention.

It was assumed that Fred would be our coach. He had played Pop Warner football for the county team and did not mind letting you know it. Even though the Scotland County Redskins were the sorriest team in the county, Fred was the only one of the Pine Street Patriots who had any experience at organized football. We needed to have a coach with "real" football experience, and Fred was our only guy who had it.

A long narrow stick served as Fred's chalk, and the dusty sand of the field was his chalkboard for drawing x's and o's.

"Now Glenn, since you're the biggest person on our team, you're going to have to play on the offensive and defensive lines," Fred said.

But before he finished barking out his orders the mutiny began.

"I don't want to play on the line. I want to play running back," Glenn protested.

"And you know who the quarterback is going to be," I chimed in.

"I'm going to be the quarterback!" Fred shouted.

"I thought you said you were the best pass catcher in the world," I replied, questioning Fred's sudden change of heart. "Why you want to change now?"

"I know the real reason you're switching positions. You just chicken that's all, Fred, because you know you might have to cover Kish Johnson," Sylvester said.

And we all knew it was true.

"I'm just trying to give us the best chance to win," Fred responded, attempting to recover his reputation. "We better stop arguing and get our plays together. If we're going to have any chance at winning, we've got to be a team."

That sounded like coach talk to me, so I dropped my protest and settled for playing wide receiver and defensive back.

Fred, who was deadly serious about his duties, was dubbed "Coach Bo Snack." He wanted our field to look as much like a football field as possible. So he prepared it before practice. He drew yard lines using sand poured from a bag with a hole in it and then used the same technique to outline, in bold letters, "The Pine Street Patriots," between the end zone oak trees.

We would show up at the field for practice with old shirts stuffed in the shoulders of our T-shirts to be used as shoulder pads and cotton in our pant legs for knee pads. Sylvester even put old clothes in the back of his pants for what he called "butt pads." That drove Fred crazy, because he did not think we were being serious enough.

"Y'all must think them boys in Washington Park are playing. I bet they ain't acting silly like y'all," Fred yelled.

"Lighten up, Coach Bo Snack," Curtis joked, causing Fred to rant and rave like a true coach.

"Y'all take that junk out of y'all pants so we can practice. I've spent all this time getting this ragged field ready—the least y'all can do is take me serious!" Fred pleaded.

"You mean take you serious like when you rode the bench in pee-wee football?" I teased.

Robert put a stop to the teasing. "Leonard, we better listen. You know we don't have that much time to get ready for Kish Johnson."

"Okay, let's go on and practice," I said, taking the clothes and cotton out of my clothes.

"I ain't taking my butt pads out. I don't care what Fred says," Sylvester defiantly said.

"Well, if you want to look like an idiot, just keep them in," Fred responded in exasperation.

"I ain't worried about how I look. I'm worried about how it's going to feel when my butt hits this hard ground."

With each practice, we grew more confident that we could give Kish's team a good run for their money, but Coach Bo Snack did not think so. He tried to run us into the ground.

"If we don't slow down and stop hurting each other, we ain't going to have enough people to play the stupid game," I warned Fred.

"Okay, crybaby, we can take tomorrow off," Fred answered, as if he were the coach of an NFL team.

The day finally arrived for the big game. There would be no chartered planes or buses to carry us to the road game against Washington Park. We had to walk across town with our cut-off T-shirts.

"I hope we win, because I sure do want to play for Laurinburg Junior High School in the fall," I said, looking back at Fred.

"It's next to impossible for an eighth grader to make the team, but I think if we win this game our chances are as good as anybody else's," Glenn observed.

With optimism and hope, we walked past the Laurinburg Milling Company and Central School.

"Let's stop by and see Spaghetti Man," somebody said from the back of the line.

"We ain't got time to be stopping to look at some old mummy," Fred responded.

"Fred, you just scared, that's all. You scared you might see Spaghetti Man in your room at night," I teased.

Spaghetti Man was a mummy that was kept at McDougald's Funeral Home. The stories surrounding his death had become part of the oral tradition of Scotland County. Everybody had their own personal Spaghetti Man story.

According to one version of the story, Spaghetti Man was a circus worker who was murdered while the circus was in town. The funeral home kept his body waiting for a family member to come to claim it. The long wait turned from weeks into months into years. They could not bury the body without the consent of his family, and when no one ever responded, the funeral home was stuck with the dead man's body. The decision was made to place the mummified body in a special airtight window display case. McDougald's funeral home would let anyone interested in seeing the body view it at no cost.

It was part of our rite of passage before attending the seventh grade at Central School. If you did not want to be teased throughout seventh grade by everybody in town, you needed to muster up enough courage at some point to go and see Spaghetti Man alone.

The memories of my first stop to view Spaghetti Man helped take my mind off the football game as I began to reminisce about my just-completed days at Central School. It was the stepping stone before junior high school, and one did not want to be in junior high having never seen Spaghetti Man. There were no excuses for any of us failing to see Spaghetti Man. We walked past McDougald's Funeral Home on the way to school every day.

I remembered my first time. My steps appeared to be calculated that day. I woke with the determination that this would be the day. I had put it off long enough, and I was tired of being teased about my fear of Spaghetti Man.

"Leonard, when you going to stop being a baby?" I heard the taunts over and over again. "You're getting ready to start seventh grade and you ain't even seen Spaghetti Man."

"Yes I have too seen him," I replied defensively. "It was between the fourth and fifth grade."

I began attending integrated schools in fourth grade—the first of which was Covington Street School. I moved to Covington thanks to Scotland County's desegregation program. It, like all White schools, was a neighborhood school located in a lily-White community.

As a fourth grader, I immediately noticed the differences between this school and the one I had been forced to attend because of my race.

Covington Street School was nestled in a well-manicured, eloquently landscaped setting. The trees were the first obvious thing one noticed walking up to the school. There had been practically no trees at I. Ellis Johnson School; at least they were not a part of the design or landscape. Maybe that was an unspoken reminder that Blacks belonged in the hot sun while Whites belonged in the shade.

It was a difficult transition for me to make. I sat there in a classroom filled with White students whose clothes and shoes were always better than mine. If I failed to recognize the difference in such an obvious manner, my fourth grade teacher always made it clear every morning that I walked into her class.

Her words greeted me each morning. "Leonard, come here. I want you to take this soap, washcloth, and comb and go into the bathroom and clean yourself up. You know you can't come to school looking and smelling like you haven't taken a bath!"

My teacher would embarrassingly admonish me in front of the whole class. She never seemed concerned about why I came to school the way I did. She never visited my home, where she would find seven brothers and sisters sleeping in the same bed. She never bothered to find out that taking a bath in my house meant building a fire in a wood-burning stove and filling wash tubs with water from a faucet that often froze during the winter. She never knew that hot water coming straight from a faucet was a luxury not afforded to me. The only hot water I knew was the kind that was heated in a tin tub on a stove.

She never bothered to discover that there was little money to get clothes washed at the nearest laundromat within walking distance.

She never knew that the closest laundromat was three miles away and that to get there you had to pile the dirty clothes on a wagon and pull it all the way.

I had thought that coming to Covington Street School would at least give me something that would help me feel like somebody. I thought that it would be a White person who would make me feel unwanted, but injustice knows no color. Why did it have to be somebody Black, and why a teacher?

My teacher was one of the Black teachers who were reassigned to a White school as a means to make integration a two-way thing for both students and teachers. I do not know if she was attempting to distance herself from me in order to make clear for her White students the obvious social class distinction between us. I had heard of "uppity niggers" before this experience. They were African Americans who did everything to let others know they were different from "lower-class niggers," as they called people like me.

I would soon learn that field trips were another one of the privileged luxuries I would get to experience now that I was in the social in-group. Yes, that was another benefit of attending an integrated school. I had never left the confines of my old, segregated school's playground and hallways, but it was a different story at Covington Street School.

Our destination one day was the Morehead Planetarium in Chapel Hill, North Carolina. I was getting the opportunity to step foot on a university campus for the first time in my life. I was leaving the city of Laurinburg for the first time. My excitement over such a venture showed in the enthusiastic way I sold bottles to get spending money.

My teacher informed us that we each would be responsible for our lunch money and any money for souvenirs.

"We will be stopping at Chips for lunch," she told us. "Make sure that your parents give you enough money. We'll spend the whole day in Chapel Hill. I've written your parents a permission slip that also explains our lunch plans. Please make sure your parents read the note carefully and send it back to me signed."

I could barely contain my excitement as I floated home down King Street toward our tin shanty. Walking in the glow of the spring afternoon, I devised plans to make money for lunch and souvenirs. I quickly that realized my only option was to do what we had always done to get money—sell bottles at Mr. Bub Stewart's store. I could not count on my brothers helping me this time. I was on my own.

As hard as I hunted for bottles, at the end of the day I could only salvage one hundred bottles, which added up to two dollars. Looking at the twenty dimes Mr. Bub counted into my open palm, I could feel the tears of disappointment welling up in my eyes. I could not let Mr. Bub see me crying, but as soon as I turned and walked out of the store, the floodgates opened. What could I buy with two dollars?

The trip to Chapel Hill was only two days away and there was no chance of adding any more money to my two dollars. I knew it was a futile gesture to ask Mama for money; it was all she could do to keep food on the table. The thought ran through my mind to ask my teacher for help. After all, she was a sister; maybe she would help a brother out. However, that option quickly disappeared as I remembered her daily routine of embarrassing me about my lack of cleanliness. I did not want to give her new weapons to use in her attacks. I would attempt as much as possible to conceal my meager funds, but there was no way I was going to miss this trip.

The day of our departure finally arrived.

"Leonard, I want you to ride with me in Susan's mother's car," my teacher ordered as we stood outside the covered walkway of Covington Street School. It would be the first time I had ever ridden in a White person's car. I guess she wanted me with her at all times, waiting for the next opportunity to embarrass and low-rate me.

Susan's mother was nice enough. The station wagon's back seat was folded down to allow extra room. Susan's mother even brought board games for us to play as we traveled down US Highway 1. I remember that at one point the radio was playing The First Dimensions' "Up, Up and Away in my Beautiful Balloon," which made the atmosphere a bit more pleasant.

Unfortunately, most of my time during the trip was consumed by thoughts of how I was going to keep everybody from finding out that I only had two dollars. I could not enjoy the ride, music, or games, not to mention what was left of the beautiful fall colors.

The Morehead Planetarium was a treat. For once, I allowed the thoughts of self-doubt and poverty to disappear. I allowed myself to be a child. In wide-eyed amazement, I excitedly walked from one exhibit to the next. I even allowed myself to join in the devious game of using static electricity flowing through the carpet to shock unsuspecting classmates. But as usual, my teacher always seemed to catch me.

"Leonard, you go to the back of the line," she turned to face me.

The planetarium was filled with students from other cities and counties. The Star of Bethlehem was a popular feature that started in late October and ran through late November for school field trips. I felt so small when I looked up into the dome as the narrator told the story of Jesus's birth. He used the huge machine in the center of the room to tell how stars in the sky played a significant part in the birth of Jesus.

The twinkling stars covered the dome, but seeing stars on the ceiling was nothing unusual for me. I had become accustomed to seeing stars through the roof. Many of my nights had been spent staring at stars from our bed before the landlord fixed the gaping hole in the roof. We had a front-seat view in our very own private planetarium. The Big Dipper or any other stars we wished to see were always in full view on cloudless nights.

However, I still sat there transfixed by this marvelous and mysterious machine that could magically and instantly cause stars to appear in broad daylight. The show ended, and the narrator reminded us that we could stop by the gift shop after the show.

Teachers scrambled to keep their classes together. I silently stood back and watched the other children buying souvenirs. I watched as my classmates purchased the popular Master the Force Gyroscopes.

"Come on, let me try to balance it on this string," I heard the boys chatter. "It says in the directions that if you spin it fast enough you can balance it on the edge of an index card."

At the planetarium gift shop, I knew better than to enter their world of excitement, because there was no way I could afford a Master the Force Gyroscope. I did not even want to touch one for fear of not being able to conceal my hurt and disappointment. I simply walked over to the glass case that held the gyroscopes. I peered through the glass at the metal objects in their attractive boxes. With my sweaty fingers, I felt the twenty dimes in my pocket. I turned and walked dejectedly away from the counter.

The bus ride to Chips hamburger restaurant became an exercise in sorrow and self-doubt. I renewed my effort to think about ways of getting my food without letting the others know I had only two dollars for lunch.

"Leonard, you come up here with me and buy your food," my teacher said, speaking the words I dreaded hearing.

Her words were like the kiss of death.

"Can I help you, young man?" The smiling face in the striped chef's hat grinned down at me.

I know my teacher could hear the tears in my voice as I responded with trembling words. "Yes, I want a hamburger and a small milkshake."

"That will be one dollar and fifty cents," the uniformed voice spoke again. I reached into my pocket for the dimes that were now moist from the sweat of my hand.

"Leonard, is that all the money you brought with you?" my teacher asked in disbelief.

"Yes, that's all that I have," I answered.

"Did you show your parents the note I sent home with you?"

"They saw it," I mumbled.

"Speak up, young man, I can't hear you." She seemed to be relishing the opportunity to make me suffer. "If they read the note, why did they send you on a field trip with just two dollars?"

"My mama didn't get paid, so I had to sell bottles to get enough money for lunch," I answered.

"Well, go on. Take your lunch and sit down over there to eat," she said, directing me to my place with the other classmates.

I sat at the back of the restaurant, where the eyes of the whole class had followed me with pity, and ate my hamburger in relative peace.

Therefore, when I learned that I would be promoted to fifth grade and would be assigned to Central School on the corner of James and McRae Streets, I was overjoyed. Finally, I would no longer be put through the hell of my teacher's torture.

When my friends challenged me for never having seen Spaghetti Man as we walked to the big game with Washington Park, I remembered that the summer before entering the fifth grade, I had talked Fred, Sylvester, and Glenn into walking up to Central with the intention of discovering who our teachers would be. I was determined to know the identity of my teacher would be so that I could be prepared, just in case I ended up with another teacher like the one I'd had in fourth grade.

"Let's stop by and see Spaghetti Man, since the funeral home is on the same street as the school," I suggested.

"I don't want to see that ugly thing," Fred replied, with a hint of fear in his voice.

"Yeah, let's stop," Sylvester and Glenn chimed in.

I could feel Fred's fear as we walked up to the funeral home's garage, which held the remains of Laurinburg's most famous citizen. I reached for the doorbell, rang it, and within seconds Mr. McDougald stood at the door.

"I guess you boys want to see Spaghetti Man," Mr. McDougald said, reading our minds.

"Yes, sir, we were on our way to see our new school and thought if it was no trouble, you could let us see Spaghetti Man for a second," Sylvester replied as our polite spokesperson.

"You boys sure you're old enough to see him without having nightmares?" Mr. McDougald asked, looking straight at me.

"We ain't scared. We're going into the fifth grade. We won't have no nightmares," I answered confidently.

"Okay, let's go!" Mr. McDougald said.

"You mean there's a dead man in that little thing?" Fred spoke.

Mr. McDougald responded by reaching up toward the gabled display case hanging on the wall as if Fred had said nothing. The door began to squeak open and each of us took a few steps backward.

"I thought you told me you were big fifth graders and were not afraid," Mr. McDougald said, smiling.

I took a baby step forward to prove I was not afraid, and while I was in the process of making that step, the doors of Spaghetti Man's final resting place swung open suddenly and without warning.

I do not know if we were plain stupid or just too afraid to run. We stood there, mouths wide open, with fear running through our spines, gaping at the remains of Spaghetti Man. I distinctly remember seeing the other tiny figures at his feet—what appeared to be mummified babies sat at the bottom of the display case.

Without speaking or mumbling a word, we ran from the funeral home on feet that would have made Mercury or The Flash proud. We did not stop until we reached Central School.

It took us a full ten minutes before we could even talk. We stood, hands on knees, gasping for air.

"You remember how we stopped by the funeral home on our way to Central School so we could find out who our teachers would be?" I said, refreshing their memories of that day when I had seen Spaghetti Man for the first time.

"Yeah, but you ain't never seen him by yourself, and you'll be the laughing stock of Laurinburg Junior High School if you don't go see him by yourself," Sylvester warned.

"Well, like Fred said, we ain't got time to stop now, cause we've got a football game to play," I replied.

Destiny awaited us in Washington Park and the journey down McRae Street continued as we passed McDougald's Funeral Home without so much as a backward glance.

"I can't wait until we get to the football field," Fred said, renewing our resolve.

"Yeah, I just want to see what's so great about Kish," Glenn said.

"Well, you'll see up close and personal," Robert prophesied.

"I don't see what you're worried about, Robert. You ain't playing defense against him," I said.

Main Street Laurinburg turned into Business Highway 74 as it crossed at the corner of James Street where First Baptist Church stood, guardian of the crossroads. Central School loomed just across the street.

Once again, I was tempted to take a trip down memory lane. The football game loomed in the immediate future, but being so close to Central School drew me like a magnet.

"Let's stop by Central and get one last look at our old school," I said.

"Leonard, what's wrong with you always wanting to stop? We ain't never going to get to Washington Park," Fred said.

"If we can't stop, let's at least walk by it," I pleaded.

"Okay, but we ain't stopping," Fred ordered.

I guess it's like that when a person moves from one transition to the next. Maybe the past gives them the courage to move into the future. Central School was one of the places in my personal journey that reminded me of Grandma Gladys's promise of silver linings.

I'd always heard of people seeing their lives flash before their eyes, but I thought it took a near death experience to trigger such a reaction. As I walked past the colonial-style building on our way to do battle with Kish Johnson and Washington Park, a flood of memories of my life at Central for the past few years swept before my eyes. It was in this building that my fragile self-esteem would gain some of the confidence that it desperately needed.

The first such boost had come during the school's annual "field day" celebration.

Mr. Stewart had already given us a list of all the events that would take place at the late spring ritual. The list included events such as the hilarious suitcase relay race, where teams would race up and down the field changing clothes from inside a suitcase with each other until a winner was declared. The relay races were among the most popular events. Another was my event, the pole climb.

"Come on, Leonard!" the cries from my fellow classmates swelled my already anxious heart. "You can do it!"

I had eliminated all the competition except my chief rival, Theodore, another lanky athlete who was as quick as greased lightning. I watched him cut down opponent after opponent with little trouble. I wondered if I would be next.

My heart pounded as Mr. Stewart's voice boomed, "On your mark, get set, go!"

Up the metal pole I scampered without taking a breath. I feared that breathing would slow me down.

"You did it, Leonard!" the voices from below greeted me as I slid down the pole.

I could finally breathe. I had defeated Theodore, the reigning pole climbing champion for the past two years.

"Leonard, how did you make it up that pole so quickly?" Mr. Stewart jubilantly asked.

"I was scared to death!" I answered truthfully.

For once in my life, I could claim the title of "Big Man on Campus."

I was the man, at least for that day at Central. I had discovered my natural athletic ability. But today, I knew I would need every bit of that ability to keep up with Kish Johnson.

Our journey of destiny continued as we followed the route I had walked for three years—one year as a seventh grade safety patrol. Walking to school was a small price to pay for having the power to stop traffic. I was now losing that power as I was preparing to enter

Laurinburg Junior High School, but I did not mind, especially if we could win this football game. Once again the memories flooded my mind.

How it happened, I could not recall. All I could remember was the overwhelming joy of being selected to be a Central School safety patrol.

I wore my white harness and badge with pride. I was even given a stop sign to hold in front of traffic. I could not help being moved by the memory of feeling so important. The disappointment of Covington Street School and my old teacher seemed light years away. I was finally somebody.

I was now ready to take it to the next level. The football game with Washington Park and Kish Johnson would be my test. I had been the man at Central and had no intention of being anything short of that at Laurinburg Junior High School.

The reminiscing came to an end as we approached the Washington Park county recreation field. I looked around at the well-disciplined players who would be our competition for the evening.

Then, in comparison, I gazed on the pitiful sight of the team we had assembled to play this game. If looking like out-of-place bandits could ensure victory, we would certainly have no trouble winning this game. We looked like alley cats that had seen our share of roughhouse fights. However, tough looks alone would not win us this game.

After weeks of practice and anticipation, I could not believe that the game was about to start. Coaches settled on the rules and quickly explained them to us. During this explanation, much to our surprise, the person who had become public enemy number one walked over and shook each of our hands. Kish walked down our bench, hand extended, saying, "Good luck. I hope y'all have a good game."

Kish's voice seemed out of character for a person who was feared by so many. To our surprise, he had the voice of a sweet, innocent child.

"He doesn't sound so tough to me," Fred said.

"Yeah, he don't look all that big, either," I added, agreeing for the moment with Fred's assessment of the man we were supposed to do everything in our power to stop.

"He sounds like a little kid," Sylvester added.

"Yeah, like he wouldn't or couldn't hurt a fly!" Robert concluded.

My grandma had always countered my low self-esteem with the proverbial words, "You can't judge a book by its cover." I did not realize that I would learn that lesson again on a grass field on a hot summer day in Washington Park.

I should have known what this day would hold right after we lost the coin toss.

"Fred, do you want me to kick it away from Kish?" asked Robert, our designated kickoff specialist.

"I think we better see what he's got right off the bat. I don't think he can run it back against us," Fred answered. Then he barked out his first order in the huddle. "Leonard, you get ready to tackle him like you did me. Hit him right in the midsection—that ought to take some of the wind out of his sail."

Kish caught the ball deep in the end zone and ran straight in my direction. I lowered my head just as I had done when Fred attempted to run me over. *I can stop him*, I said to myself. *He ain't as big as Fred. This should be a piece of cake.*

The move Kish made was effortless; he sidestepped me and, with the speed of a deer, outran our entire team.

"Leonard, I thought you had him!" Robert yelled.

"I thought I did too, but he's too fast," I replied, trying to justify my failure to stop Kish.

"Let me play defense on him the next time they have the football," Fred said. "I'll show you how to put a stop to him. It's our ball now; let's get ready to play some offense! We've got to score on them before this thing gets out of control quick."

It did not take us very long to realize that things were already out of control. They had been so since the minute we walked onto the field.

"We've got to go with our best play now," Fred spoke in the offensive huddle as he drew the play with his finger on the ground. "Leonard, you and Sylvester line up as wide receivers on the corners. Run your patterns down the sidelines." He confidently pointed his skinny finger at us. "Once you get in the end zone, you crisscross and I'll throw the ball to the one who is in the open."

It was our bread-and-butter play. It had worked before, and we saw no reason why it would not work now.

Down the field we raced, easily out-running Washington Park's front line of defense. Just as Fred had drawn it, Sylvester and I crisscrossed, but as soon as Fred released the football, Kish came out of nowhere, intercepted the ball, and ran into the opposite end zone for a Washington Park touchdown.

"They stopped our best play," Sylvester shouted at an already-livid Fred.

"I hope this game ends quick—I'm tired of chasing Kish up and down this field," I said exhaustedly.

Mercifully, the game finally ended. We learned the painful truth that the sound of a person's voice and how he looks can be deceiving.

The team from Washington Park, true to form, ran us ragged.

Once again, Kish surprised us by coming over and, without gloating in victory, thanked us for coming to play against them. Kish's gesture of compassion lifted our spirits after such a devastating loss.

I broke the silence of a dejected group of would-be warriors as we made the painful trek back to Newtown.

"They kicked our butts, but Kish ain't half bad."

"What do you mean, he ain't half bad?" Robert responded.

"He almost single-handedly whipped us," Fred said, still fuming.

"No. I mean he's a nice guy," I clarified.

"Yeah, you can afford to be nice when you're that good," Sylvester added.

"Well, I just think it was nice of him not to rub defeat in our faces. You know if we had won, we would never have let them live it down," I said.

"Well, I guess we can kiss any chance of making the Laurinburg Junior High School football team goodbye," Glenn stated.

Fred finally spoke. "I ain't giving up so quick."

"Yeah, I'm still going out for the team," I added.

"I don't think Coach McCracken will hold this loss against us, if he even hears about it," Robert said.

Our depression over the defeat at the hands of Washington Park disappeared with the beginning of football tryouts at Laurinburg Junior High School. We received the necessary medical physicals at the county health department and were cleared for tryouts. It was good that we had a doctor's clearance before going out for one of Coach McCracken's teams, because he tried to kill us on the first day.

"It's got to be a thousand degrees out here!" I complained while Coach McCracken was drilling somebody else on the dreaded blocking sled.

"Leonard, you knew it wasn't going to be easy," Fred said as we stood waiting our turn.

"Well, I didn't know he'd try to kill us out here in the hot August sun," I replied.

"Fairley! Fred!" Coach McCracken's words shot through me. "Come on! Let's see what you got left in your tanks today!"

"Fred, you better do your part on this blocking sled; I don't want to be running no extra laps after practice today," I warned Fred as we ran toward the sled.

"When I blow this whistle, I want y'all to hit this sled like it owes you money," Coach McCracken bellowed as the whistle was already making its way up to his mouth. The whistle blew and was followed by Coach McCracken's chatter. "Come on! Is that the best you two can do? My grandma can hit harder than that! Dig deeper! Push! Put your shoulders into it, little girls!"

Coach McCracken yelled at us in sprays of words and spit.

Satisfied that we had moved both him and the sled far enough, Coach finally called on two other potential team members. Fred and I went back to our places on the sidelines with a mixture of sweat, dirt, and Coach McCracken's spit running down our faces.

"Okay, boys, take five laps around the field and hit the showers!" Coach shouted.

At the time I thought these were the kindest words anybody could every say. It was all we could do to make the walk home from practice. Each step was a trial by fire. I felt pain in places I never knew existed in my body.

"You going back tomorrow?" I asked Fred.

"Yeah, you doggone right, I'm going back. I know I can make the team," Fred confidently responded.

"I don't know," Glenn added. "It was pretty tough out there today."

"Yeah, the only person that didn't seem to be working hard was Kish," I wondered as Fred's explanation rang through the air.

"Maybe Coach just wants to save his star player for the upcoming season," Fred replied.

"That still don't make it fair—Coach trying to kill us while Kish stands on the sideline with that big grin on his face."

The complaints about injustice and favoritism did not keep us from trying. The next day, all of us were right back on the practice field for more punishment.

The tryouts lasted almost three weeks. After Coach McCracken was certain that he had drained us of every ounce of strength, he instructed us to watch the board on the field house door for the cut list.

"I just got one thing to say," Sylvester said after the final practice. "I better make this team. Every bone in my body hurts and I need something for my troubles."

No one said a word as we made our way to the field house, hoping to see our names among the elite. I never wanted to see my name in print so badly. The crowd was already gathered around the field house door, and many people were leaving dejected. However, those who made the team stayed around to see who else was lucky enough to make it.

Glenn was the first Pine Street Patriot to read his name. Glenn could not control himself. He was leaping into the air in jubilation.

"I made it! I made the team!" he screamed over and over again.

Fred and I reached the list at the same time and began frantically searching for our names, but no matter how hard we searched, our names were nowhere to be found.

"Well," Fred spoke with the hint of tears forming in his eyes. "I guess we didn't make it."

Glenn was the only Pine Street Patriot to make the team, and we knew that even in our disappointment we needed to show our support of him. Indeed, we were proud of Glenn, but now we would have to attend Laurinburg Junior High School with little chance of being noticed. It would be a hard pill to swallow not being "the man."

I thought it would be even harder to face Mable. Why would she want to be seen with a loser?

But Mable's response was just like her love for me—non-judgmental.

"Leonard, I don't love you any less because you didn't make the team," Mable said, consoling my broken ego as only she could. "I love you even more because you tried, and that's good enough for me."

Once again I was forced to wonder if Mable had dropped from some cloud in heaven. Although Mable was a junior at Scotland High School, an age difference that presented its own anxiety, her words made my first day at Laurinburg Junior High School the long-awaited joy I expected it to be.

It did not matter much that I was not "the man." I was Mable's man, and that was more than enough to soften the blow of not making the football team.

"There's always next year," Mable told me. "It's like that at Scotland, too. First-year students almost never make the team."

If not for Mable's love and wisdom, I would have given up on sports altogether. But thanks to her, I kept going.

If not for Mable, I never would have been in the Laurinburg Junior High School gym on that fateful day when all hell broke loose.

Chapter 10

Fire

Growing up with little supervision and spending most of the time outside playing in the streets, swimming in creeks, and climbing trees made us what you might call true natural athletes, even though Coach McCracken did not recognize it. I could jump like a rabbit and run like lightning but was never given a chance to play organized sports. I believe this denied privilege caused me to miss making the football team at Laurinburg Junior High School.

It was just another confirmation of poverty's deadly reach. There had been no one to get me back and forth to practices when they were not within walking distance. There was no money to buy the equipment needed to participate in organized sports, anyway.

The closest thing to organized sports competition for me was the daily intramural basketball games played in the Laurinburg Junior High School gymnasium during physical education class.

It had become the popular activity for students to attend during free period. The gym would be packed with students watching their favorite teams playing. There was nothing different about the beginning of the game on the 7th of March; it began like all other intramural basketball games. We gathered in the usual manner to play.

"I hope we win today. I'm tired of coming in here and getting whipped," Fred whined.

Fred was always trying to prove he was more than just a natural athlete, always trying to prove he could hold his own against the big boys.

"Fred, all you're going to do is sit the bench like you always do," Sylvester teased, knowing his words would infuriate Fred all the more.

"I bet I'll get in the game before you do," Fred struck back.

"Not if Kish is on his game," I said. "You know Coach McCracken will play him the whole game."

"Let's get ready to play!" Coach McCracken shouted over the crowd gathered in the gym. "This team will be skins today," he pointed in our direction.

I hated being skins, because it meant that the whole world would be looking at my bony chest. Reluctantly, I pulled my school-issued P.E. T-shirt over my head and felt the cool breeze from the gym's ceiling fans blow across my non-existent chest. I wondered why Coach McCracken was making us take off our shirts, knowing that the chances of us starting the game were slim to none.

"I ain't sitting on this bench with my shirt off in front of all these people," I frowned in Sylvester's direction.

"There must be two hundred people in here today," Fred said.

"Yeah, and here we are catching splinters when we should be out there playing some ball," I responded.

"Look at Kish! He thinks he's God's gift to the world," Sylvester noted.

The game was barely seven minutes in when Kish appeared to trip and fall on the court. Coach McCracken immediately blew his whistle for play to stop as Kish picked himself up off the floor.

"Fred, get that shirt off and go in for Kish!" Coach yelled as he removed Kish from the game.

"Johnson, you all right?" Coach McCracken asked Kish.

"Yeah, I'm okay. I just feel a little dizzy," Kish answered.

Coach McCracken checked Kish out to make sure his breathing and his reactions appeared normal.

"Johnson, you sure you're all right?" Coach McCracken asked again.

"Yeah," Kish answered, still startled over his fainting spell. He even laughed at himself for falling down on the court.

"You just stay here in the bleachers for the remainder of the game," Coach told Kish.

The game started again. Fred ran onto the court with a gleeful grin plastered across his face as he looked back at us poor bench riders.

The sound appeared to echo throughout the fifty-one-year-old gymnasium as Kish fainted again in the bleachers.

"Go call the rescue squad!" Coach McCracken yelled to his assistant coach as he leaped to the bleachers and started mouth-to-mouth resuscitation.

When Principal Burnette arrived, he helped to coordinate CPR efforts to revive Kish. The stunned crowd grew so silent one could almost hear each breath Coach McCracken blew into Kish's still body.

The rescue squad arrived and transported Kish to Scotland Memorial Hospital.

However, Coach McCracken's face bore the truth—Kish was already dead.

Principal Burnette cleared the gym and assured us that he would share any news from the hospital whenever it became available.

The scream could be heard all the way down the hall in Mr. Isler's Science class when Mr. Burnette shared the news with Wanda, Kish's younger sister.

Kish Aaron Johnson was pronounced dead on arrival at Scotland Memorial Hospital. The unofficial opinion indicated death may have been the result of a heart attack.

The walk from school that day was filled with questions for which none of us seemed to have the answers. How were we supposed to make sense of such a senseless thing? A heart attack at fifteen . . . What kind of joke was God playing on us? A fifteen-year-old ninth grader . . . the best athlete in the whole school.

What kind of God would do such a thing?

"It don't make any sense," I broke the silence. "You saw how Kish could run. He was in good shape."

Sylvester ventured an explanation. "Well, Leonard, maybe it was just his time."

"My grandma told me that when a person dies it's just God's will and they ain't nothing you could do when your number is called," Fred added.

"Yeah, I've heard that too," Glenn said.

"Y'all must be crazy. I can't believe God would do such a thing, and if he did, then he's not much of a God." I fumed as I pictured how crazy it would look for God to be picking death numbers for people.

"Leonard, you better be careful how you talk about God," Fred warned.

"I don't care. It's just not right."

I had started to cry. The tears brought no answers.

Where was God while Kish lay there in the bleachers with his life slipping away? Where would I find answers that would help me deal with the anger, sorrow, and righteous indignation I was feeling toward a God who was supposed to be all powerful and loving?

The only place I could think of going was to Grandma Gladys. This was before she had passed away, and I knew she would have some good wisdom to share. After all, she was the one who was always talking about silver linings. I hoped she could shed some light on this awful miscarriage of justice. Yes, that's what I would do—I would ask the person who had assured me that God had once saved me from the grip of death.

Kish's death was the talk of Laurinburg. Everybody in Newtown had heard the news. Mable was standing there in my front yard, already sensing that I would need her.

I fell into her arms, definitely needing the embrace and the touch of somebody special. I did not need words, and Mable seemed to sense that. She simply pressed her lips against mine, and for a moment the pain was gone.

"Mable, I need to walk over to Beta Street and talk to Grandma Gladys," I finally spoke as the spell of the kiss began to fade.

"I'll ask Alta Maria if I can go with you," Mable said.

I was overjoyed when Mable returned with the news that her older sister and guardian said it was all right for her to walk with me across town. Hand in hand, we walked the familiar route toward Beta Street. Mable offered none of the easy answers I'd heard on my way home from school. She seemed to realize that her presence was all I needed at this point.

Grandma Gladys, like everyone else in Laurinburg, was aware of the events that transpired in the Laurinburg Junior High School gym.

"Come on in, honey," Grandma said as she held the screen door open for us. "Hi, Mable. How you doing? I'm glad you came with Leonard. I was expecting you to come. I've got some ice cream for both of y'all. Sit down at the table while I get y'all some spoons," she said in no great hurry.

Grandma Gladys always took her time when teaching important lessons of life, and this was one of those times.

"Grandma," I started. "Where was God today? Was God in the gym when Kish got sick?"

"Yeah, Leonard, God was there," Grandma assured me.

"If God was there, why didn't he do something to keep Kish from dying? Fred told me his grandma said it was the will of God and it was just Kish's time."

I spoke these words in almost one breath, afraid that if I did not, they would get stuck in my throat and never come out.

"Honey, God's ways are not our ways, but I do know that it is never God's will that anybody should die," Grandma said, still picking her words with care.

Grandma Gladys seemed to realize this was a fragile time in my life. She understood that this event would help shape my view of God, as well as my belief concerning silver linings.

"I want both of y'all to pay attention to what I'm going to say," Grandma said. "God was there in the gym. God was just as upset and hurt as anybody in that gym today. Think how you felt watching Kish die and how you feel right now. Well, magnify that feeling a million times and still your anger and your hurt could not be as painful as it was for God."

"If God hurt so bad, why didn't he prevent it? He saved me, didn't he?" I asked.

Although my grandma could not read or write, what she said next let me know that she was the greatest theologian I would ever meet.

"Leonard, God can do everything, but God will not do everything. I know that sounds like I'm letting God off the hook, but in those moments when God does not intervene, it does not mean God is not there. It is in times like these when God is nearer."

How could a sharecropper know such things, and how could she explain them so clearly? Although Grandma Gladys's explanation never answered all my questions, what little she did say helped ease my heart. I think Grandma left part of the mystery unanswered for another place and another time.

I could not bring myself to attend Kish's funeral that Saturday at one o'clock at Cool Springs United Methodist Church. Laurinburg Junior High School administrators had already planned to hold a memorial service for Kish in the school's auditorium on the following Monday morning. That would be the place and time to deal with a concept that seemed as alien to me as visitors from the planet Mars.

Human death had never been a part of my personal vocabulary. I was too young to speak that word. There was too much life yet to be lived. Why did it creep into my life now? Death was the one thing that held the power to turn any silver lining into dark clouds too thick for light to penetrate. Of course, I had heard adults talk about death. I had been to my father's funeral, and I had heard lots of talk about funerals, but I thought death was a distant journey not to be reached until one had at least smelled, touched, tasted, and drank the bounty of the world's joy and sorrows.

It was so unfair. Kish would never marry. He would never get the opportunity again to do what it appeared he was born to do—run gracefully through opposing defenses as he had done against us on the football field of Washington Park. Yes, I had already heard the clichés from his funeral about playing football in heaven. Heaven was the last thing on my mind as I tried to prepare myself for the impending memorial service.

"Lord, I don't want to go," I prayed.

I was already getting the treatment from the Pine Street Patriots for not attending the funeral. "Leonard, you should have gone," they said.

The only words that came to my mind were, "In my own time," as I tried defending myself against the criticism.

"God, don't make me have to go," I prayed before falling asleep.

I was not expecting God to answer such a prayer so quickly with such force and wrath.

The old Zenith radio was blaring away the news before we even had time to wipe Sunday night's sleep from our tired and weary eyes. The announcer was saying something about a fire at a junior high school.

I had grown up listening to the fog horn alarm that sounded whenever there was a fire in Laurinburg. I knew how to count the number of times it sounded. I knew what each number meant. One could always tell the location of the fire by counting how many times the horn blew. The residents of Newtown knew exactly when and where fire struck in the Black community. Therefore, when the horn sounded, no adult paid it much attention because it was not in the community. It was not in our community, so who cared?

Being the resident newsperson, Mrs. Lucy certainly was curious. She was always alert for any information no matter where it happened. Once Mrs. Lucy counted the fire fog horn and determined the location of the fire, she immediately woke Fred, ordering him to get down to the junior high school.

It was never questioned as to who would have the scoop on this second tragedy that rocked our world.

"I bet Fred already knows everything that happened," I agonizingly said to Curtis.

"But they said it happened late last night," Curtis said. "You know

Fred wouldn't be outside that late at night."

"Now, you know if Mrs. Lucy figured out that the fire was at the junior high school, it would not matter what time it was—she would find out what happened," I countered.

"Well, what are we waiting for? Let's go talk to Fred and find out what really happened," Curtis said.

We found Fred standing in the middle of Pine Street, the center of attention, telling all the things he saw to a group of confused and shocked junior high students.

"I don't know what we going to do about school," Fred said. "The building burned to the ground, and the only things standing from the main building are the pillars."

"You mean there was nothing left?" an anxious voice spoke.

"Nothing. It burned so fast," Fred answered. "The auditorium caved in first, and flames leaped through the classrooms."

"Well, I'm glad the gym burned," Sylvester said. "I bet it was the ghost of Kish that set it on fire."

My face grew hot as I lit into Sylvester with both barrels.

"What crazy house did you escape from, fool?" I shouted. "In the first place, there is no such thing as ghosts, and I don't believe Kish would do such a thing even if there were ghosts."

I was ranting now. "Why can't y'all let Kish rest in peace! Ever since he died, y'all been 'round here talking nonsense. Anyway, I heard the radio announcer say they think the fire started in the art room."

"That's Mr. Sherman's room, ain't it?" Robert said, jumping in the conversation.

"Fred, are you sure there was nothing left?" I asked.

"Man, I'm telling you, ain't no way nothing could have been left," Fred answered. "I was standing right there. Don't you think I would know if something survived the fire?" he added, angry that I would question his retelling of the events.

"It was dark outside," Sylvester noted, not intimidated by the tongue-lashing he had received.

"I know what I saw, boy," Fred said. "There were so many fire trucks with their lights twirling that it would take a blind man not to see what was happening. Fire trucks came from Wagram, Gibson, Maxton, Hamlet, and even from McCall, South Carolina. Now tell me—with all those lights, how could I miss the action? There was even a man in one of those lift buckets from the CP&L Company spraying water on the fire."

"Fred, what about the gym and the cafeteria? They weren't part of the main building, so they shouldn't have burned," I reasoned.

"Oh, yeah. I forgot," Fred answered ashamedly.

We later learned from the newspaper that the adjacent buildings, which included the gym, the band room, cafeteria, and home economics classrooms, were undamaged by the intense heat of the fire's fury. But the dreams of the summer of 1972 were shattering right before my eyes.

Had I really wanted it to happen this way? In anger over Kish's death, I'd prayed for this. Was God answering that prayer? It certainly appeared that my selfish dreams had come true. These thoughts were running through my head as I wearily walked back into the house, attempting to steady myself for the force of other bad news coming from the radio.

I'd come to the conclusion that if Fred could not even remember what buildings were left standing, I had gotten all the accurate information I was going to get from him for now. I'd heard enough talk about how Kish's spirit was somehow connected to this new jolt. With morning's light filtering through the semi-darkened room, I wondered if this was indeed poetic justice for a life taken so early.

But if this was justice, if this was an answer to a prayer, why didn't God just burn down the gym and leave the school?

We knew there would be no school that day, so we attempted to catch up on lost sleep by going back to bed, but sleep never came for me. I was haunted by the thought that I'd prayed for this to happen, and now there would be no school because of my selfishness. I would be careful about what I asked God for from now on, because it might just happen. I had prayed that I could somehow avoid attending Kish's memorial service, and God had fixed it so that I would not have to go.

It seemed to take the school leaders forever to determine what they would do with six hundred eighth and ninth graders. It was not that we could not find something to do with the almost three weeks it took them to come up with a reassignment plan. We spent the time doing what we usually did—getting into trouble. It was a great opportunity to spend the mornings with the Pine Street Patriots and the evenings with Mable.

Glenn was the only Pine Street Patriot with a basketball court in his backyard, and we spent lots of time honing our skills there. However, there were two drawbacks to playing in his backyard. The first was the laundry his mother hung on the clothesline to dry. We would kick up a lot of dust, causing the product of her hard work to suffer. We left Glenn to deal with his mother's anger when she came home.

The other problem that confronted us was the ordeal, test, and adventure of getting to Glenn's house by means of the white picket fence bordering Mr. Isler's backyard. The fence was a formidable obstacle. The fence already suffered from the wear and tear of many crossings. It was always in disrepair, but Mr. Isler was never able to catch the culprits.

It was just our luck that Mr. Isler happened to be one of the teachers at Laurinburg Junior High School, so he, too, was on extended holiday because of the fire. Mr. Isler also happened to be my science and health teacher.

"Boy, what you doing crossing my fence?"

The voice froze me almost in mid jump. *Why, of all days, did I have to pick this one on which to be the last person to jump?* I could have easily done what I had always done—forced my way to the front of the line—but no, I let everybody go in front of me today.

I stood, like a fool, watching everybody else cross the fence and make it safely to Glenn's backyard.

The only options left for me under the present circumstances were to turn around and run or give some kind of answer.

"It's the only shortcut to Glenn's house," I stammered.

"Well, do you think that your need for a shortcut makes it right for you to vandalize somebody's property?" Mr. Isler responded. "Say, ain't you that Fairley boy who's in my science class?"

I was cold busted. There was nothing else to do but confess and ask for forgiveness.

"Mr. Isler," I began in my most sorrowful voice, "I'm sorry that I helped break down your fence."

What happened next was unexpected.

"You don't have to stand there like you're scared to death of me," Mr. Isler said.

I had not noticed that my fear was anchoring me to the same spot. However, there was something in Mr. Isler's voice that let me know I had nothing to fear.

"Where do you live?" he asked.

"I live right behind you on Pine Street."

I pointed through the gulf of trees that separated our houses. I don't know what caused me to be drawn to Mr. Isler, but he was the first male professional who had ever talked to me with concern and understanding.

"Why don't you answer questions in my class? I know you're smart," Mr. Isler said. "I've read the answers you write on your tests."

It was the first time an adult with standing acknowledged that I was more than just a trashy, nappy-headed kid running the street. Mr. Isler saw something in me that even I was afraid to acknowledge.

I constantly heard through my grandma that I was special, but that was Grandma, and that's what grandmas always say. I expected her to say things like that. Therefore, when Mr. Isler spoke similar words, they sounded as if I was hearing them for the first time. I loved my grandma, but somehow Mr. Isler's words of affirmation were the validation that would help turn my life around.

It was almost too good to be true. Somebody in authority believed in me.

Mr. Isler became the male mentor in my life—yet another silver lining. Jumping the fence became for me a jump into another world. Mr. Isler would cause me to look beyond my social status and to truly not judge a book by its cover.

"Well, you go on across the yard, but I want you to come over here tomorrow and help me repair my fence," Mr. Isler said calmly.

"Leonard, what did Mr. Isler say to you?"

The questions immediately flew at me when I got to Glenn's yard.

"I thought he was calling the police on you," Glenn said. "Mr. Isler don't take no mess."

"Yeah, did you tell it on us?" Sylvester nervously asked.

"I didn't tell it on y'all. I know better than that," I assured Sylvester. I knew the code of the Pine Street Patriots: If you get caught, just give rank and serial number.

"Well, I know he must have said something," Fred said. "You were over there an awful long time. We thought you'd chickened out and run back home. So tell us what he said."

Everybody kept pestering me.

"He said I was smart," I proudly answered.

"I know Mr. Isler must be crazy if he thinks you're smart," Robert said.

"Well, that's what he said. He said I answer most of the questions on test papers right," I responded.

"Since you're so smart, tell us what are they going to do about school for us?" Robert asked.

"He said I was smart. He didn't say I was a prophet." That shut Robert up.

"I heard somebody say they were going to reassign us to another junior high school," Sylvester said.

"Boy, you crazy! Where the students at that other junior high going to go to school?" I asked.

"Let's play basketball and forget about all this school stuff. It don't matter to us what Mr. Isler said," Glenn said.

Our brief vacation was over almost before it started. The ruling was handed down from the main office. We would be reassigned to

I. Ellis Johnson, the segregated school I'd once attended—the school located "Cross the Creek."

History, it appeared, was repeating itself. I had moved from this school when integration became the law of the land. I was now going back to the place where I learned so many unpleasant lessons about injustice. Injustice had kept people separated by race, but now, some of the White students would get an up-close and personal view of Black community living. They would get an education on racial injustice.

I was sure that many of my White classmates had never set foot in a Black community. The communities in which they lived were insulated from this kind of life. It took an actual fire to move them into a place they'd rather not be. It has been said that fire purifies. It forges and molds the hardest steel. It would be an interesting three months in which to see if the steel of racism could be purified in this fateful move.

I was glad my White classmates would see how we were forced to live. I just did not like the idea of attending classes in shifts. The shifts were scheduled to begin in April. The students already at I. Ellis Johnson would attend classes from eight in the morning until one in the afternoon, and the students from Laurinburg Junior High School would use the same facilities from one until five in the afternoon.

It was an idea that in the beginning had promise. We could sleep late, for one thing, but I soon learned to hate our shift because it cut into time I spent with Mable. Mable was a Scotland High School student, and she came home from school at the usual time while I was still stuck in classes at I. Ellis Johnson.

The second disadvantage of attending school at such a weird time of day was the missed opportunity for the one meal we knew we would get, because all of us qualified for free school lunch. It was understood that there was only one meal at home, and that was supper.

We supplemented this loss by selling bottles and buying the popular candy known as Now and Later. We would load up on the square multiflavored candy. I know the janitor at I. Ellis Johnson cursed us out every night because the desks at I. Ellis Johnson were filled with not only Now and Later wrappers but also spit-out sunflower seed shells.

From April through June, this was our Monday through Friday daily routine. There would be no more evening games of kickball in the middle of Pine Street. There would be no more evenings of sitting on Mable's front porch and no more evening walks around the block. I hated it and saw the solution as a punishment.

We would wake up every day and begin trying to sell enough bottles before one o'clock. The conversations began the same way each day. "Where we going to get bottles from today?" We had probably found every lost bottle ever thrown out in Laurinburg by now, but every day we started again, knowing this was for our lunch.

"I'm tired of this crazy shift stuff. Whoever thought up such a solution must have been half drunk," I complained.

"Leonard, we know why you hate it," Glenn said. "You just want to hang out with that old girlfriend of yours."

"Yeah, I kind of like waking up late," Fred added.

"You just a lazy dog, Fred. You wouldn't wake up if your grandma didn't threaten to whip your big butt," I said.

"I bet y'all haven't tried those new rum-flavored Now and Laters," Sylvester said, changing the subject.

"Sylvester, you ought to know they ain't going to sell no rum candy," I countered.

"Man, it ain't got no alcohol in it. It just tastes like it does," Fred answered.

"Well, we ain't going to taste no flavor of candy if we don't sell these bottles before eleven o'clock," I said. "That's why I hate this shift mess. We don't have time to do nothing."

"We ain't got no choice, so we might as well make the best of it," Robert concluded.

Making the best of it would prove difficult for all of us, because every time we walked down the halls of I. Ellis Johnson School, we were reminded of why we were there. Kish was dead, and Laurinburg

Junior High School was gone.

However, there were glimpses of joy. P. E. class continued to be a thrill. I guess Coach McCracken attempted to keep us busy, hoping it would take our minds off Kish. He allowed us to use different pieces of gymnastic equipment. I suspected the new physical education lesson plan was also done to replace the usual intramural basketball games that were a tradition at Laurinburg Junior High School.

The trampoline proved to be my favorite piece of equipment. I had never seen a trampoline; the closest I ever got to jumping on one was the old worn-out bed mattress springs we used to bounce up and down on. We wore out bed mattresses fast in our house. They wore out even quicker because my younger brothers and sisters peed in the bed every night. The old mattress was carried out to the woods and dumped until both weather and bacteria rotted what little cloth was left on the springs. When the forces of nature had completed their job, we moved in to jump on the exposed springs to our hearts' content. Therefore, it was no surprise that I was a natural on the trampoline.

I looked forward to P.E. class every day. The fire at Laurinburg Junior High School had wiped out all the state-issued blue and white physical education uniforms. Coach McCracken allowed us to wear shorts from home. I would soon learn that this was a mistake when I climbed upon the trampoline with my worn out, hand-me-down shorts. I heard the rip as I attempted a flip, and then came the laughter of my classmates.

"Fairley!" Coach McCracken laughingly called out as he threw me a towel. "Tie this towel around you so that you don't have to walk around school today showing everybody your underwear."

I vowed never to get on the trampoline ever again, but the next day I was right back jumping as high as I could with my sewn reinforced shorts.

There were rays of joy at I. Ellis Johnson. Once again, my grandma's words about silver linings were made apparent. Mr. Isler's willingness to see potential in me caused me to come alive in his class. I quickly gobbled up any new thing he taught us. Mr. Isler even let the class know that I was the smartest person in the room.

I do not think he realized what those few words did to move me closer to places my Grandma Gladys always knew I could go if only I believed in myself.

The journey had begun in, of all places, I. Ellis Johnson, a onetime segregated school that I once thought inferior, and with, of all people, an African-American mentor. I was now becoming grateful for getting caught jumping Mr. Isler's fence. As long as I had Now and Laters or sunflower seeds, the shifts were not so bad.

Mr. Isler, true to his word, helped me repair his fence and even paid me for the task.

Soon I no longer had to sell bottles, because Mr. Isler allowed me to do little jobs for him, including keeping his lawn and hedges cut.

The remainder of our time at I. Ellis Johnson rapidly concluded, and summer took its place. Summer once again was a time of anticipation—the anticipation of returning to our beloved Laurinburg Junior High School.

The summer of 1973 brought with it new adventures and brighter opportunities, because I was now working steadily for Mr. Isler. Stank, my mama's live-in boyfriend and common-law husband, had also been blessed with a job at Eaton's Golf Pride factory. Therefore, the summer of '73 was a time of celebration, and there were always people at our house. I guess it's true that when you have money, friends come out of the woodwork.

We had never been fortunate enough as a family to have the finer things of life. Therefore, Mama and Stank had no clue as to what to do with their newfound wealth. Mama was now receiving a decent amount of Social Security benefit money for each of my deceased father's seven children, and along with Stank's increased pay at Eaton, there was more money coming into the house than we were accustomed to having. We were not rich by any stretch of the imagination, but these new developments were a quantum leap from where we had been.

No matter what extra money came into the house, there was never enough of it to move us from Newtown, but there was enough to at least enjoy life a little. And enjoy it we did.

We understood that the winds of fortune could easily turn and blow us back into abject poverty. Therefore, we lived the summer of '73 with the epicurean philosophy of eat, drink, and be merry, for tomorrow we may die. Stewardship was the last thing on our minds. We were like the grasshopper in the Aesop's Fable of "The Ant and the Grasshopper."

"Leonard, my daddy wants to know if y'all are having a cookout today," Fred asked.

Mr. James was one of the many people who frequented our house on those warm summer nights. He knew there would be plenty of food to eat and whiskey to drink.

"I don't know, Fred," I answered. "I think Stank went to Pete's after work."

In East Laurinburg, Pete's was the place where most people purchased their steaks. The butchers always custom-cut your steaks. It became part of a new Friday ritual that usually lasted through Saturday. Stank would travel to East Laurinburg and buy enough food to feed everybody on Pine Street. He would also stop by the ABC Store and buy gallons of liquor.

The yard would be made ready and the stereo placed outside for music. The summer evenings would be a block party. We never had to send written invitations; all that was required was the beat of the music from such stars as Smokey Robinson and The Miracles, The Temptations, and Mr. James's favorite, Junior Walker and The All-Stars. Once the neighbors heard these tunes, they came like cartoon characters floating on the mist of aromatic smells of good food.

"Yeah, Fred, I think we might have a party tonight," I said to Fred. "I saw Mama pulling out the records; I guess that's a good bet there will be a party tonight. But you better tell your daddy he better not get so drunk that he can't walk home. I don't want to have to help carry him home again."

I knew they were vain words. It never failed. Mr. James and Stank would sit there in the same spot under the pecan tree listening to Junior Walker and The All-Stars pretending that they were playing the saxophone while getting drunk.

"James Thomas, listen to Junior Walker blow," Stank would say.

"Yeah, man, he's pumping it, ain't he?" Mr. James would add.

The next minute both their jaws would be filled with wind as they mimicked every movement a saxophone player might make. The men were not the only ones who got caught up in the atmosphere. I remember the crazy idea my mama and her sister Odessa conceived during one of the parties. They decided it would be a good idea to tape a Winston cigarette filter butt onto a Pall Mall cigarette. It was the craziest thing I'd ever seen. They would each try to smoke the taped cigarette. Of course, each attempt ended in the cigarette falling apart; when that happened they would fall apart as well, rolling on the floor in unabashed laughter.

The world's conventional wisdom would have said, "Save some of that money for a rainy day," but what the world failed to realize was that we had already seen our fair share of poverty's cruel rain. How could we not celebrate our liberation?

I also wondered why my mama did not put some of the money in the bank. What was wrong with them? Didn't they know we couldn't keep this up? Didn't they know that as soon as the money was gone, there would be no friends? It just did not seem to matter to them. Today was all that mattered.

In my boldness, I ventured to become a sane voice in the midst of this seemingly wasteful joyride.

"Mama, why don't we save some of this money?" I asked.

The answer did not make sense.

"Leonard, you don't understand," my mama began. "Have you forgotten what it was like living in that tin house on Evans' Quarter?

Don't you remember the times y'all had to beg for food? Don't you remember eating cereal with water instead of milk?"

She rattled off reason after reason why it was good to celebrate now.

"We deserve some happiness," she said with triumph in her voice. She spoke as if we were getting rewarded for enduring the suffering of poverty.

All those things were indeed true, but I still could not see the logic in her thinking.

"What's going to happen when we're right back where we started from?" I countered.

My mama's next lines of justification began. "Leonard, tomorrow is not promising anything to anybody. You've got to learn to live one day at a time," she said.

"Why don't we find another place to live?" I asked, not knowing if I really meant it.

I certainly did not want to leave my friends. I was only trying to find some words that would shock my mama into reality.

But there were no words that could stop her desire to live for the present. It was as if she had waited for this moment all her life and nothing, not even the future, was going to change her mind. This was her promised land.

The parties continued. At our expense, people were offered at least a little piece of heaven in the midst of hell.

I found my inability to sway my mama to what I viewed as "the proper course of action" as an excuse to spend more time with Mable. I was spending so much time at Mable's house that her sister would often have to make me leave.

"Leonard," she would say in the sweetest voice she could muster. "Don't you think it's time for you to go home?"

Sheepishly, I would walk to the front door with Mable, who would always give me a much-anticipated kiss. I would at least leave with something to sleep on, besides the noise of Junior Walker and The All-Stars wailing in my ears.

The summer of '73 could also have been called the summer of Bruce Lee. Mable and I must have seen every Bruce Lee movie fifty times. We remembered every move and scene of *Fist of Fury* and *Chinese Connection*. During walks back home from the Gibson Movie Theater, the habit of retelling the entire plot complete with sound effects was as entertaining as watching the film itself.

Mable was a great companion for a young man just discovering himself. However, I never wanted her to see my reaction to Bruce Lee films when I watched them with the Pine Street Patriots. We would leave the theater trying to kill each other with the kicks and punches Bruce Lee threw at the bad guys. The flying kicks were my favorite technique, and Sylvester became my favorite target for practice.

"How many of y'all believe that I can jump high enough to land a flying kick up beside Sylvester's head?" I asked.

"I'll believe it when I see it," Fred replied, which provided me with additional motivation.

The Pine Street Patriots were not aware that after first seeing the Bruce Lee movies with Mable, I had been practicing my moves on trees and bushes. I became good enough to see if practice made perfect. Sylvester was also skeptical of my ability and was so sure I could not do a flying kick high enough to reach his head that he became a willing subject.

"I dare you, Leonard," he said. "I won't even move a muscle because I know you'll never make it near my head."

"Stand back and give us room," I commanded everybody.

They willingly stood back eager to see if I could master this technique.

"Now remember what you said, Sylvester. You ain't going to move, are you?" I wanted to make sure that Sylvester was truly willing to let me try to kick him up beside his head.

"Like I said, you won't make it that far, so why should I move?" he responded.

I took a few steps back to gain the momentum I needed for the kick. I leapt into the air, and within a split second, I made contact with the side of Sylvester's head.

"Man, that was just like Bruce Lee," the voices echoed.

"I told you I could do it, didn't I?" I apologized to Sylvester while helping him up from the ground.

I would have never tried such a thing in Mable's presence. She might have seen it as a childish thing to do, but with the Pine Street Patriots, it was a never-ending game of trying to succeed at every challenge made.

"Leonard, how did you learn to do that?" Robert asked.

"I been practicing," I answered.

Everyone then begged, "Can we practice with you?"

"I don't care, but y'all better not laugh at my equipment unless y'all want me to use kung fu on y'all," I warned.

I had gone out and bought some of those slippers that look like the kind Bruce Lee wore in his movies. I never took the time to realize what I was purchasing. I did not care that they turned out to be a pair of women's elastic bedroom slippers. I even sawed an old broom stick in half and made myself some num-chucks. I would go to any length to be like Bruce Lee, as long as Mable didn't see me.

I had never realized that Mable was just as crazy about Bruce Lee as I was until one day, when we were sitting on her front porch, she said, "Leonard, I bet I can do more Bruce Lee moves than you can do."

I could barely contain my enthusiasm. It was too good to be true. Mable did not mind getting down and dirty when it came to kung fu.

How many more times would this girl surprise me? I wondered to myself as we matched Bruce Lee moves on her front lawn.

The summer was going too quickly. I had begun to open up myself fully to Mable. I shared my passion for science and in particular, archaeology. Mr. Isler opened my mind to all kinds of possibilities, and it was his class that gave me the idea to try to put together a chicken skeleton like true archaeologists reassembled ancient dinosaur bones.

I shared my idea with the Pine Street Patriots and tried soliciting their help, but they laughed so hard that they cried.

"Leonard, you must be crazy. Where you going to find all the bones of a chicken and how are you going to make the bones stay together?"

The Pine Street Patriots teased me endlessly with their questions.

"Well, if y'all don't want to help me, I'll save the chicken bones myself, and I'll use coat hanger wire to hold my chicken skeleton together and upright."

I was so determined to prove them wrong again that after every chicken dinner on Sundays, I saved all the chicken bones I could get my hands on for my experiment. If Mable did not think my practicing kung fu moves was crazy, maybe she'd be interested in my half-assembled chicken skeleton. I don't know if she was truly impressed or just being kind. Whatever the case, she seemed awestruck. But by the time I'd decided to share everything with Mable, the summer was rapidly slipping away.

It was now time to focus our attention once again on what school would be like. We had received only scant information about what the rebuilt Laurinburg Junior High School would be like. We only knew we would be returning in August.

The return was traumatic. Gone were the stately Greek-style columns. It looked nothing like the school of my dreams. The principal and teachers called them mobile classrooms, but to us it did not matter what words they used to try to dress it up; they were trailers. The only vestige of the old Laurinburg Junior High School left standing besides the gym, home economics classroom, cafeteria, and band room were the tops of the columns cemented at the front entrance of the trailers. I guess they thought this would at least give us something to remember about the grand old school, but all it did was remind us that nothing, and certainly not trailers, could bring back Kish Johnson or the building.

I guess the only thing that helped me through this ordeal was my newfound love for learning, thanks to Mr. Isler. However, my thirst for knowledge was a silent one. I did not want to bring attention to myself.

I had been told ever since I was a child that I would never be anything. I'd even been labeled a "special needs child"—the term used to define a child with a learning disability.

The only thing I saw as a disability was the lack of belief on the part of society and the school system that a person from the ghetto of Newtown could be intelligent. The generalization was so strong that I kept my love of learning secret, and no one without a keen interest could detect otherwise. Mable always knew because I would help her with her homework. The special needs classes were a bore, and I passed each one with little effort.

"What's the name of that book you're reading?" Mr. Laviner, my special needs English and language arts teacher, asked me one day.

It was a habit of mine to spend time in the library going through the bookshelves searching for my next novel to read.

"It's called *Shackleton's Valiant Voyage*," I answered.

"Tell me, what's it about?" Mr. Laviner asked.

He had now lifted the book from my desk and was examining its cover.

"It's about the British explorer Sir Ernest Henry Shackleton and his exploration of the Antarctic," I nervously said. "It's a story about the way he and his men survived the bitter cold and their other adventures in Antarctica. Shackleton was born in 1874 and died in 1922."

Mr. Laviner immediately asked me to follow him to the principal's office.

"Am I in some kind of trouble?" I asked.

Mr. Laviner never said a word until we reached the principal's office.

"Wait here, Leonard, until I get back," he mysteriously said.

I did not have much choice. I had been taken to the principal's office for God knows what, and I was not about to cause more trouble by getting up and walking out.

The principal came out of his office and looked me up and down. "I don't believe it," he said, looking at me in disbelief.

I must have done something mighty bad, I thought to myself. *I hope they get this over with quickly before Fred or somebody I know catches me sitting in the principal's office.*

"I tell you it's the truth," Mr. Laviner said. "I think we've made a big mistake."

"Where do you live, son?" the principal asked.

"I live in Newtown," I answered.

I was now scared to death. What had I done to bring on this treatment?

"Let's go to the guidance counselor and check his records," Mr. Laviner spoke. "I'm sure there's some kind of mistake."

"A mistake about what?" I wanted to ask, but this was teacher talk, and I was already in enough trouble.

"Can you pull the file on Leonard Fairley, please?" the principal asked the guidance counselor.

He looked through my file folder for a few moments.

"See, I told you his test scores would prove he's in the right place," the principal said.

"Yes, I know that's what the scores show, but when I asked him to tell me what this book was about, he gave me complete details," Mr. Laviner said, holding up my library copy of *Shackleton's Valiant Voyage*. "The scores don't reflect what is in this young man's head."

I knew those books were going to get me in trouble one day, I told myself.

"I just don't believe you mean he could tell you what it was about." The principal was still not convinced I could read and comprehend such a complicated novel.

"We can test him today and find out his reading comprehension," the guidance counselor said.

"Leonard, you're not in any trouble," Mr. Laviner finally assured me. "All they want you to do is take this test."

"What test?" I asked.

"Just a simple test for reading comprehension," he calmly answered. "It won't hurt you, and you can take it now. It won't take long."

I just wanted to get out of the office as quickly as possible, so I relented. The test was quick and easy.

"Leonard, just sit here for a minute while they grade your test," Mr. Laviner said to reassure me that everything would be just fine.

The guidance counselor and principal walked from her office with mystified looks on their faces. Mr. Laviner followed behind them with a triumphant smile of "I told you so" scrawled across his face.

"Leonard, do you want to know what this is all about?" Mr. Laviner asked.

What kind of question was that? I'd been marched down to both the principal's and guidance counselor's offices, made to take a test, and now this man had the nerve to ask me if I wanted to know what it was all about. I don't know why people in power do such things to others. They do what they please to you, and then explain afterward what happened. Even if it is for your own good, it should not give them the right to treat you like an object. I guess people in power feel they can treat poor people any way they choose without explanation, and if and when they feel like it, they might explain.

"Yes," I answered, trying not to reveal my indignation.

"Well, because of low test scores, they put you in the wrong class. You don't belong in any special needs class," he explained.

Tell me something I don't already know. I thought y'all were the smart ones, I said to myself.

Mr. Isler already knew what these teachers were just discovering, but it took a White teacher to convince the system that a person from Newtown could indeed be intelligent. It took Mr. Laviner's word before they even considered taking me out of special needs classes.

I wondered how many more people had been placed in such classes simply because they came from the wrong side of town and were the wrong color. I was told that the main reason I'd been placed in such classes was because of my unwillingness to talk or answer questions in class. It was ridiculous that teachers thought I was dumb because I was quiet.

Mr. Isler was the only teacher who thought otherwise but knew no one would believe him.

Laurinburg Junior High School would be different now that I was all-of-a-sudden smart. The school had indeed changed. The magnificent structure that once held me spellbound was now replaced by trailers, and the restrooms were like sheds. We were now biding our time until high school came calling, but there were still things in this trailer-park school that kept ninth grade exciting with each new discovery.

The auditorium, where all our assemblies were held, had been destroyed in the fire. Therefore, all assemblies were now held in the school gym. It was hard to focus in a place where death had forced us to grow up so quickly. The reminder of Kish's death was made apparent every time we walked into the gym. It was an unspoken tradition that no student sat in the bleacher Kish died in. This was our memorial to him.

I guess it was fitting that one particular assembly would be in the gym. The evangelistic group known as the Fellowship of Christian Athletes was our assembly guest that spring afternoon. They were all college-aged students dressed in 1970s-style apparel, and their most impressive attribute had to be that they traveled as an inclusive group. It made us sit up and take notice as we entered the gym.

"I wonder what they're going to talk about," Sylvester said.

"I don't know, but I bet it's another one of those assemblies to help us deal with what happened last year," I replied.

"Why you say that?" Fred asked.

"Look at them! They're young," I stated. "They got Black, White and Asian students. Don't you think something looks fishy?"

"Yeah, we ain't never had a group like this at our school. Ain't that a Bible one of them is carrying?" Sylvester perceptively commented.

"I hope this ain't some church thing," I responded.

I'd only been in church once, and that was when my father died. Grandma Gladys was all the church, preacher, and spiritual advisor I needed. Other than Mrs. Almeta in Evans' Quarter, that is. That was the way I liked it.

There was nothing those hypocrites in church could tell me. There were churches all over Laurinburg, but they never offered us any kind of help except at Christmas and Thanksgiving. Where were they the other 363 days of the year, when we almost starved to death? The church was never in the forefront of any social issues, so why were they all of a sudden showing up at area schools of all places?

It was not that I did not believe in God; I was just having a hard time reconciling the God that Jesus talked about with the actions of God's so-called people. I had tried going to church on my own once, but when I got to the door, the ushers made me leave.

"You can't come in here dressed like that," they said, looking down their noses at my bare feet and ragged clothes.

I don't have to come here to be looked down on, I thought. I vowed at that point never to set foot in another church. Surely God did not expect me to go through such humiliation just to worship. If I needed God, I would do what I'd always done—just talk to the creator where I was. I did not need nor did I care to seek God in a place where I was not welcomed.

"Leonard, go on in," Fred pushed me through the door of the gym for the assembly.

I tried to sit as far away from those people as I could get. I had no intention of listening to their self-righteous pleas to get people to become Christians.

The principal introduced our guests. The person with the Bible called each student from his group forward to give their personal testimony. They each told in their turn about how God had changed their lives and how much salvation meant to them. After each person's testimony, one of the college students played the guitar while the others sang praise songs.

In an attempt to get us closer to the action, the leader summoned us down from the bleachers and onto the gym floor.

After Kish's death and the fire, it always felt strange in the gym, but this had to be the weirdest feeling. It was almost as if you knew something extraordinary was going to happen.

"Why they calling us down there?" I nervously asked Fred.

Fred was already on his way down front with almost half the people in the gym. *What in the world is happening?* These people had come into our school and cast a spell on everybody. I decided I might as well go down front. I finally convinced myself to go.

As soon as I touched the gym floor, it happened. The wind blew through as I heard the first groan. We were reliving the Day of Pentecost. Something strange was happening, that was for sure. As I looked across the gym, there was Charles McClennahan sprawled prostrate on the floor. What started as a groan slowly became wailing cries.

"What's wrong with him?" I asked a student standing beside me.

"I think he's got the Holy Spirit," he answered.

Charles's body began to jerk as his cries filled the gym, and by now, one of the guest speakers was kneeling down beside him. The college students were now milling through the crowd, talking to individual students and even praying for some of them. It was a scene right out of the early church.

The Apostle Paul would have been proud of these college missionaries who had come to help us find Christ. Maybe it was what we needed after so much tragedy. *Could it be that God had indeed sent these students as an answer?*

I watched other junior high school students with tears in their eyes talking to our guests, but I could never bring myself to such a public show of emotion. Therefore, I was not "saved" on that day. That was the term they used at the close of the assembly.

"Who wants to get saved?" they asked.

Charles walked forward. Something must have happened that day, because Charles certainly began to change. He was never the same after that day. I thought to myself, *Have I missed something? Was God trying to prepare me for what was coming next?*

"Man, didn't you feel something in there today?" Fred asked anyone he thought would dare answer.

"I don't know what it was, but there was something in the gym," Sylvester answered.

"Maybe it was Kish's spirit come to haunt us," Glenn said.

"Glenn, you ought to know better than that. Once a person is dead there ain't no coming back," I responded, trying to be the voice of reason. "Those people just came and got everybody worked up about God. That's all they did."

"I don't know, Leonard. I think there might be something to what Glenn said," Robert replied, refusing to let reason prevail.

Fred added to the mystery. "We all know how much Kish loved playing in the gym, and most people believe it was more than an accident that the school burned down right after he died."

"Don't tell me that you believe Kish came back and burned down the school?" I asked incredulously.

"I'm just saying something mighty fishy is going on around here, and I can't wait until this year is over so we can go to Scotland High School," Fred replied anxiously.

"I'm with you, man," Sylvester added. "It's getting to the place that you don't know what's coming next, and I don't want to be around with the next tragedy happens."

"Y'all crazy! That's all. There ain't nothing in the gym," I responded to the almost tribal fear circulating among the Pine Street Patriots. The fear had been present ever since we stepped foot back on the grounds of Laurinburg Junior High School. "I'm not about to let what happened in the gym scare me," I announced.

I kept on talking. "If there was anything in there today, I believe it was the releasing of unanswered emotions surrounding Kish's death and the school fire. If God was trying to say something to us, I believe he was just letting us know that everything will be okay; like he was saying 'Go on. Don't be afraid to be teenagers.' We can't walk around here looking for Kish around every corner."

I'm not sure if my attempt at philosophy and psychology had any impact on the rest of the Pine Street Patriots.

Laurinburg Junior High School had certainly been a time of unexpected challenges. We were forced to deal with issues that pushed us to the brink of understanding. We were truly tried in the fire; if we could make it through this fire, certainly we could make it through whatever came next. Who knew that this was just the quiet time before the storm? We were junior high kids trying to live and adjust to a world that we were discovering sometimes made no sense. The world could throw you curves with no questions asked and no apologies given.

I was discovering that if there were indeed silver linings, finding them would mean struggling through the thick clouds of suffering and sorrow. The tragedies at Laurinburg Junior High School caused something like a fire in my heart—a fire that would suddenly spread out of control.

I was not aware that this fire meant the darkest clouds were now forming just over the horizon.

Chapter 11

Out of the Fire and into the Frying Pan

I should have known that nothing good lasted forever. The descent started gradually, and nobody took the time to see it coming. We were too busy living the good life—if one could call the life we were living "good."

I think the slide started with Grandma Gladys's death, and the downward spiral continued when my other first love moved away.

"Man, look at Ronnie flooring that Roadrunner! He's putting the pedal to the metal!" Essie screamed in wide-eyed amazement at the incredible speed of his brother-in-law's olive green, oversized engine automobile.

Ronnie was attempting to outrace the police car that trailed in his dust down Brizzle Street.

"What is he trying to do?" his wife, Alta Marie, shouted as she ran to the front porch with Wendy, her newborn daughter, hanging from her hip.

"If that policeman catches him, he's going to jail!" Mable said.

Ronnie's reputation as a drag racer around City Street was notorious. He had already been warned several times that if he was caught racing again, his driver's license would be revoked. The warnings went unheeded. There was no question about it; Ronnie had racing in his blood. It never crossed his mind that if he ever lost his license, it would limit his ability to find a good job. Ronnie risked everything for the thrill of speed—including, most importantly, his life.

"I hope that fool makes it in the driveway before that cop catches him," Mable anxiously said.

It was everybody's prayer that Ronnie would stick it to the "man" by outracing him home. If Ronnie could just make it to the driveway, there would be nothing the police could do. We'd watched Ronnie do this a million times—race down the same dirt road with a cloud of dust behind him.

However, this time the misty gray cloud of dust appeared to loom like a tragic premonition, a bad omen. I could not get the words out of my mind—the old proverbial saying of "where there is smoke, there is fire."

Alta Marie had tried over and over again to talk some sense into her husband's head—reminding him his luck was going to run out one day and the law would throw the book at him. Today would be the end of Ronnie's lucky streak in outracing the police.

"Oh, my God!" Alta Marie screamed in unison with the gasps coming from the crowd gathered in the street. "They finally caught him!" she said, shielding the eyes of her daughter from the scene yet to come.

The pursuit squad car had evidently radioed for backup help. We stood in surprised amazement as a second squad car pulled in front of what must have been an equally astonished Ronnie. The second car cut Ronnie off just before he could make the anticipated right turn onto Pine Street.

It was a scene no child should have to witness but unfortunately was one that Black children in Newtown saw countless times. It was a fact of existence. The police never came near Newtown unless it was to arrest somebody, and they never came alone—always in twos, and most times fours.

The four policemen jumped from their cars with drawn guns. It puzzled my already bewildered brain that they needed four guns to apprehend one man who was still sitting in his car.

The police ordered Ronnie to step out of the car slowly with his hands up.

"Get out the car!" they repeatedly yelled.

"Y'all children get out the street and go home!" Mrs. Lucy commanded.

Mrs. Lucy kindly attempted to spare us the pain of injustice. In spite of her continued attempts, Mrs. Lucy's words fell on deaf ears. We were determined to see for ourselves what was getting ready to go down. What we were witnessing now might be a lesson that would save our lives in the future.

I'm staying right here. I ain't going nowhere. I want to see what they going to do to Ronnie, I said to myself. I had heard stories all my life about how the police treated Black people, and here was my first opportunity to see it firsthand. *Who knows, one day it could save my life,* I thought.

Alta Marie had seen enough; in tears, she ran back into the house.

"Why the hell they got to treat him like that?" Essie flew into one of his infamous cursing streaks, only this time nobody attempted to shut him up.

The scene of another Black man being brutalized by the police seemed to justify Essie's foul language.

Ronnie's face was smashed and rubbed against the hood of one of the police cars so roughly that we were certain the car's paint was painfully merging with his flesh. Handcuffs were mercilessly clamped across Ronnie's wrists, and he was thrown into the back seat of the car.

"What are they going to do with him?" I asked, as the police cars sped away with lights flashing and sirens blasting.

"I don't know, Leonard, but I sure wouldn't like to be in his shoes," Curtis answered.

The look on Mable's face was a visual reminder to each of us that Ronnie was in a boatload of trouble.

I tried to console her. "Mable, don't worry."

"But Leonard, you don't understand. If anything happens to Ronnie we might have to move back to Charlotte with my daddy."

Through her tears, Mable spoke words that froze every inch of my body.

I soon learned all too painfully the truth of Mable's words. It took only two weeks for my world to crumble. Not only had Ronnie lost his driver's license, but he was sentenced to six months' active jail time as well. It was a grave injustice in more than one way. I was now sentenced to life without my first love.

I hid behind the house and cried like a baby as all the family's belongings were loaded into the station wagon parked in front of Mable's house. Mable was moving to Charlotte with her dad. Alta Marie had done her best to provide for them, but she could no longer support Mable, Essie, and Fern with Ronnie in jail.

I was discovering all over again how much love could hurt. For three years, Mable had been a part of my life, and now I was losing her. The pain was so great that I dared not try speaking to her for fear of breaking down like a baby before her. In hindsight, I could have at least gotten her address.

But I just stood there with eyes full of tears, watching my first love leave. I was tightly clutching her high school identification card, which she had given me so I would have a picture of her to remember her by.

Stank used the major portion of his good fortune to buy a 1969 Super Sport Chevy. I had already learned firsthand how much trouble and pain a hot rod car could bring. Therefore, when I watched Stank pull into the driveway with his '69 S.S. Chevy, I knew things were quickly going to hell in a handbasket.

It would not take long to feel the flames. Stank had already been driving through the streets of Newtown like a bat out of hell. All he needed was another fool to race.

Calvin fit the description perfectly. Calvin was an Army sergeant stationed at Fort Bragg, North Carolina, who had seen active duty in Vietnam. Like most soldiers in Fayetteville, he was a frequent customer of Hay Street. Hay Street was notorious for its late-night activity. A soldier could indulge himself in any carnal activity that crossed his mind on Hay Street. All of the oldest professions in the world were practiced on this godforsaken strip, but prostitution was its forte. Prostitution brought with it homeless cutthroats, beggars, and all the other violent or ill-refuted crimes—stabbings, shootings, and drug deals.

It would be on the mean streets of Fayetteville that Calvin would meet the woman determined enough to convince him to marry her.

The small town of Laurinburg was always too slow for Barbara Ann, like most teenagers looking for something to do. Barbara Ann was determined to get away from this hick town as soon as she was old enough to make her own decisions.

The decision came sooner than Barbara Ann thought it would. Her teenage pregnancy took care of that. Fayetteville was the most promising place to kill two birds with one stone. Here was the city life Barbara Ann longed for and the job she would need to take care of her son, Robert.

Barbara Ann found herself forced into an adult position of making life-changing decisions that would affect not only her life but her son's life as well.

Her first decision was to leave Robert in Laurinburg with Mrs. Lucy while she tried finding work in Fayetteville. Unfortunately, change of location does not bring with it an automatic personality change. The same restless spirit followed Barbara Ann to Fayetteville. Before long, she was pregnant again. Her daughter, Charletta, was soon shipped to Laurinburg to join Charletta's brother, Robert, and Barbara Ann remained in Fayetteville.

Mrs. Lucy never questioned where the money came from, just as long as it kept coming. Barbara Ann began her first job of prostitution on Murchison Road, the deadliest place for such employment, but before long she had become a pro and was promoted to Hay Street. Barbara Ann always made her annual summer trip to Laurinburg to see Robert and Charletta.

"My mama coming to see me!" Charletta would scream with delight.

Charletta was not old enough to distinguish one month from another, but she knew when the time was approaching for Barbara Ann to come. On the other hand, Robert had grown distant from his mother and called Mrs. Lucy "Mama."

I cannot begin to think about Barbara Ann without seeing Charletta's face. It is often said that little girls look like their daddies and little boys look like their mothers, but in Charletta's case, God must have gotten things mixed up. Charletta was the spitting image of her mother; maybe that's the reason Mrs. Lucy could not look her straight in the eye without getting upset. It must have been extremely difficult for Mrs. Lucy. Every time she looked at Charletta, it was like looking into the face of Barbara Ann.

It proved to be a deadly combination of emotions. Obviously, Mrs. Lucy still struggled with her anger over Barbara Ann getting pregnant and dumping two children on her. Charletta became the object of Mrs. Lucy's frustration and wrath. She was punished for the least trouble she got into and sometimes for things she did not do. Mrs. Lucy did not care what object she used to whip Charletta. Whatever object was closest was used to discipline her.

"If I can't punish Barbara Ann, I'll get the next best thing or the person who looks like her," Mrs. Lucy seemed to be saying.

A day did not go by that you did not hear Mrs. Lucy yelling at this beautiful three-year-old who did not ask to be born the spitting image of her grandma's source of anger.

"Charletta get in here and pick up this trash you left on the floor! I thought I told you to clean up behind you yourself. You're trifling just like your mama!" Mrs. Lucy never passed up the opportunity to remind Charletta of how no good her mama was.

Mrs. Lucy did not bite her tongue in letting Charletta know what her mama was doing in Fayetteville either.

"You going to end up just like your mama—selling your body to every Tom, Dick, and Harry that comes along," Mrs. Lucy would rant. "Barbara Ann knows she wasn't raised like that," Mrs. Lucy would lament to anyone willing to listen.

Mrs. Lucy's words proved to be a deadly foreshadowing. Charletta would not live to see her twenty-fifth birthday. She was raped and killed over a drug deal, and her body was thrown in a ditch in Fayetteville on the same streets her mother had worked as a prostitute.

Barbara Ann, in what to me was far from justice compared to what would happen to her daughter, was lucky enough to meet someone who would rescue her from the streets of Fayetteville. We first met Calvin demonstrating his self-defense moves to Stank.

"My new daddy knows kung fu," Charletta said with delight.

"Yeah, that's right," Robert boasted. "Calvin knows some moves that will break a person's neck in one second."

"Man, Calvin don't know no kung fu," we countered.

"How do you think he made it in Vietnam without getting killed?" Robert replied.

"Yeah, that is right," Sylvester accepted Robert's logic.

"I bet he can't take down a man big as Stank," I challenged.

It did not take much to get these two grown men to test their wills against each other—both of them were just boys in men's bodies. What began as a test of strength soon became a constant battle between Stank and Calvin to outdo each other in whatever they did together. Calvin soon became a part of the summer ritual of backyard parties at our house, and there he and Stank tried to outdrink each other.

It did not take a rocket scientist to realize that Calvin would end up being the man who would push Stank to illegal drag racing.

Calvin at least had a good reason for his foolishness. His having seen active duty in Vietnam convinced us that it had affected his mental state of mind. We were sure that such action had warped his brain. It was a treat to sit around Calvin when he got drunk enough to tell stories about his time in Vietnam.

"Come on, Calvin, tell us what happened over there," we would prod when we thought the vodka had loosened his tongue.

Calvin began relating the grizzly details of life and death in the jungles of Vietnam.

"Man, I've seen people get their heads blown slam off their bodies. I've seen children younger than Charletta come to greet GIs and have bombs hidden in their underclothes—killing themselves along with the GIs who were crazy enough to get close to them," Calvin would explain. "So y'all ought to be thankful y'all ain't living in Vietnam," he finished, letting us know how fortunate we were.

We might not have been in the jungles of Vietnam, but living in Newtown had its own set of war rules for survival.

"I wouldn't go if they told me I had to go fight in Vietnam," I said to Fred, with all the seriousness of being willing to be like Muhammad Ali.

"I ain't going to die in nobody's foreign country," Fred added.

"You don't have to go to Vietnam to get shot and killed," Sylvester said. "You can go right down to McDuffie Village and get killed."

Sylvester was right. McDuffie Village was the Dodge City of Newtown, and a week never passed without news of somebody getting stabbed or shot in this Black war zone. McDuffie Village's reputation was so terrible that when the call went out for the police to go investigate a shooting, it seemed like the entire police department showed up.

"If y'all don't want to hear no more about Vietnam, then stop wasting my time," Calvin said, getting the present conversation back on target.

"See, Sylvester you 'bout to make us miss hearing about Vietnam," I said.

"Yeah, why don't you keep your big mouth shut and let Calvin finish his story," Robert said.

"Tell us some more," I begged.

"I'm just glad I'm back stateside," Calvin sighed. "I was getting sick and tired of smelling burning flesh and looking at guts and brains spattered across the ground. I remember some young punk trying to play the hero got his brains sprayed all over my army fatigues."

Calvin was a hero to us, even though he was a little bit of a nut case. I concluded that he had to be crazy to marry Barbara Ann.

The only good thing that came from their marriage, as far as I could tell, was the picnics we would share with them on family outings to Fort Bragg Army base.

"Let's go to Smith Lake on post this weekend," Barbara Ann suggested.

It sounded harmless and safe enough. It sounded like a great idea.

"Yeah, I'm getting bored with having parties in Stank's backyard," Calvin said.

"I don't know," Mama hesitated. "I don't think it's a good idea, especially if y'all going to be drinking."

"Doretha, I can handle my liquor, if that what's you're scared of," Stank fumed.

"I don't think nothing is going to happen, Doretha," Barbara Ann assured Mama.

I dared getting into grown folks' business. "It's going to be nice this weekend. Come on, Mama. Let's go."

"Who asked you to say anything?" Mama turned on me. "You need to take your little skinny butt and go somewhere and sit before I knock you down."

I'd taken the necessary precaution of staying well out of range of Mama's arms. Mama had a habit of throwing punches while she fussed at you.

I hated to get a whooping from my Mama; she'd always talk to you in between licks. I could recall the many times she would say over and over again as she whipped the tar out of you, "I thought I told you not to do that? Why don't you listen when I tell you something?" she would ask. If I had not been afraid of getting a worse whipping, I would have stopped her in mid-swing and said something like, "Mama, just go ahead and whip me, but don't make it any worse than it already is by talking to me in the middle of the whipping."

When the decision was finally made to make the trip to Smith Lake on Fort Bragg's Army base, I could barely contain my joy.

However, if I had been able to see into the future, I would have stayed home with Curtis.

The day of departure started out pleasant enough. The early spring day was ideal for a picnic at the lake; there was not a cloud in the sky, nor were there any threats of rain clouds over the horizon.

"Curtis, you're going to miss all the fun," we teased Curtis, who was still determined to stay at home.

"I'll be glad just to have some peace and quiet," Curtis responded to our teasing.

"Well, you stay here. We'll tell you about it when we get back," I answered.

"Come on here, Leonard, and help me get this cooler in the trunk of the car," Stank ordered.

"What's in this thing?" I asked my brother Willie as he helped me lift one of the coolers that seemed to weigh a ton.

"You know what's in there. You know good and well Stank ain't going nowhere without his beer, gin, and juice."

I knew immediately what Willie meant; there must have been at least a case of Budweiser in those two coolers.

"I wonder where all the food is," I asked Willie.

"It's over here," Robert spoke. "Come and help me get it into our car."

Stank agreed to transport all the liquor and beer. Calvin would transport the food.

"Y'all come on here and get in the car," Mama yelled after giving Curtis instructions about taking care of the house. "There's food on the stove for supper. Curtis, don't you let nobody in this house, and don't you get in no trouble."

It was not Curtis that my mama needed to be worried about. With all the beer and liquor in the car, she should have been lecturing Stank.

The drive up to Smith Lake was uneventful. It was the calm before the storm. The trees whizzing by the car even seemed to be warning us about impending danger. One minute they would be perfectly still, then all of a sudden, with no apparent winds blowing, leaves would dance chaotically to some unseen force.

Calvin led us on a quick car tour of Fort Bragg before heading for the lake.

"Man, look at all that water!" I screamed as the car pulled into the picnic area of Smith Lake.

The cloudless sky and green trees reflected off the black waters of the lake. At any minute, I expected God's face to show up in this brilliant natural mirror.

"Look at that big sliding board," Diane yelled, pointing at the abundance of playground equipment.

"It looks like a rocket ship," Robert said.

"Is that a real jet air plane over there?" Charletta asked her mother as she was helped from the car.

"I don't know," Barbara Ann answered. "Go ask your daddy."

"Yeah, that's a real jet," Calvin answered. "Now go play while I put the charcoal on this grill."

"Don't y'all get out here and lose your mind," Mama instructed us. "I don't want to catch none of y'all down near that water. You know you can't swim," Mama yelled behind us as we scattered in all different directions.

What Mama did not know was that we had been swimming in the Kenny Pool without her knowledge. We could swim, but what she did not know would not hurt her.

"Where's the music?" Barbara Ann asked.

"Come here, boy," Stank called as I ran by him trying to get back on the high rocket ship slide.

"What does he want now?" I mumbled under my breath. *He's going to make me miss my turn on the slide,* I fumed silently.

"Go look in that bag over there under that tree and bring me those eight-track tapes," Stank said.

Stank never asked you to do anything. He always ordered it as if your sole purpose in life was to be his instant fetching dog.

"Take my car keys and put them in the ignition switch and make sure you turn the key back toward you," Stank began his instructions.

I held my hands out to receive the car keys, but they fell to the ground because I was paying more attention to the fun everybody else was having. *Why he always got to stop somebody from having fun?* I asked myself.

The slap on the back from Stank's heavy hand jolted me back to attention.

"What's wrong with you, boy? I hope you're listening to what I'm telling you because if you mess up my eight-track player, I'll skin your little narrow butt alive," Stank warned. "Go put this Junior Walker tape in the player."

I hope this tape melts, I again wished under my breath. *I'm getting tired of hearing this mess.*

I knew I'd have no such luck. It was standard practice to put a piece of paper underneath the eight-track tape if it started to skip. Those tapes were like cats with nine lives; they never died. The horns of Junior Walker blared into my face as I slipped the tape in the player following Stank's instructions.

"Turn it up some, baby!" Barbara Ann yelled.

Who's she calling baby? I thought. *I ain't her baby.*

The sound of Junior Walker's horn blasted louder as I felt the soft hands of Barbara Ann slip around my waist.

"Come on, let's dance, baby," she spoke into my face with beer breath.

The constant struggles to break away from this crazy woman were in vain. Barbara Ann's grip was like an octopus holding onto its favorite food.

"Don't you like to dance?" she said between my attempts to escape. "Come on. You can be my boyfriend. Calvin won't mind. Come on. Give your girlfriend some sugar," she said with pursed lips.

I was not about to kiss Barbara Ann. I was not going to ruin lips that had been kissed by Mable on some woman who had lost her mind.

I finally managed to escape and started running like a mad man away from Barbara Ann's clutches.

I tried to stay as far away as I could from Barbara Ann when it came time to eat. I did not trust myself around her anymore. It wasn't that I was going to do anything like kiss her or something like that. I was not so sure that I might not just rear back and hit her if she tried that mess with me again.

The time was quickly approaching for us to start the journey back to Laurinburg. While we loaded up the cars for the return trip, I noticed the furrows form across my mama's forehead letting me know that all was not well.

I could hear her whispering to Calvin. "Calvin, I don't think Stank's in any kind of condition to be driving home. He ain't sloppy drunk, but I still worry about him driving such a long way."

"I'll talk to him," Calvin reassured her.

"Stank, you just drive behind me on the way back to Laurinburg," Calvin suggested.

"Man, I don't have to follow you nowhere; I know how to get back home."

Stank took Calvin's concern as an attack on his manhood. Stank was appalled at the idea that he needed somebody to lead him back to Laurinburg.

I should have known better than to believe anything Stank said.

"I'm not going to drink anything, Doretha. You know I'm driving." I think those are the words I heard him use as they were loading all the liquor into the cars.

It was a temptation that could not be overcome. We should have known that if liquor was anywhere within eyesight, it would sooner or later find its way past Stank's lips. One beer quickly turned into two, and beer soon gave way to liquor.

"Stank, you need to stop. You know you're drinking too much," Mama had implored over and over again. "You know what you promised," she ventured, appealing to Stank's principles as a man.

After all, a man's word was supposed to be his bond, and what man would lie to his wife and family?

"Doretha, I ain't drunk," Stank kept repeating, but you could hear the liquor in his slurred speech. One could hear him struggle to put words in proper sequence. "I can drive home," he spoke before heading toward the car.

By now not only was his speech slurred, but his legs were no longer paying attention to his brain.

"Please, Calvin, talk to him again," Mama begged. "I don't want me and these kids to get killed out on the highway. I only came down here because Stank said he would not be drinking."

It appeared that everything was settled after Calvin attempted one last conversation with Stank.

"Stank will be trailing me back to Laurinburg. I think he can do it, if he stays behind me." Calvin's words seemed to slightly soothe my mama's anxiety.

"Okay, Calvin," Mama trustingly answered. "But don't you be driving too fast."

"I'll be driving the speed limit and that ought to keep Stank behind me." Calvin spoke the only words that could have convinced Mama to begin such a foolhardy and life-threatening venture.

Driving through Fort Bragg Army base was a piece of cake. Stank followed Calvin without any major altercations. He obeyed every traffic light, stopped at every stop sign, and at times drove well below the posted speed limit.

However, when he saw the speed limit sign on Highway 401 indicating fifty-five miles per hour, his liquor-impaired brain snapped. Stank zipped around Calvin's car, which was traveling about forty-five.

"Stank, what are you doing?" Mama screamed. "You promised to stay behind Calvin!"

Calvin sped alongside Stank's Super Sport and motioned out the window for Stank to pull over on the shoulder of the road.

"What in the world do that nigger want?" Stank said as he pulled onto the shoulder.

The two men got out of their cars and began a heated conversation.

"What you trying to do, man?" Calvin asked. "You know if the cops stop you and smell all that liquor on your breath, you going straight to jail."

"Nigger, you can't tell me how to drive," Stank shot back at Calvin. "I'm a grown man, and I don't need no Army punk telling me what to do. You must think you somebody's daddy since you been to Vietnam and know a little bit of karate."

"Man, I'm just trying to keep you from killing your family and getting into serious trouble with the police!" Calvin tried to reason.

Stank and Calvin returned to their automobiles. For the moment, Stank seemed to have paid attention to Calvin's words. Once again, he started driving down Highway 401 toward Laurinburg with Calvin in the lead.

But the effects of the liquor soon returned with a vengeance.

"I don't know who the hell Calvin thinks he is," Stank began to angrily mutter. "I been driving longer than he has and I ought to know what I'm doing. The speed limit is fifty-five, and he's driving forty-five. He must think I can't drive the speed limit."

Stank's words became more hostile. "I'm going to show that punk I can drive," he said as his foot proceeded to smash the gas pedal to the floor.

Within seconds, we were accelerating past Calvin's car. I could see the knuckles on my mama's hand almost tear through the skin as she gripped the door handle of the car with all her strength.

"Stank, you better slow down!" she screamed.

However, her words had the reverse effect. The more she screamed, the faster Stank appeared to go.

"You're going to kill us all!" Mama tried using the threat of death.

But not even the fear of death could cause Stank to slow his speed.

"Man, we doing ninety!" Darryl shouted.

"Boy, if you don't close your mouth, I'll throw your little stupid butt out of this car," Mama warned Darryl to stop giving Stank encouragement.

The S.S. Chevy appeared to float off the road as we were now reaching speeds of almost one hundred miles an hour. Darryl was still thrilled with the speed but knew better than to voice his excitement.

"Man, did you see that raccoon?" Willie yelled with astonishment. "We nearly hit him!"

"If anybody else back there in that backseat says another word, you ain't going to know what hit you!" Mama's quivering voice yelled. "Don't y'all know every last one of us about to get killed? This ain't no game!"

I watched my mama's hands form the familiar shape of prayer, and with closed eyes, she began to pray. I tried reading Mama's lips. I could make out the words: "Please, Lord, send your angels to protect us."

The blue light appeared to come out of nowhere as the Highway Patrol squad car pulled Stank over onto the shoulder of the road. The curse words began spraying from Stank's mouth as the state patrolman made his way toward our car with his flashlight beaming.

The light from the patrolman blinded us as he shone its bright light in the backseat of the car.

"Can I see your driver's license?" the patrolman ordered. "Mr. Avery, what are you trying to do—kill your family?" the patrolman asked while he read the license.

Stank's breath must have smelled like a liquor factory, and there was no way the patrolman could have avoided smelling that much alcohol.

"You were driving all across the road back there. Traveling at such a high rate of speed and crossing the center lane like that could have caused a tragedy," the patrolman said. "Mr. Avery, I'm going to have to take you to the Hoke County Jail in Raeford and lock you up. Mrs. Avery, my partner will drive the car to the jailhouse, and you can use the phone to call somebody to pick your family up from there."

These were words of salvation to my mama.

"I don't know where y'all came from, but I know God sent you to save us," Mama acknowledged her thanks.

The silence inside the squad car made the hum of the tires rolling across the asphalt sound like thunder. The unspoken truth of police authority was quite evident. Mama did not have to warn us to be quiet. We knew better than to talk while in the presence of the man.

The ride to Raeford took what seemed to be forever.

"Mrs. Avery, you can come inside and telephone somebody to come pick you and the kids up. You can wait inside your husband's car until somebody comes to get you," the officer offered.

Inside the familiar confines of the red Super Sport Chevy without the officer, the conversations and joking between my brothers began where it left off.

"Man, I mean we were flying down the road." Darryl started.

"I bet we would have made it home before Calvin if that patrolman hadn't stopped us," Willie added.

"No, we would have been dead," Mama said. "Y'all just need to thank God for saving us."

"What's going to happen to Stank?" somebody finally asked.

"Why won't they let him out so we can go home?" Darryl asked.

"Yeah, I'm getting tired of sitting out here in front of this courthouse," I said.

"They ain't going to let Stank out of jail tonight," Mama explained. "I already called for somebody to come pick us up and y'all just need to be patient."

I could tell by the sound of her voice that Mama had taken about all she could take for one day and to push her any more was asking for trouble.

"Y'all just wait until we get home. I'm going to tell Curtis what he missed," Willie said over the ever-present chirping of crickets.

The night grew into morning, and the conversation grew into sleepy murmuring as heads begin to sway with the heaviness of sleep. I thought I was dreaming when the hand reaching in the window finally fulfilled its purpose of waking me up.

"Are we still in Raeford?" I asked rubbing my swollen eyes.

I proceeded to attempt to get the blood running in my cramped arms by stretching them without regard to who was in arm's length. Suddenly a shout let me know the destiny of the much-needed stretch.

"Leonard, why did you hit me?" Willie screamed.

"I didn't mean it," I half-heartedly apologized.

"Well, you need to keep your stinking arms down," Willie said.

I tried to justify what must have been a powerful odor of musk flowing from my armpits. "I hope you don't think my underarms are supposed to smell like roses after being crowded in this car with y'all animals all night."

"Leonard, don't y'all start that mess," Mama spoke in a hoarse voice. "I know that everybody needs a bath. Now that Calvin has come to pick us up, y'all can wash up when we get back to Laurinburg."

I was not too thrilled that it was Calvin who had come to get us at four-thirty in the morning. Was it not his fault that we were even sitting here in the parking lot of the Hoke County jailhouse?

"Why did he have to come get us?" I grumbled, stepping from the back of Stank's Chevy.

"What did you say, Leonard?" Mama asked.

"I'm just ready to go home," I lied, well aware that my mama had reached her breaking point and one more word from a whining child would cause her to explode.

"What's going to happen to Stank?" Darryl asked.

In total darkness, one could feel Mama's eyes burn through Darryl as she turned toward the sound of the question.

"I don't think he's coming home until they have his trial," Calvin answered. "Why don't y'all just be quiet and give your mama some time to think."

Who was he to tell us what to do? Why did he not think of all that before we decided to go on this godforsaken trip? The anger inside my head was forming like hot molten lava about to reach the critical stage of eruption, but Mama's eyes kept it in check. I might have a said a few choice words to Calvin if Mama was not around, and if she, herself, had not already passed the boiling point. Darryl's daring question was the last word spoken on our journey home.

The tension seemed to disappear as we drove up North Pine Street. We finally heard the familiar sound of our driveway gravel being crushed under the car wheels.

The sound of that familiar driveway caused a long sigh of relief to escape from my yawning mouth.

I dared to break the silence with words. "Curtis must be asleep."

"Yeah, all the lights are off except the kitchen light," Willie rationalized.

"Y'all just get out the car and head straight for bed. This is one night you don't have to worry about washing up," Mama said.

"Curtis," my mama yelled through the house. "We're home."

"I'm in here," an anxious voice responded from the kitchen.

"What's wrong with you?" Mama intuitively asked.

The voice that came from the kitchen had the sound of fear in it, and we followed Mama into the kitchen.

The water in the foot-tub looked like somebody had filled it with red food coloring.

"What you trying to do, dye your foot red?" I said.

Curtis lifted his foot clear of the water, and it was then that we realized the water was red because of the deep gash in the bottom of his foot.

It was obvious from the furrows etched across Mama's face that this was only the beginning of exhausting and anxious days awaiting us. But the weight of the world would have to wait another day as Mama doctored Curtis's injured foot.

Mama always had the ability to tune out everything else when it came to taking care of her children. It must have been an inherited trait. I had watched Grandma Gladys do the same thing. No matter what struggle or problem reared its head, Grandma Gladys exhibited that "go ahead" mentality.

I was now watching that same determination as Mama blocked out the troubling events of the day. The face of anxiety and worry transformed to one of tender care the minute she started wrapping Curtis's foot.

Assured that Curtis would be all right, Mama then forced her tired body to fall across her rickety bed. Sleep came for all of us without struggle.

The peace and comfort of sleep disappeared with the sun's bright rays streaming through the window. With the immediate acknowledgment of Stank's absence came the realization that the events of yesterday were no dream.

"Wake up, Leonard. I want you to walk with me over to T.C.'s house and see if he will drive us over to Raeford for Stank's first court appearance," Mama called.

"Mama, I'm tired. I ain't even slept a good three hours," I whined.

"If you don't get your butt out that bed, you ain't going to sleep tonight either," Mama warned. "We've got to be at the courthouse by eleven o'clock, and you're going to ride with me."

Realizing it was senseless to fight, I rose and rubbed the sleep from my eyes. I immediately reached for the tattered Scotland High School identification card picture of Mable. I slept with that picture beneath my pillow. It was the last thing I saw before sleep and the first thing I looked at in the morning. If the world around me was changing, I needed at least one thing to remain constant. Mable was gone, but at least her picture was a comfort that made things somewhat tolerable.

Our walk to T.C.'s house began in thoughtful silence. Silence had the tendency to drive me crazy. I guess it's one of the many emotional side effects of low self-esteem and lack of self-confidence. It never failed; even though I was by nature an introvert, it killed me when no one spoke to me or acknowledged my presence.

Therefore, it wasn't long before I broke the silence with a question.

"Mama, why are we going to the courthouse in Raeford?" My voice cracked the still air of nerve-racking silence.

"We've got to go see if they going to let Stank out on bail," she answered, almost relieved to speak the words that had been churning in her head.

"Does bail mean he might get to come home today?" I asked.

"Yeah, if we can get the bail money."

I knew we should have saved some of that money we were getting, I thought to myself. It was now my turn to go silent while trying to process this new information.

T.C.'s house seemed to rise from beneath the ground as I raised my head to start my next series of questions. Before I could get the words through my teeth, we had already begun our ascent up the four cinder block steps that led to T.C.'s front door. I knew instinctively that I would never know the answers to my questions, because Mama's brain had switched gears. Her thoughts now would be occupied with trying to get T.C. to drive us from Laurinburg to Raeford.

Mama's slender hands formed a tight fist that twitched as she slowly and deliberately knocked on T.C.'s door.

"Who is it?" spoke a voice with hints of sleep in it.

"T.C., it's Doretha," my mama answered in her most desperate voice. "I need you to do me a favor, and I'll pay you," she called through the closed door, loudly enough for the words "pay you" to penetrate.

The voice that answered was now growing stronger and more alert.

"Wait a minute, let me slip on some pants and a shirt," T.C. said.

With uncombed hair and eyes that revealed pupils still trying to adjust to daylight, T.C. blinked as he opened the door.

"What favor you talking 'bout?" he inquired.

"I need somebody to drive my son and me to Raeford for Stank's first court appearance for DUI," Mama pleaded.

I instantly wanted to know what DUI stood for, but I held the question in my head for another place and time.

"How much will you charge me?" my mama asked, revealing her willingness to pay whatever was necessary.

"What time y'all got to be there?" T.C. asked.

The talk of money had brought T.C. to full attention, and now that he was fully awake he began negotiating with this desperate, anxious woman who showed up unannounced at his front door.

The bartering continued back and forth through the screen door. T.C. stood there in the blur of the wire mesh screen.

His eventual answer was joy to my ears. "Yeah, I'll take y'all. Let me slip on some shoes and crank up the car."

I'm sure T.C. had no idea that his simple yes was like lifting the weight of the world off my mama's shoulders as well as the weight off my tired feet.

"You don't know how much this means to me," Mama spoke in a whispered sigh.

We got to ride all the way to Raeford in that thing? T.C. owned an old powder blue station wagon that sounded like it would barely make out of his driveway. The only part of this clanking clump of metal on wheels that worked properly was its radio. The vibrations of the bass line from Marvin Gaye's song "What's Going On" rattled the junky interior of the station wagon that was to transport us all the way to Raeford and back again.

I hope we don't end up parked at the side of the road in this piece of junk, I told myself.

"Leonard, you go on and get in the back seat," Mama said.

"There ain't no seats back here!" I cried.

The rear seats of the station wagon had been folded down. It did not take a rocket scientist to realize that the car had been used for some other purpose. The wood chips scattered throughout the car were a dead giveaway that the car had apparently been used as a truck to haul firewood.

"I'm going to get dirty lying back here. I'm going to end up with wood chips all over my clothes," I said, looking at Mama with pleading eyes.

"It ain't nothing but wood chips," T.C. responded in an annoyed voice. "You can brush them off with no trouble."

When adults reason like this, there is only one thing for a child to do no matter how stupid the instructions are. The only safe course of action is to do as you are told.

I crawled into the deep blue chasm of the back of the station wagon. I knew what Jonah must have felt like when he was swallowed by the whale or big fish—whatever it was that ate him.

There must be enough room back here for fifty children my size, I thought. *I could hide or get lost back here and nobody would ever be able to find me.*

"Can't this thing go any faster?" I yelled from the canyon of the powder blue interior.

"Boy, you ought to have enough of going fast after what happened to Stank," Mama said, turning around and breathing the words out like a dragon breathing fire.

"I was just asking. Everybody's passing us," I said.

"We'll make it there in plenty of time," T.C. added.

Certain that if I said another word Mama would crawl in the back seat and whip the tar out of me, I decided to keep quiet. There was certainly enough room in the backseat of this car for her to do some damage to my skinny butt.

I spent the remainder of the drive without speaking another word. *Yeah, this is what it must have felt like for Jonah in the belly of the whale,* I thought to myself and hoped that this car would spit me out of its mouth. The only thing that made my stay in the belly of this beast tolerable was that I had something that Jonah did not have. I had Mable's picture to keep me company, and I did not remember Jonah having a girlfriend or a wife.

I must have looked at that high school identification card a million times as we traveled down Highway 401 toward Raeford. Mable was gone, and this card with her picture was the only thing I had left to comfort my broken heart. The edges were crumpled, and the laminated covering was beginning to slowly peel away. Yet despite its deteriorating condition, I treasured its warmth. I knew this tattered photo identification card could never replace the real thing, but it gave me hope as I watched our lives cascade back into the valley of abject poverty.

"I told you we'd make it in time," T.C. said as we drove into the parking lot of the Raeford Courthouse.

The building looked much different in the daylight. I knew the building was only made of steel and stone, but it felt threatening. This building seemed as if it could swallow you up and never spit you out. Courthouses had been known to do just that to the countless Black men who were unfortunate enough to have to enter their walls.

"Come on here, Leonard." Mama had to yell twice.

This building gave me the creeps. Something inside me told me that this was the place where everything would change. Raeford Courthouse would steal all our dreams of a better life. This building would strip us of the little piece of heaven that was now ours.

I knew it had already begun when they brought Stank out for his court appearance in handcuffs. The people in this building spoke a different language; it was like being in a foreign country. I know now how the children of Israel must have felt when they were taken into exile. I was lost in this unfamiliar environment with its incoherent language and rules. I vowed that I would never put myself in a position to be standing in front of people like these in handcuffs like a slave.

I tried to remember every detail. The judge sat behind a big bench looking every bit like a priest standing behind the altar ready to offer a sacrifice. The judge was dressed in a priest's robe with his gavel in hand ready to strike the sacrificial offering if it moved. The jury sat near him facing the audience like a church choir. They even had a scribe to record all the action on what looked to me like a mini typewriter. The scene was almost identical to church services I had attended once in a while. The preacher in those services only spoke about God's judgment at the last day, but I would soon discover that this judge spoke of judgment that took effect immediately.

I was frightened beyond belief and afraid to breathe in this pristine atmosphere of justice. But there I stood, watching the wheels of justice grinding like a great machine dispensing judgment.

The judge had the bailiff or somebody call out the next case on the docket: "The State of North Carolina versus Franklin Avery."

The words vibrated off the walls of this hallowed room. I almost did not recognize whom they were calling. I had called him "Stank" all my life and most likely would have never recognized his given name in this foreign place.

Stank and his court-appointed attorney stood together.

The judge read off the charges in some language I could not understand.

"How do you plead, Mr. Avery?" the judge asked.

Plead. Maybe if Stank pleaded this whole thing would be over.

Stank stared straight ahead and answered, "Guilty as charged, your honor."

That did not sound like pleading to me; it sounded more a like man ready to accept punishment.

"Mama," I whispered. "He said he did whatever the judge said he did, so does he get to come home now or will that man in the robe punish him?"

"I don't know what they're going to do. You just need to sit still and wait and see like everybody else," Mama answered.

It would not take long for us to find out as the judge started to say something else. I hoped that he would speak in plain English. I was getting tired of trying to figure out this courtroom language.

Stank's lawyer was asked to approach the bench. Whatever they were whispering about did not do Stank any good, because he was ordered to be held over in jail without bond.

The look of disappointment and confusion spread across Mama's weary face.

"Next case," the judge called banging down his gavel.

Stank and his lawyer spent a few minutes discussing their next move before the sheriff came to lead Stank back to his jail cell. Stank looked over at us with an expression of resigned acceptance on his face.

The court-appointed attorney walked toward us and began to explain in everyday language about what the judge decided and why Stank would not be granted bail.

"Mrs. Avery, the judge will pass sentence on your husband tomorrow, and Franklin informed me that he'd rather spend the night in jail rather than spend the money on bail. I think he made the right decision."

"Well, what kind of sentence do you think he'll get?" Mama asked. "Franklin has another DUI charge on his record and that won't help him."

"I think you're looking at the judge revoking your husband's driver's license for at least three years."

The lawyer's words fell like a pall on my mother's narrow shoulders. I thought for sure her knees would buckle, but Mama was strong.

"Thank you for all your help," she said, and reached out for my hand as we walked out of the courthouse.

I, for one, was glad to be leaving and never wanted to come back.

"Stank can kiss his job goodbye." My mama tried mumbling underneath her breath so I could not hear.

Stank had already missed several days from work, and I'm sure the people at his job knew of his arrest.

"I don't know where he's going to get a job with no way to get work."

Mama did not care now about what I heard because she was so angry.

The worst was realized at Stank's sentencing the next day. The judge revoked his driver's license for three years. It made no difference that Stank pleaded for mercy when he was asked if there were anything he would like to say before the judge passed sentence.

"Your honor," the words trembled from his throat. "I have a wife and nine children, and I need to be able to drive back and forth to work. Can't you do something to help me feed my family?"

I had never witnessed a grown man almost reduced to tears. If this was how justice affected a person, I knew I would never be pleading for the mercy of a judge.

The judge dropped his court demeanor and began speaking to Stank like a father reprimanding a wayward child.

"Well, son, you should have thought about your family before you put their lives in jeopardy on the highway."

The court-appointed attorney reached over and touched Stank's hand, prompting him to give up his attempt to sway the judge. The judge's decision was final.

In just a few moments, that judge had changed the lives of not just one man but a devastated wife and nine young children. The "good life" was over. We had already been living on the edge, and now we had been pushed off.

Chapter 12

Explosion

"I don't know what we're going to do."

The words filtered through the thin walls of our house on Pine Street for several weeks after Stank's conviction. These words would be the beginning of discussions that would start out as conversations about what the future held but then quickly escalate into late-night arguments.

"Doretha, if I knew what to do I'd be doing it. I know I lost the job at Golf Pride. You don't have to keep reminding me of it. I'm getting sick and tired of you always throwing it up in my face. I know I made a mistake," Stank argued. "I'm trying my best to find a job that's in walking distance. I just need you to stay off my back and give me some time."

Mama refused to let the matter drop. "We don't have time! These children need food, and what are we going to do during the winter without heat?"

Jobs were hard to come by as it was, and for Stank, now unable to drive and with his record scarred by a DUI conviction, finding a job within walking distance was a nightmare. Nevertheless, he kept looking.

The backyard block parties were gone and so were the friends.

It was a struggle for my mama to keep the bills paid and food on the table with just the Social Security check she was receiving for us.

Once again, meals became few and far between. It became necessary for us to supplement these shortfalls by scavenging grapevines, apple trees, and local freshwater fishponds, and by making always-dangerous yet popular raids on gardens.

Laurinburg Milling Company rose like a giant scepter in our community. The tall, rambling, fifteen-story building on the corner of James Street and Railroad Street had been manufacturing flour and feed grain for more than fifty years. The residents of Newtown woke every morning in the shadow of Laurinburg's tallest building. If for any reason (of which the only one I can think of would be blindness) you missed seeing it, you would still know it was there by the smell of cooking feed grain, which permeated every room in your house. The horrific odor of burning grain let everybody in Newtown know that a feed processing plant was located less than a block from where we ate, slept, and played.

The Laurinburg Milling Company had been the source of my love affair with pigeons. I never thought that Stank would end up working there. I'd always wondered why such an awful-smelling plant had been built so close to a community. I did not understand why the county health inspector allowed the risk of sickness and disease. Where were the voices of reason? I never heard anyone speak out on behalf of Newtown residents. I never saw the signs of "not in our backyard," not that it would have mattered. The city council voted to build such a God-awful plant right in our backyard, claiming it would bring jobs to our depressed area. I do not think anyone cared or thought about the death it would ultimately bring.

The damage was done. We'd learned long ago that voices like ours were, almost without thought or question, drowned out by more powerful and politically savvy voices whispered in some dark boardroom with shades drawn.

"While niggers are still in the bed sleeping, White folk are meeting somewhere planning their next move," Stank often warned us.

Laurinburg Milling Company became just another part of the

scenery in a community that was doomed to be the armpit of the city. What further damage to an already historically rundown ghetto could the appearance of a feed processing plant do?

The Scotland County Courthouse and the jailhouse were only yards away from the milling company.

"You know why they built the courthouse and the jailhouse so close to Newtown?" Stank would say during one of his now frequent verbal attacks against a system that was slowly destroying him and everybody living in Newtown. "They built it there so they wouldn't have far to drive to transport all the niggers they lock up."

The physical premises seemed to point out the truth of his statement. Scotland County Jailhouse was filled with more than its share of Black men and women. Mr. Leo Avery shared with us part of the historical stigma of Newtown, which had such nicknames as "blood field" and "the bottom." According to his stories, Newtown had been corrupt from the start with its drink houses, whorehouses, and the like.

Horrified and shocked by his accounts, we'd often ask, "Why didn't the police do something about it?"

Mr. Leo would answer, "They were getting rich off their cut of protection money."

Newtown had sold its soul to the devil in order to survive, and it was still paying the price in 1974. I could understand why Stank hit the roof when Mama suggested that he try getting work at the Laurinburg Milling Company. It was a job, and the plant had indeed kept a lot of families from starving, but what self-respecting man wanted to work at such a place? It was a heavy enough burden to be seen as half a man because you could not get a good job. It added to that burden to be working at a plant you could not avoid seeing every waking hour. It became your sunrise and moonglow because of its domination of the skyline of Newtown.

Stank kept resisting Mama's strong suggestions that he apply for a job at the mill.

"I'll work digging ditches before I step foot in that hellhole!" Stank would shout. "Doretha, ain't you ever seen the men when they leave that place? Look at them sometime. They work like dogs and leave a day's work with nothing but feed grain dust in their hair and all in their clothes. That ain't no way to treat a man. Doretha, I know you don't expect me to work in that hellhole."

Stank gave every reason why working at the Laurinburg Milling Company would kill him. We had all been witnesses to the truth of his argument. Most, if not all, of the men who worked at the feed mill lived in Newtown. They indeed walked through the streets of Newtown after work looking like ash-colored zombies from Michael Jackson's "Thriller" video. The men went to work with black hair and came home appearing prematurely gray within the span of eight hours. The gray hair and pronounced limp caused by back-breaking labor made it difficult to determine at the end of each work day if these were the same men who had started the day vibrant but who now appeared to be senior citizens.

"Stank, you know winter is just around the corner, and we've got to have gas in the tank for heat or else we're going to freeze to death," Mama said, refusing to listen to Stank's argument.

"I'll get my daddy to let us borrow his wood-burning stove for the winter," Stank countered.

"What do you expect me to cook on? You know the kitchen stove is gas, and what do you think we're going to eat if you don't take that job?" Mama asked with desperation in her voice.

I was certain Stank would not take the job at the feed mill, especially when I saw the big potbelly stove sitting in the middle of the floor.

"What's that thing doing in here?" I asked as I walked into the house after school.

"That's what we're going to use for heat, and your mama is going to cook on it, too," Stank answered.

"Why can't Mama cook on the stove in the kitchen?" I asked, afraid of the answer I would receive.

The kitchen stove was Mama's pride and joy. I had learned that lesson firsthand.

Calvin, as usual, made one of his great discoveries. He figured out a way to climb onto the roof of the house from the back porch. Each of us eventually rose to his challenge, or should I say his dare, to climb up on the roof.

It was not enough for me to be satisfied with completing Calvin's dare. I had to do something stupid. *I wonder where this dark hole leads,* I said to myself as I stared down the chimneystack. The only way to find out was to drop something down the chimney and see what would happen.

Removing one of the loose bricks from the chimney, I proceeded to drop the brick down the hole. A dark cloud of ash soon poured from the open kitchen window. I do not remember what I realized first. Did I hear the crashing sound first, or did I see the ash cloud? It did not matter. I just knew I'd broken something in the kitchen.

"What's going on in that kitchen?" the voice vibrated thorough the tin roof and shot through my feet and into my heart, causing it to almost stop.

"Leonard is on top the house!" Diane yelled as she looked up at my rigid body still frozen in the act of letting the projectile slip from my hands.

"Get off the top of that house and get in this kitchen!" Mama's voice trembled with anger. "Just look at this mess!" she yelled, her words piercing right through my body as I made my way through the back door and into the kitchen.

The white stove was covered in soot, and the walls were taking on that smutty look as well. I learned without a doubt where that hole in the chimney led. It led to the opening that once was used as the stovepipe ductwork that carried smoke from a wood-burning kitchen stove. It was obvious that whoever lived in the house years ago must have had a wood-burning stove.

Mama spoke the words that always sent me running.

"Leonard, you're going to clean this mess up, and when you finish,

I want you to go cut me a switch."

It took me hours to clean up the mess, and I deliberately took my time trying to delay what I knew was coming next—a good old-fashioned butt-whooping. I truly paid for my inquisitive nature and could barely sit down after the price was paid.

I knew Mama loved to cook on that stove, and to cook on a potbelly wood stove was a hard pill for her swallow.

"Doretha, you just going to have to adjust to cooking on a wood stove because I ain't taking no job at the feed mill," Stank said, standing firm. "What do you think people cooked on before gas came along?"

The winter came and Stank, true to his word, did not take the job at the milling company. It fell upon our narrow shoulders and empty stomachs to cut wood for the potbelly stove.

However, cutting wood is an understatement. We had no axe, no manual saw, and heaven knows no chain saw. We gathered old dead tree limbs and used our weight by jumping on them to break them up into sizes small enough to fit into the stove.

But as usual this became a game for us. We used this chore to practice up on our karate skills, and often before we knew it, there was enough firewood to last all night and to start a fire for the morning.

"Boy, you know that piece of wood is too big for you to break," the conversation would start.

"No, it ain't! Don't you know I'm Bruce Lee?"

This was the answer to any and all karate questions. If the branch proved too big for the first challenger, we each took turns trying to break it.

The pushing and shoving would begin for a crack at proving ourselves more skilled than the previous karate master. This kind of competition went on for hours, starting the minute we arrived from school and slipped out of our good clothes.

"You can load me up some more," I commanded Calvin.

"Boy, you know that's enough wood in your arms," Calvin warned. "How you going to see with that armload of wood covering your eyes?" he asked through the mountain of dried tree branches spread out across my chest and above my neck.

"Don't you worry about that. I got it all under control," I snapped back. "I'm ready to get this over with—it's getting cold out here."

As I spoke, my exhaled breath became the only thing visible through the branches stacked up to my face.

It was both dangerous and amazing to watch Stank build a fire. He would take the most flammable object handy to start the fire. It did not matter what it was. Stank would use old roof shingles, kindling, and even pieces of rubber from old discarded automobile tires. But the weirdest thing I ever saw him use was old cooking grease. Stank would take grease and pour it over the firewood in the stove and set a match to it; before you knew it, the fire was burning and the house was being heated.

Our family had become the ultimate survivors. Mama would take the eyes from the top of the potbelly stove, place her pot over the open fire, and cook whatever happened to be in the kitchen to eat. The food cooked on the wood-burning stove was often better than anything cooked on her fancy gas-burning stove. Stank said it tasted better because we put our backs into helping prepare the fire to cook it.

I understood what he meant. I could eat anything after working up an appetite gathering fire wood.

But my mama started back in on Stank. "Those children can't be out there all winter dragging up old dead tree branches. You should have swallowed your pride and taken that job at the milling company."

Then she asked the question no one had taken into consideration: "What if we get some snow this winter?"

I could see the wheels starting to turn in Stank's head.

The after-school chores soon changed, because Stank once again found a remedy for our ongoing problem of finding fuel for our fire.

"Y'all take my daddy's wagon and go down to the train dock and pick up some of that coal left on the ground down there."

It was becoming increasingly evident that all the places and things we once viewed as play things were now becoming important in our daily struggle to stay alive through the winter. We rode around Mr. Leo's house a million times in that old wagon, and we wore it out. Mr. Leo had to replace every part of it, including its tongue. The wagon was a sight for sore eyes with its mismatched wheels and its tongue held together by wire clothes hangers supplied by Rummie's mama from her job at Terry Brothers' Dry Cleaners, where she worked as a steam-press operator.

"Get in, Rummie! Let's race around the house!" were the only words needed for us to tear out like bats out of hell with Rummie sitting in the wagon. It was always a certainty that Rummie would fall out of the wagon or it would turn over on him, adding some new injury to a body that already seemed covered with every kind of wound possible.

"Rummie you can't drive. Let somebody who knows what they're doing take a shot at it," Curtis shouted over our laughter as we pulled the wagon off Rummie.

"Curtis, you can't drive no better," somebody would shout.

It never failed, and sure enough the wagon would be going so fast that the next rider would fall out of the wagon or let it turn over on him.

I watched Mr. Leo use the wagon to walk to Marge's store to purchase coal and kerosene for his wood-burning stove. I never thought we would be using the same wagon for gleaning coal at the Laurinburg and Southern train dock. This was the last straw, or as they say, "the straw that broke the camel's back."

Mama waited until the opportune time to slap it in Stank's face. There we stood, unloading what seemed like the millionth wagonload of coal onto a pile almost a mile high.

"I'm tired of seeing those children leave this house and come back in here covered with coal dust just because you too proud to go get a job at the feed mill."

There was no way Stank could get out of this one. His eyes darted from one place to the other. He'd look at Mama and then at us.

He knew the only answer that could speak to such a harsh predicament was yes.

"All right, Doretha, I'll go apply for a job at Laurinburg Milling Company tomorrow."

It broke my heart to watch Stank moving in slow motion. His movements were those of a dejected, trapped animal forced into a corner with no way out.

The next morning was brutally cold as he rattled the grate at the bottom of the potbelly stove, shaking the ashes from last night's fire into the ash pan. Gone was Stank's usual excitement of experimenting with different methods of starting a fire. The fire had truly gone out of his eyes.

"Bring me a piece of coal and one of those shingles," he mumbled in my direction.

"It's cold out there!" I said from beneath the blanket that was tightly wrapped around my skinny body.

"If you don't do like I tell you, I'll heat up your lazy butt with my belt and you won't have to worry about being cold."

It was dangerous to fool around with Stank when he was in a foul mood. I had learned from firsthand experience not to mess with a trapped or injured animal.

When I was on safety patrol at Central School, I was usually assigned to the McRae Street post, along with Kevin and Charles. Many times during our patrol hours, a particular automobile drove down the street.

"Look at that car with the Batman fins," Kevin shouted as the blue-green automobile first came into sight.

"No, that's a kitty cat car!" I yelled.

"Whatever it is, I don't like the way it looks," Charles said.

Kevin started our innocent game. "Let's see if we can touch those fins when it drives by us," he said.

"Kevin, why you want to mess with that car? Don't your grandma drive a Deuce and a Quarter with fins like that?" I asked.

Kevin spoke his dislike for any car that remotely looked like his grandma's. "I have to wash that thing all the time, and I hardly get to ride in it."

To further express his displeasure, Kevin grabbed a hand full of dirt and threw it at the passing car.

"Kevin, you must be crazy! You're going to cause all of us to get into a world of trouble with Mr. Stewart," Charles warned.

Two days of this behavior must have been all the poor owner of the "kitty cat" car could withstand.

The next time Mr. Stewart saw us at our patrol post, he demanded, "Kevin, Charles, and Leonard, I want to see all three of y'all in my office immediately."

"I wonder what he wants to see us for?" I asked the others as we followed Mr. Stewart to his office.

"I bet that lady told him we were throwing dirt at her car. I know we're being thrown off the safety patrol list," Charles answered.

"I ain't been throwing nothing at that old ugly car. Kevin, you've been the only one doing that mess," I said.

But it did not matter which one of us did the throwing; we were all guilty by association, and that's all that mattered to Mr. Stewart.

"I'm not going to kick y'all off patrol duty this time, but the next time I hear of anyone doing something like this again, I will remove you from the squad. I'm not only going to throw you off the patrol, but I'll have you suspended as well." Mr. Stewart's words cut like a knife, and he was not even finished dishing out the punishment. "I'm moving y'all down to Vance Street."

"Vance Street!" Charles yelped. "That's the sorriest post to work in the whole school," he finished his complaint.

"Well, it's Vance Street or nothing." Mr. Stewart gave us our only choice, if you could call it a choice.

"Kevin, we ought to wring your bony neck. Look at the trouble you got us into throwing at somebody's car. All because of your stupid butt, we've got to walk all the way down to Vance Street."

"It won't be that bad," Kevin said, trying to patch things up. "I walk that way from my house every day."

"Well, it ain't like walking all the way from Newtown," I said.

Even though we were upset that we'd been demoted to Vance Street because of our deviant behavior, the adjustment of walking to our new patrol post did not take long for our young legs, and before we knew it we were looking for some new devilment.

The opportunity presented itself in the form of a squirrel sprawled out in the middle of Vance Street like a squirrel skin rug, but still alive.

"I bet I can catch that squirrel," Charles said.

"Man, who do you think you are? I know you don't think you're The Flash," Kevin spoke in disbelief.

"Watch me!" Charles yelled as he made a dash in the squirrel's direction.

Before Charles could get within ten feet of the creature, it darted across the street and up the trunk of one of the huge oak trees that made living arches over the streets of Laurinburg.

"I told you you would never catch a squirrel. They're too fast," Kevin said.

"Wait a minute, I see him out on that limb," Charles replied. "Leonard, I'll give you a quarter if you climb up that tree and push the squirrel down."

I was not about to change my usual response to a challenge. I'd try anything at least once.

"How you going to catch the squirrel when I push him out of the tree?" I asked, not wanting to risk life and limb for nothing on such a risky venture. "I'm not going to break my neck and y'all mess around and let the thing get away, so y'all better be ready when that squirrel comes flying to the ground."

"We'll be ready. You just knock him down," Charles said.

"If I get him down, I want to keep him for myself, and you can keep your quarter," I added.

"You can have the old squirrel. I don't want him anyway," Charles agreed.

"Yeah, I don't want him, either. My grandma won't let me keep him. I know she'd have a heart attack if I brought something into her house that looks like a giant rat," Kevin said.

So up the huge oak tree I went. It did not take long for me to reach the limb where the squirrel sat huddled.

"Leonard, hurry up!" the shouts rang from underneath the tree.

I was able to distinguish each voice as the sound echoed through the tree's branches.

"I hope Mr. Stewart don't come by here," Kevin said. "What are we going to tell him if he ask 'Where's Leonard?'"

Mr. Stewart never deviated from his usual route to school. He had worn a path through what grass remained on the shoulder of the road on Vance Street. I think he had moved us there just so he could keep an eye on us.

The words were barely out of Kevin's mouth before I turned and saw Mr. Stewart through the branches.

"Here he comes!" I said, loudly enough for Kevin and Charles to hear me but not Mr. Stewart.

"Just don't move when he gets here, Leonard," Charles warned.

"Please don't fall out of the tree, either," Kevin added his own warning.

Why did he have to mention falling out of the tree? It now became one more thing to worry about besides getting caught. My whole body shook as I gripped the oak tree's branches with all my strength.

"Where is Leonard?" Mr. Stewart asked as he approached Kevin and Charles.

I might have known that if anybody could think up a lie that would satisfy Mr. Stewart, it would be Kevin. Kevin had lying down to a science. It was a necessary art he'd used over and over again as a tool to get out the house and skip chores. Kevin's grandma strictly ordered him to stay away from my house, but Kevin never let that stop him from thinking up a lie. We all knew he had come up with a good one any time we saw him riding up our driveway on his banana seat bike.

"I think Leonard walked back up to the school to get another patrol badge. He left his at home," Kevin calmly replied.

"Okay, y'all hold down things until he gets back," Mr. Stewart answered.

"That was close. Now I better get down to business," I whispered to myself.

I could understand now why Charles and Kevin wanted me to climb up the tree. I must have looked like an inchworm as I slowly crawled toward the squirrel. The closer I got to him, the further out on the limb he climbed and the smaller the branches became. *Man, I'm glad I don't weigh much*, I thought, wiping the sweat from my face. *I hope this squirrel realizes there's nowhere else to run and jumps off this limb. I don't think I can go any farther.*

The squirrel was now on the end of the branch, which swung out over the road. I could see it in his eyes—he was trying to figure out which way to go. The squirrel could not run back toward me.

"I think he's getting ready to jump. Y'all get ready to catch him!" I yelled down to Charles and Kevin.

Immediately an argument broke out over what they were going to use to catch the squirrel.

"Kevin, let's use your jean jacket," Charles said.

"Man, I ain't letting you catch no stinking squirrel in my jacket. My grandma will kill me if she smells squirrel on my jacket."

"Kevin, unless your grandma is part bloodhound, how is she going smell squirrel scent on your jacket?"

"I don't care what y'all use. I know y'all better not let this squirrel get away or I'll kick both y'all butts for having me climb way up here and risk my neck," I shouted again.

I shook the branches and yelled at the squirrel, "Jump! Jump!"

Sure enough, the squirrel jumped, and Charles caught him in Kevin's jean jacket.

"Did y'all get him?" I called toward the ground as I started climbing down the trunk of the tree as fast as I could.

"Let me hold him," I cried over the squirrel's yelps and struggles to get free.

"You better watch his teeth. I think he's trying to bite somebody," Charles warned me as I reached for the tiny animal.

The squirrel's head was already lunging toward me with teeth exposed. The next sound that came from my mouth was a cry of anguish and pain. I felt the sharp teeth of the squirrel sink into my finger, but I was determined to hang on to him no matter what.

"Man, that thing has got some sharp teeth, and he don't mind using them," Kevin said. "Leonard, don't let that blood get all over my jacket," he added, more concerned about his jacket than about my bleeding finger.

"We better hurry up and get this squirrel up to Mr. Stewart's classroom before he bites Leonard again," Charles said.

"Yeah, Mr. Stewart will give us something safe to put him in. I think he'll be glad to use the squirrel for science class," I anxiously said, hoping this would be the case.

We managed to get the squirrel up to the school.

"Fairley, what's that you got in that jacket?" Mr. Stewart asked.

"It's a squirrel we caught. I thought you might be able to use him for class today and maybe I could take him home with me after school," I explained.

Mr. Stewart grabbed the first thing he could get his hands on as the squirrel started to struggle again.

"Leonard, put him in this trash can. I'll make some holes in the lid. Just make sure you tape it down."

Mr. Stewart quickly started giving orders that would ensure both the squirrel's safety and ours. The classroom was filled with eager students who'd gathered as close as they could in order to get a glimpse of the tiny squirrel. The chatter of so many excited children made the squirrel struggle harder.

In spite of all the clamoring, we finally succeeded at getting the frightened animal into the trash can. However, we continued to hear him struggling to escape from this cage. It was apparent this squirrel meant to be free.

Eventually, the lid of the trash can blasted from its place like a bullet shot out of a gun.

"Look out! He got out!" The voices screamed as the squirrel went berserk.

Mr. Stewart tried to regain control. "Somebody close the door before he gets out in the hall!"

When the squirrel realized its only means of escape from the room had been eliminated, it started jumping from desk to desk, becoming a blur of yelping fur. The squirrel even landed on the top of some student's head during its frantic attempt to escape.

It was like watching Keystone cops running around in fast motion as people were trying to avoid this maniac squirrel. It must have taken us most of the class period to catch the squirrel and put him back into the trash can. The lesson of trying to keep a wild animal inside a trash can with a room full of excited children taught us to be extra careful. Therefore, we taped the lid down with duct tape and placed books on top of it as well.

Mr. Stewart turned his attention to my injury.

"Leonard, you're going have to go see the school nurse and get that finger checked out. It looks like a very nasty bite the squirrel gave you."

The nurse dressed my wound and told me I would need to have my mama take me down to the health clinic for a shot just in case the squirrel had rabies.

The possibility of getting rabies was the last thing on my mind as I walked home with the trash can and squirrel. Once at home, I put the squirrel in a cage Stank built to keep baby chicks in.

The squirrel refused to touch the food I attempted to feed it, and he began to rapidly weaken. Maybe if I take him out and let him walk around he'll get better. I'll take my belt and make a loop to go around his neck and walk him, I said to myself.

I proceeded to open the cage, stepping inside with belt loop in hand. The squirrel just sat there a minute, carefully watching me slowly approach him.

I would soon learn that the squirrel was not watching me but was keeping his eyes on freedom's door. I had forgotten to close the gate behind me. It was no wonder the squirrel was looking at me with what appeared to be a grin on his face.

He waited until I moved further away from the door and then slowly started moving toward me.

In a flash, the squirrel jumped and dashed across my back as I bent over to put the belt loop around his neck. I had never seen an animal move so fast. Up the nearest tree he sprinted, looking back as if to laugh at me for being such a fool for thinking that I could keep him in captivity. This squirrel seemed bent on teaching me that his will to be free was stronger than my desire for a pet.

I was learning that a wild caged animal would do anything to be free, including trying to bite my finger off.

When Stank ordered me to bring him the shingles and coal, I saw the same look in his eyes as those I saw in the squirrel's when he was trapped. I did not want to cross Stank and suffer the consequences of dealing with his feelings.

I walked to the back porch and brought enough shingles and coal to make sure I would not have to go back outside in the freezing cold.

"Go find the matches for me," Stank ordered.

I now began to regret being the first to wake up. It was hard to tell if it was colder outside or inside as I made my way to the kitchen to find some matches. Another task accomplished—another order carried out. I was now ready to crawl back into bed or wake somebody else up so they could feel the wrath of Stank.

As I was heading back to bed, Stank's rough voice spoke again. "Don't you get back in that bed. I still might need your help."

I stood there freezing to death, watching the flames lick themselves around the dead tree branches and listening to the coal pop and sizzle. "Come on, fire, hurry up and get hot," I whispered to myself. I certainly did not want Stank to hear me. *I ain't going to be so stupid tomorrow*, I promised myself.

Eventually, the fire did get hot enough, and my cold body finally started to thaw out. But I would still not get a reprieve.

Stank ordered me to go out into kitchen and fill up a foot tub with water, and put it on the stove so that he could have hot water to wash up in.

"What's taking you so long in there?" He yelled into the kitchen where I labored to lift the foot tub clear of the sink.

"This tub is too heavy for me. I ain't never had to carry it by myself before," I answered to the voice yelling from the other room.

"That tub ain't that heavy, and you better get it in here quick. I've got to get down to the feed mill and apply for a job, and you better not make me late with your complaining."

So that was it—that's why Stank was in such a dangerous and foul mood. I knew immediately that Mama must have been able to talk him into doing the one thing he had vowed never to do.

One would think a man who had not worked in months would be happy about finally landing a job.

However, when Stank returned from the mill, there was understandably no joy in his voice as he announced, "I got the job and I start tomorrow."

Already you could see the gray dust of grain residue in his hair. The grain was scattered across his broad shoulders as well. The grain looked like flakes of dandruff.

Stank dejectedly shared the details of what he would be doing.

"I'll be working in the bag sewing room up on the second floor. It will be part of my job to sew the tops of bags on dog, chicken, cow, hog, and horse feed." He abruptly ended his explanation and said,

"I'm tired now and need to lie down for a while."

We knew immediately this meant we needed to go outside so that the noise of children at play in the house would not disturb an already crestfallen and weary soul.

We heard the familiar refrain of Mama's voice calling into the backs of our heads.

"Y'all be back in this house before dark."

Stank hated his job but vowed to make the best of it. The muffled voices of Stank and Mama filtered through the wooden non-insulated walls as bedtime arrived.

Stank began the conversation trying to keep his voice down.

"Doretha, you should see what they got me doing at the feed mill. I sit on this little three-legged dunce stool and sew the tops of bags for eight hours. I get all this dust on my clothes and in my hair from the machine that pours the feed into bags and from the processing part of the mill way up on the sixth floor."

"Well, Stank, it's just temporary," Mama answered.

"That's what the rest of the men working on the second floor said, and all they do is cough all day long from years of inhaling all that dust into their lungs. Doretha, that place is a death trap."

"There must be someplace else you can work in the mill besides in the bag room?" Mama asked.

"Don't you think I already asked somebody about that?" Stank said. "The only other job is driving the delivery truck."

Mama tried to ease Stank's anxiety and anger. "Why won't you drive trucks?"

In her attempt to console him she'd apparently forgotten why Stank was in this predicament in the first place.

"Woman, you don't know nothing about driving no truck. You can't get up behind the wheel of a truck and call yourself a truck driver. It takes training and a special driver's license."

Before Mama could cut in and cause him to lose his train of thought, Stank quickly started talking again. "Even if I had a license, I would have to wait on others who have seniority. I'd be put on a waiting list a mile long behind men who've been there longer than me."

This cleared up for me what "seniority" meant.

"Why don't you go on and apply for your truck driver's license? If you just try, and stop feeling sorry for yourself, you don't know what might happen," Mama said.

Stank brought Mama back to the reality of the situation. "You know I can't get a driver's license for three years. What am I supposed to do in the meantime, just sit on that dumb stool and watch bags pass me by?"

It never failed. Every day, Stank returned home from work with stories we dubbed "idiot stories." The story always centered on the fact that any idiot or moron could do his job with their eyes closed. The only thing that kept Stank sane was the new hobbies he would work on during the weekend.

I suspect it must have been a combination of things that caused Stank to become interested in raising chickens. Stank's first job had been catching chickens, and now he'd come full circle, it seemed. While the endless stream of chicken feed bags passed before his face at the feed mill, the dormant seed must have germinated subliminally, with each chicken feed bag whispering, "Breed chickens!" I would not doubt that Stank had heard a bag or two clucking every once in a while. If his job was as mundane as he claimed it to be, anything was liable to cross his mind on that three-legged stool.

Working at the Laurinburg Milling Company, no matter how boring or stupid, did have some perks, if you could call them that. Laurinburg's dominant and wealthiest family, the McNairs, owned the milling company. The company processed the grain they grew on their huge corporate farms to feed their enormous cattle, poultry, and hog interests.

The perk that all McNair Company employees received were discounts on purchases made at McNair's Hardware Supply Store or

The Laurinburg Department Store, both owned by McNairs. Therefore, it was never a question as to where the creosote poles, chicken wire, and everything needed to drill a hand water pump came from. I did not need to guess where the strainer and all the items came from. We would grow to hate all these items that cluttered the ground in our backyard where twin outside toilets once stood.

Once Stank got it in his head to start raising chickens, he gave us instructions about how to dig a trench in the shape of a box, and then every day for the next three weeks we spent digging four of them.

"I don't know why we got to come out here and dig these stupid trenches," we would complain.

"Yeah, everyone else is playing, and we're out here busting our butts for something that don't even make no sense," Calvin said, venting his anger.

"I'd like to know what all this mess is going to be," I said with frustration but also some curiosity.

When we finally thought we'd guessed what all this strange junk would eventually become, Stank threw us a curve. He literally brought in the kitchen sink and the bathtub.

"Stank has really lost his mind," Curtis whispered.

"Yeah, sitting on that idiot stool has caused him to flip his wig," I agreed.

We watched Stank stand on the back of the porch and begin to drill a hole deep enough for the pump strainer to draw water.

"I don't know how he expects water to reach all the way out here from up there, if that's what he has on his mind," I said.

"I just know one thing," Calvin said. "I want to know why he brought that sink and bathtub out here."

It was amazing to see Stank's plan unfold before our eyes. Whatever he had envisioned sitting on the dunce stool must have been able to occupy his mind so strongly that he could not think of anything else.

Stank did not even try to verbalize for anybody what was in his head; he simply gave orders and, by his expression, dared us to ask any questions. So no matter how insane all this work appeared, we simply did what we were told.

Stank did all the detail work himself as he measured and cut lumber. We were his "fetch-and-go" grunt workers. We were the worker ants, never knowing for certain what was to become of all our sweat and blisters.

Little by little, the wooden frame that would hold the kitchen sink took shape.

"I know what he's going to do with that sink now. He's going to pump water into the sink and make it go into the fence," I proudly deduced.

"I bet you still don't know how the water is going to get all the way out here," Darryl teased.

"Well, I know what that bathtub is for," I fired back.

The bathtub was placed inside the chicken wire fence strung between the creosote poles and nailed to the baseboard and poles.

It had been Willie's job to dig a trench from the pump and sink on the back porch down into the chicken wire fence ending at the bathtub. Stank plugged the holes in the bathtub with tar, making sure the tub would hold water.

"Well, since you so smart, tell me what the sink is for," Willie said.

I'm sure Willie wanted to know why he'd dug that big trench. I'm sure he did not want all his work to be in vain.

"It will bring water from the pump and into the tub," I explained.

"Leonard, you're just as crazy as Stank. There ain't no way in the world water's going to fill up that tub from the back porch," Willie said. "Can't you see the bathtub is sitting too high off the ground for that?"

"I don't know how Stank is going to do it, but I still say water from the pump will run through the sink and out into the bathtub," I spoke, unwilling to give up my idea.

It did not take long for my theory to prove true. Stank brought yards of PVC pipe home the following day and attached one end of the pipe to the drain of the sink. The other end reached through Willie's trench and into the bath tub.

"I told you, Willie," I gloated triumphantly.

Although we could clearly see the chicken wire fence, we still did not know what would go into it. It did not take a genius to figure out that whatever Stank intended to put inside the fence would include large numbers. Whatever they were, they would be alive and need lots of water.

Maybe that idiot stool was not such a bad place to think, after all. Stank had devised an ingenious plan that would keep plenty of fresh water to drink for whatever was to live in the wire fence. Stank knew that when we got tired and thirsty, we ran back and forth to the pump for a cool drink of ground well water.

I was amazed by the ingenuity of it all and would often stand behind the pump pumping water and watching it run into the bathtub yards away.

Each day, Stank teased us by adding another piece to the chicken wire puzzle; he brought home a fifty-gallon drum feeder one day, and the next day, he brought home something that looked like puppy houses constructed of mesh wire just tall enough to clear the ground.

"I wish he'd tell somebody what he's doing," we mumbled back and forth.

It had become a guessing game for us as we took turns trying to be the first person to correctly figure out where all this was leading.

I heard the chirping before I saw the almost one hundred golden chicks, or "biddies," as Stank called them. The golden glow of the chicks was almost blinding against the clear blue sky of late spring.

My hands were just itching to touch one of those balls of golden energy. I knew before that ever happened, I would have to endure the lecture from the CEO. I would have to endure the telling of the entire vision from start to finish. I would learn how Stank intended to eventually start an egg-selling business.

"I don't want y'all playing with these biddies. We're going to make some extra money selling hen eggs, and I can't afford the loss of even one of these biddies," Stank warned.

Handling the small bundles of velvety chicks as if they were indeed priceless gold, Stank demonstrated the proper way to lift these chirping balls so as not to injure them.

We placed the chicks one by one into mesh wire cages.

"All of y'all going to get a chance at making sure they get fed and have plenty of water," Stank said, causing arguments to start about who would be the first to care for the chicks.

"I want to be the first!" I yelled. "I know how to take care of birds. Remember how I took care of Snowflake and Moses."

"Okay, Leonard, you can go first. Make sure you put this amount of chicken feed in each feeding tray," Stank said, scooping out the desired amount from the open chicken feed bag. "Always make sure they get fresh water, too."

The golden specks with wings and beaks danced before my awestruck eyes, and for a second I was overwhelmed by the thought of caring for so many baby chicks. Caring for one bird had been no trouble, but caring for one hundred was a different story.

I can do this, I convinced myself. We each took our turns at being surrogate mother hens, but the excitement of it all eventually wore off. It was a glorious day when it came time to release the much larger chicks into the chicken wire fence.

"I'm glad we don't have to feed and water these things no more," I said as we released them into the self-watering, self-feeding environment of the chicken coop.

In the heat of celebration, one can sometimes lose touch with reality. The chicks had indeed grown large enough to liberate them into the wide-open spaces of the chicken wire fence. Stank was no longer concerned about them slipping through the holes in the wire mesh fence.

Yet with the first appearance of the gray clouds looming overhead, we learned that our mother hen days were not behind us just yet.

"Y'all go out there and put them chickens in their houses before they drown!" Stank yelled.

I thought turkeys were the only birds stupid enough to stand out in a thunder storm and drown themselves looking up into a pouring rainstorm.

"Come on, Shelia and Vanessa, y'all can help us get these chickens into the chicken coop!"

We jumped into the pouring spring shower and started herding the chickens toward the chicken coop.

"Y'all get your crazy selves into the coop!"

We ran around through the quickly forming mud yelling at the stupid birds. I do not know who looked stupider, the chicks or us. It was a sight for sore eyes—chickens scattering with frightening chirps and children screaming through raindrops that were getting larger by the second.

I guess it was exhaustion as a result of running around in wet clothes that caused us to begin chasing down the remaining chicks. We started scooping them up into our hands and physically putting them in the chicken coop.

"Vanessa, what are you doing, girl?" I stood in amazement watching Vanessa holding a chick in one hand and a switch in the other.

"Didn't I tell you to get in that house? I'm tired of y'all not doing like I tell y'all to do." Vanessa said, mimicking my mama stroke for stroke as she came down with the switch across the struggling chick's back.

Vanessa imitated Mama's habit of always talking to you while she whipped the living daylights out of you. It never appeared enough punishment to get the whipping in the first place. Mama always talked to you in the process of carrying out her punishment.

Vanessa tried to justify her treatment of the helpless chick. "I'm tired of running down these hardheaded chickens."

"You better put that chick down before Stank sees you," I said.

"Yeah, if Stank catches you hitting that chicken, you know you're going to get the same thing but worse," Shelia warned Vanessa.

The chickens were all safe inside the coop, but we were soaking wet.

Unfortunately, bad weather never prevented us from doing the chores that waited for us every day. The minute we changed our school clothes, we went right back to work.

Our days continued to be centered on taking care of the chickens. The workload continued until we saw the red combs begin to grow on the tops of several of the chickens' heads. It was easy to distinguish the two Rhode Island Red roosters from the two Dominick roosters. Stank made sure we knew the names of each breed in this chicken kingdom. It was important to him that we be up-to-date on this new business that would bring extra money into the house.

It was obvious from the expression on his face that Stank somehow understood the frantic clucking of the hens. The chicks had grown to adulthood, and it was only a matter of time before the egg-laying started in earnest.

"Go out there and see which hen laid that egg," Stank commanded.

"How does he know one of those hens laid an egg? He ain't no Dr. Doolittle," I mumbled to myself as I walked out to the chicken coop.

It was like trying to find a needle in a haystack, walking from one hen's nest to the next. *I know Stank has lost his ever-loving mind if he thinks he can speak chicken.*

But there it sat. The brown speck stood out in the messy nest of straw, and there was no doubting that Stank knew his stuff.

"I found three eggs right here in the straw!" I proclaimed my discovery loud enough that the whole neighborhood could hear.

"I know one thing, you better not drop those eggs," Stank warned me as I ran without stopping.

I jumped up on the back porch holding high my prize.

"Doretha, I want you to write an ad for the Laurinburg Exchange newspaper," Stank said as he took the eggs from my hands.

"What kind of ad you talking about?" Mama asked.

"I already told you we going into the egg-selling business, and this is only the beginning. I want folk in Laurinburg to know that we sell the best eggs in town. Come on now, write that ad; all you got to do is tell people the address and they'll come running. We'll charge a fair price. The word will get out and folk will be standing in line to buy Franklin Avery's famous eggs," Stank boasted.

If Stank had a little education, he could have been a broker on Wall Street. It was amazing to see the light in his eyes as he explained how he planned to carry out his business. Stank talked about the details with all the seriousness of a business executive on Wall Street.

Stank spoke the truth when he said this was only the beginning. The hens started laying eggs by the dozens, and before long it seemed like millions. Our after-school ritual now included gathering eggs from more than ninety hens that were suddenly on an egg-laying frenzy. It fell upon the shoulders of the boys to gather the eggs and the girls to package them.

Once again Stank had been prophetic; people from all over town started showing up at our door looking for eggs. The extra money did come in handy.

Shelia was the first to notice that something drastic was happening.

"Look at that chicken. It looks like something ate its tail feathers off. I know chickens ain't supposed to look like that."

It was apparent that something did not make sense. Unnatural was what it was. We began to notice other chickens walking around with the same affliction.

"I want y'all to keep a close eye on those chickens," Stank instructed us.

We could not believe it as we watched in stunned horror as the chickens seemed to become cannibalistic.

"They're eating each others' butts off!" Vanessa screamed.

It appeared to be some kind of contagious evil. Once one started, the others seemed unable to resist the temptation.

Stank did not appear too overly concerned about this shocking turn of events going on in the chicken coop.

"I asked somebody on the job about why chickens sometimes plucking each others' backsides, and they said it was because they need calcium in their diet." Stank seemed more than satisfied with this answer.

He started spreading calcium pellets on the ground of the chicken coop, and for a short period of time it seemed to work.

However, within weeks somebody discovered the body of a dead chicken in the chicken yard. I'd never seen a chicken with its insides completely gone. It was obvious that another chicken or chickens had pecked this chicken to death and then picked out its insides.

Stank was beginning to worry about his investment.

"I ain't never seen anything like it in my life."

Mama spoke up. "I don't know what's going on either but the other day I saw Rene feeding those chickens something out of a spoon through the fence. Now I don't believe in roots or nothing like that, but I know Mrs. Lucy believes in roots. I've seen her outside spreading sulfur around her back door to ward off evil spirits. I bet she told Rene to give those chickens something that's got them eating each other like that."

Mama's chilling explanation made us all begin to wonder if it were indeed possible to place a spell on chickens that would turn them into cannibals. I would not put anything past Mrs. Lucy.

The whole community knew that Mrs. Lucy's personality lent itself to prying. Mrs. Lucy also had her ways of attempting to control other people's lives. Mrs. Lucy was the kind of person who was all up in everybody's business. It was also common knowledge that she would do anything to disrupt somebody else's attempts at trying to make life better for their family.

"I don't think Rene gave them chickens nothing to make them start doing what they're doing to each other," Stank said. "I do know that I need to put some more chickens in there, but I'm scared to put more in with those crazy ones. I'm already getting eaten out of my profit. I don't know what I'm going to do. I just can't afford to buy anymore chickens right now."

Stank was at the end of his rope and needed the winds of luck to blow in his favor. It did not take long for the wind to blow in the right direction.

Stank gave voice to what appeared to be the answer to our problem. "I found out yesterday there's a woman up in the Sandhills that has some bantam chickens that she wants to get rid of. I hear she's willing to give them to anybody willing to take the time to catch them. I just need to get my hands on some of those chickens. They make good watchdogs, and the rooster will keep these crazy hens in check."

I could not believe that people living out in the country often kept yard chickens, of which bantams were the favorite.

If I had known what it would take to catch bantam chickens, I would have adamantly protested going to the Sandhills in the first place. I was not a chicken expert like Stank. I had no idea that bantam chickens were wild. But I would soon learn why people used them as watchdogs.

I happily hopped into Stank's friend's pickup truck and went chicken catching.

The white house with the rusting tin roof stood in the middle of an already harvested soybean field with rows that went on for what seemed like eternity. It was all you saw for as far as the eye could see— nothing but soybean stubble.

As we approached the house, the whining of the truck's engine caused the chickens to cluck wildly. The sound of all these chickens could have raised the dead. I could see why people used them as watchdogs. There was no way on God's green earth that anybody could have made it past this alarm system.

Bantam chickens started darting in all directions.

"I don't know how Stank expects us to catch them wild things," Curtis cried.

The bantam chickens were about the size of a large pigeon, but man, they were fast. I had never seen chickens with such bright colors. The roosters looked like flames as their colors flared in a blur of speed.

"Let's go!" Stank yelled out the window of the truck.

I could feel everybody's uneasiness about this chore as each one of us slowly climbed from the bed of the pickup truck. Stank tried demonstrating the art of catching chickens, but we had already determined that those instructions would get us spurred to death. It did not matter how many chickens Stank could catch during his chicken-catching days; he had never tangled with this kind of bird.

"Those roosters got spurs like switchblades," Calvin said. "I ain't about to be trying to catch them things by the feet. I'll jump on their backs before I get my hand caught up in those sharp spurs."

The chase was on as Calvin started running behind a bantam hen at top speed.

"I got it!" Calvin shouted in mid jump before eating dust. "I thought for sure I had that chicken," he said, spitting dirt from his mouth.

"Man, those things can fly!" Willie was the next person to realize how difficult our task would be when the chicken he was chasing suddenly took flight into the nearest tree.

Curtis accepted the challenge of going after one of the roosters.

"Curtis, you got him!" voices rose in support of Curtis's certain victory.

"Look out, he's coming after you!" Calvin screamed.

Upon discovering he was about to be cornered, the rooster suddenly turned and began to ruffle up its neck feathers—a sure sign that it was about to attack.

Curtis cornered the rooster beneath the old farmhouse near what must have been the kitchen. Dust could be seen flying from beneath the house as Curtis fought it out with the bantam rooster. The iron skillet made a loud clank that echoed through the dust. Curtis was lucky enough to have found an iron skillet and did not hesitate using it as a weapon to knock the rooster unconscious.

Curtis crawled from beneath the kitchen porch holding his prize rooster in one hand and the skillet in the other. Curtis stood in triumph, looking every bit like David after his dramatic defeat of the giant Goliath.

"Curtis, how did you get that crazy rooster off you?" I asked.

Curtis brushed the dust out of his hair and off his clothes and eagerly began to recount his story.

"That rooster was all over me. He was trying to spur me in the face, but I turned my back to him and kicked him up against one those big floor beams, and that's when I saw this iron skillet. Before that chicken knew what hit him, I laid him out good with this iron skillet," Curtis said, shaking his weapon.

Curtis's victory renewed our resolve to catch these wild birds. Fortunately, we possessed something they did not—brains. However, even with all our brainpower, it took the entire day to round up all the bantam chickens. They were indeed worthy adversaries.

For all our troubles, Stank's experiment did not work. The domestic chickens seemed to instinctively realize that they were no matches for the bantam chickens and promptly left them alone. But our domestic chickens kept dying. It did not take long for one hundred chickens to become fifty, then twenty-five, and soon all that remained were the bantam chickens. The egg business still suffered—no one wanted the tiny eggs of a bantam hen.

As a result, Stank's dream of being the owner of his own business went down the drain.

I never would have thought that being forced out of the egg-selling business would be such a blow. Stank put his whole heart and soul into this venture. Therefore, failure caused him to sink into deep depression. The words must have constantly run through his mind: What kind of example am I, a man who can't keep a driver's license? What kind of man am I, working at a feed mill? What idiot couldn't raise chickens?

The slide into the chasm of worthlessness and despair was swift and the drinking heavy. Stank's behavior became predictable and familiar. We had watched our biological father go through the same thing. The pattern of abuse was different in that Stank never fought our mama, but his words became as violent as any physical blow could have been.

Stank took out his physical anger on other objects. He often came home from some drinking binge and would begin throwing pieces of furniture out the back door.

"Stank, what are you doing?" Mama screamed the first night he pushed furniture out the door and set it on fire. "You know we ain't got nothing now, and we don't need you acting the fool by burning up what little bit of stuff we do have."

But as usual, Mama's words were in vain. There was nothing she could say or do that could fill the void in Stank's manhood. The unworthiness burned its way into Stank's soul.

The wounds were just too deep. I remember the weekend Stank staggered back home from God knows where and literally fell into the house repeating over and over again, "Doretha, feed me like a dog. Nobody cares about me; I'm just a dog. Doretha, feed me like a dog out on the back porch."

Monday would arrive, and Stank would start the cycle all over again. He'd work the whole week sitting on the idiot stool and get paid on Friday. He always kept enough money to get drunk. I guess spending the week sitting on that stool thinking of his failure became too much for Stank to endure. Therefore, the bottle became his escape.

But by now, painful and tragic things were the least of our concerns. Summer was just a few days old, and once again we were free to roam Newtown looking for the next big adventure.

What kind of adventure would placate teenagers with the intoxicating magic of hormones running through their veins? The days of swimming in creeks and riding on stick horses were long gone. The summer would prove our readiness to leave behind childish things and prepare for high school.

It would be especially difficult for me because my one true love was no longer living in the house located in front of me. Mable was miles away in what might as well have been a different country.

Surely there must be something in town that would be able to occupy the minds of restless youth. I was coming of age, and it would prove to be crucial in more than one way. I had already watched other teenagers' lives take a dramatic turn for the worse. We were learning that teenagers needed excitement in their lives. Many of our peers found that excitement in drugs, alcohol, and sex.

The conversations of the summer would be about which teenager had become pregnant or which had gotten into trouble with the law. Options for the summer would be limited. There would be no vacations to Disney Land—not even a trip to an amusement park.

The complaints begin to flow from the lips of more than one Pine Street Patriot, and summer was only a few days old.

"There ain't nothing to do in this sorry town. What are we going to do today?"

These types of questions became a daily refrain that constantly reminded us that living in Newtown could quickly become a death trap for restless teenagers with nothing to do.

One day, Sylvester offered a potential solution to our boredom.

"I hear there's a party in McDuffie Village tonight."

"Man, you know if your mama ever caught you stepping one foot into McDuffie Village, she'd whip the skin off your back. Didn't you hear about that boy who got killed down there last summer?" I said, trying to quickly shoot down Sylvester's dangerous idea.

"Well, you tell us what we going to do, and don't you dare talk about going fishing or swimming. I'm tired of that baby stuff," Sylvester retorted.

McDuffie Village became the section of Newtown where one could live life in the fast lane. If there was anything exciting happening, especially violent or criminal, it happened in McDuffie Village. City police gave this community its own notorious nickname, "Dodge City." McDuffie Village's reputation was so bad that police never answered a call to go there without backup.

Whenever an officer was called about criminal activity in Newtown, they never came alone. The local newspaper, the Laurinburg Exchange, was loaded with news about shootings, stabbings, rapes, and drug deals gone bad. McDuffie Village was a war zone on weekends. One could always count on news from McDuffie Village to spice things up a little.

McDuffie Village was the place Stank often frequented to drown his sorrows. Stank encountered his share of dangers in McDuffie. If we needed proof of how dangerous McDuffie Village truly was, all we needed to do was remember how Stank was once robbed there in broad daylight. Therefore, it was understandable why we made every effort to heed Mama's warning: "Y'all don't need to be hanging around a place where you might get killed just by being in the wrong place at the wrong time."

The proof of Mama's words was made vivid to us as we watched the ambulances and police cars race up and down Dickson Street. The flashing lights and blaring sirens transporting both victims and perpetrators alike to the hospital or jail were constant on weekends.

It was always believed that nothing happening in Laurinburg could overshadow the news coming out of McDuffie Village. The news of Kish's death and the fire at Laurinburg Junior High School were rare exceptions, when the front page of the newspaper carried news about something other than who got shot or stabbed in McDuffie Village. It was a sad commentary about life for people like us who just happened to be born the wrong color and on the wrong side of the tracks.

We learned that there were only two ways to make the news—either as a criminal or by becoming a sports star on the local high school scene. If you did not make news in either of these ways, you were just out of sight and out of mind. The world, along with the city, appeared to relegate us to the status of invisible nobodies.

I'd paid little or no attention to these things in the past. Why were they now becoming a part of my thought process? In the past I had no need to worry about such injustices. Mable always eased the pain. Could it be that we'd built walls of insulation for each other as the Pine Street Patriots? Whatever the reason, I had never paid much attention to the obvious degradation of spirit that resulted from our status in society. I simply accepted this as my home, and as long as there was a sense of community, nothing else mattered.

But now, for the first time, I began to look at the foundation of that community with different eyes, and what I saw was not pretty.

What else can happen? I wondered. The clouds were becoming darker. The silver linings were becoming increasingly harder to see. Things, I thought, could not get worse.

But I was wrong.

Stank followed his usual routine of trying to drink away his sorrow one weekend in mid-June. As he returned to work the following Monday, he had no idea what was about to happen. He was unaware that things were about to take a more drastic, painful, and ugly turn.

The sound of the explosion that would forever change our lives rocked Laurinburg on Wednesday, June 19, 1974.

"What in the world was that noise?" I screamed from the backyard, where we usually gathered for our routine discussion of the latest happenings in McDuffie Village.

"Look at that cloud of smoke coming from the feed mill!" someone cried.

I could only pray that our eyes were deceiving us. The mushroom cloud ascending from the Laurinburg Milling Company could be seen for miles, and the explosion rocked the city for several blocks.

"The feed mill blew up! Run, Leo, and see what's going on!" Mrs. Hattie's hysterical shouts could be heard traveling behind Stank's seventy-year-old father, who was already on his way to see what was happening.

The ominous cloud was starting to settle over the community. One could smell the grain dust. The sting and stench in our nostrils told us that something terrible had happened.

However, the cloud and the smell were nothing compared to what we saw as we stood at the edge of Railroad Street. The explosion had ripped the whole second floor of the Laurinburg Milling Company apart. There was nothing left of the second floor except a small portion of the wall.

"What's going to happen to those people on the third floor? If somebody don't do something quick, they're going to be stranded up there in all that fire," Fred shouted.

"Lord, there ain't no way nobody could be alive if they were sitting on the second floor!" the voice of a spectator cried from the sea of people who had gathered to witness the devastation.

"Wait, I see somebody hanging on to a piece of the remaining wall," another voice cried.

"I wonder if he's going to jump," another voice echoed dismay.

"Yeah, I think he is going to jump!" a female voice answered.

The lone figure clinging to the last remnant of hope suddenly let go of the wall. We witnessed him descending through the clouds of dust and falling bricks. He had made a heroic struggle for survival, but his exhausted burned body had no strength left. The only thing we could do was watch in horror as the man dropped to what for him must have seemed like certain death. His was the choice of being burned to death by the rapidly approaching fire or taking his chances of meeting death by the fall.

"Why are they hosing down those men over there by the ambulance?" I asked a weary and anxious Mr. Leo.

"Boy, can't you see them men are on fire! They got to put them out somehow!"

"But Mr. Leo, they blowing the skin off them! Ain't they hurt enough without having the fire hoses turned on them?"

The scene was like a war zone. Fire officials and rescue emergency workers were moving frantically trying to answer the death-curdling screams of smoldering bodies.

"Ain't that Stank walking over there?"

Mr. Leo disregarded the boundary guard placed in front of the spectators to keep them out of danger. There was no way the police or anybody else was going to stop Mr. Leo from getting to Stank.

Stank was walking around in a daze.

"Somebody give me something to kill me! The pain is too much;

I just want to die!" Stank screamed over and over, louder and louder.

"It's going to be all right. Come on; let's get to the ambulance over here," Mr. Leo replied, coaxing Stank closer to a waiting ambulance.

Stank was so disoriented that he had wandered away from the medical attendants.

The men working on the second floor were so badly burned that they could not even be placed on stretchers. The men, including Stank, were placed in the ambulances in sitting positions with a row of intravenous bags filled with fluid. The EMS workers were desperately trying to replace fluids that were disappearing quickly from these burned bodies. However, keeping up with the rapidly emptying bags was beginning to prove an impossible task. The bags were empty almost as soon as they were started. It was as if the fluids were being run through a strainer. The walls of the ambulance could not muffle the screams of men whose bodies were trying to adjust to hell's fury.

"Doretha, please tell them to give me something that will kill me." Those were the last words I heard Stank speak before the ambulance sped out of sight.

"Leonard, y'all go on back to the house! I'm going out to the hospital!" Mama yelled over the sounds of spraying hoses and wailing sirens.

Standing there watching, horrified at the scene being played out before my eyes, the words "That place is a death trap" sent chills down my spine. How could anybody have guessed that things would play out like this?

The dust and grain in the milling company proved to be a deadly combination. The same dust that each man brought home with him in his hair now became a death net. The same dust and grain that was a chore to wash from their clothing was now a magnet drawing the fire through their defenseless bodies. The same dust that made them feel worthless and had taken the light out their eyes was now threatening to destroy them physically.

There was no other way to describe what was happening. It had always been said that lightning would not strike the same place twice.

I stood there wondering who ever said those words had never lived Laurinburg. In a brief span of time, lightning dared to strike twice. We stood helpless as fire and death were once again ripping our world apart.

"Man, this can't be happening! Laurinburg must be cursed!" I spoke what others certainly must have been thinking.

"Well, at least it looks like all the men on the second floor somehow got out alive," Robert said.

"What kind of foolishness is that? I know you ain't blind. I know you can see the meat dropping off them men. I want you to tell how anyone could live through such a thing for very long?" I said, noting what was clearly evident as the water from the fire hoses continued to strip away chunks of burned flesh from the bodies of the screaming men.

"Robert, there ain't no way those people are going to survive all that fire. I think they're just in shock right now," I added.

"I wonder what caused it to explode like that."

Already the rumors were beginning to stir about what started this horrifying accident.

"I just heard somebody say a man was welding and made a mistake and left the hot torch on the gas tanks," Curtis said.

I responded to the rumor that Curtis had picked up somewhere out of the crowd.

"You better make sure you get it straight before you start talking like that. You know the company ain't going to never admit that."

"Leonard, it does make sense," Fred justified. "It don't take a genius to know that if somebody messes around and leaves a hot torch on a gas tank, it will blow up."

"If that's what happened, all that grain dust would have made it worse. Anybody in his or her right mind should have known better than to do that."

Stunned and horrified by what we had witnessed, we staggered back home. Our school had burned down, and now the mill had exploded and burned.

The thoughts whirled through my head like the flames consuming the mill. *Would Stank survive? And even if he did, what would his life be like now with those horrible burns? What would happen to us? Oh God, why did this happen?*

I could no longer seek comfort and answers from Grandma Gladys and Mable; they were gone. Mama was at the hospital with Stank.

That night, I could only go back home to my brothers and sisters and try to seek solace in sleep.

Chapter 13

Healing Dreams

By the next day, the people investigating the accident confirmed the cause of the explosion that had circulated as a rumor the night before: A welder had left a hot torch too near a gas tank.

Stank and the other three men sewing bags were sitting in the room where the welding was taking place. They did not have a chance when the torches ignited the gas, dust, and grain.

Scotland Memorial Hospital wasted no time determining that three of the men were burned so badly that they needed to be transported by helicopter to the University of North Carolina Hospital burn unit. The burns were so critical that they were again transported from UNC's burn unit by helicopter to Bowman Gray Medical Center in Winston-Salem.

It was a small blessing that Stank, lying in bed with more than thirty percent of his body suffering second- and third-degree burns, would remain for his treatment at Scotland Memorial Hospital. Hospitalized in Winston-Salem were Stank's work partners on the sewing bag line: fifty-four-year-old Carl Williams, fifty-two-year-old Edward John, and forty-two-year-old Thomas David.

"Mama, when can we go see Stank?" I kept begging the day following the horrific explosion.

The smoldering ruins simmered for days, and the Laurinburg

Milling Company looked naked with its second floor blown away.

"Y'all can go out there tomorrow, but Stank won't look the same and you might not recognize him," Mama warned us without going into any detail.

As I prepared to leave for the hospital the next day, Mama said, "Now, Leonard, don't you tell Stank about them other men."

I promised my mama that I would not tell Stank that the other three men who worked alongside him in the bag room were already dead or dying. I knew from reading the newspaper that two of the men were, in fact, already dead, and the other one was not expected to live much longer.

Walking to the hospital located in front of Covington Street School gave me time to gather my nerves. If Stank was burned beyond recognition like Mama said, I would have to be ready for the shock.

"Don't be nervous," I kept telling myself as I pressed the elevator button and the doors slid open.

I pressed the number four and the elevator jerked its way upward toward a scene I would never forget. I had never seen a person with thirty percent of their body burned; despite Mama's warnings, nothing could have prepared me for what I saw.

Stank's head appeared to be swollen twice its normal size, and his hair looked like burned animal fur. The blisters covered his swollen body; the hospital had covered these with some kind of white cream. I could hardly make myself walk across the room to Stank's bedside. He looked like something out of a horror movie.

It took what seemed forever for me to reach his bed.

"Leonard, give me some of that water on the table." The voice spoke just above a whisper.

If it had not been for his pointing, I would have asked him to repeat himself. But that would be unnecessary torture, because even his lips were swollen and blistered over.

"I'm glad you were brave enough to come see me. I know you're scared, but it's all right. I was scared too when they let me see myself in a mirror for the first time," Stank assured me.

Whenever Stank moved his eyes you could see some of the debris that had gotten into his eyes from the initial blast. It could have easily happened when he decided to jump right in the midst of all those falling bricks and dust as the wall collapsed. I was not sure where it came from, but you could clearly see it moving around inside his eyes.

"You don't have to say anything," the words rolled from my mouth.

I was now over the shock of seeing how the fire had transformed Stank into somebody that I could only initially recognize by voice.

I wanted to tell Stank about the other men so badly. *I owe it to him*, I said to myself. But a promise is a promise, so I did not breathe a word.

I walked out of his room knowing things would never be the same. I knew in my heart that Stank would be dealing with the trauma of this event for the rest of his life. However, I don't think any of us were prepared to deal with just how dramatic a change it would be.

There was never a time during visits that Stank did not ask about the other three men who sat with him every day sewing those feed bags. They might have been sitting on idiot stools, but on those stools, friendships were forged. It did not take a rocket scientist to realize how close these men had truly become. It was evident with the frustration and anger that clearly showed up on Stank's face when we tried to avoid answering his inquires.

"Have y'all heard anything about the other fellows?" were the first words Stank uttered as he climbed into the waiting car upon his release from the hospital.

For Stank it must have been like living through hell over and over again every day. I could visualize him lying in his bed worrying about his friends. It was evident that he spent a lot of time thinking about how they were doing.

Several times each day, Stank would accuse us of withholding information about his co-workers—which of course we were.

"What the hell y'all trying to hide from me?" he would say. "Y'all can't keep it from me forever. I'm going to find out what happened to the fellows sooner or later so y'all might as well tell me."

Stank was experiencing all sorts of reactions to the trauma of the explosion. I do not think anybody in the entire household got any rest the first two weeks of Stank's release from the hospital. The nightmares kept Mama up at night, and the short fuse of his temperament kept us always trying to avoid Stank on his bad days.

I started noticing how he'd jump every time he heard a banging sound. Simple things that never got on his nerves before now drove him crazy, and he became increasingly self-conscious about his looks.

"Is my hair growing back? How does it look? Is my skin color coming back, or do I still look like a freak?"

The barrage of questions came rapid fire at anyone unlucky enough to be in listening distance. However, the constant questioning and worry were minor when compared to Stank's almost violent nature. Stank asked every question with an undertone of violence. I often thought that if Stank had full use of his hands he might try to pick up the nearest object and kill somebody with it.

He was at his most violent when he felt you were hiding something from him, and so Mama finally made the decision to tell him that his friends had died in the fire. Instead of easing the tension and helping calm his now violent moods, the revelation of the loss of his friends drove Stank deeper into depression. It became too much for him to handle. The revelation of the loss only caused more frequent mood swings. Often in the middle of a conversation, Stank would start to weep uncontrollably and no matter what you said he cried harder.

Stank began to imply that his suffering was my mama's fault.

"Doretha, I tried to tell you that place was a death trap. I wish I hadn't listened to you when you told me to go over there and apply for that sorry job."

"Now, Stank, you know nobody knew that place was going to explode," Mama would respond, trying to put up a front of strength.

But I knew it hurt her very deeply. It especially hurt her to think her actions were in any way responsible for Stank living through this hell.

"If I could have predicted that the building would explode, I wouldn't have asked you to work there."

But no matter how much Mama tried explaining, I think Stank in some way thought she was responsible for all this.

It became clearer each day by the way Stank started to treat Mama that he blamed her. The verbal abuse became so intense that Mama sometimes lost control and started crying.

"Mama, what you crying for?" one of us would ask.

"I just can't take it anymore," was the answer that emerged between sobs. "I already feel guilty for the deaths of those other men. Why does he have to make it worse?"

I could only guess how difficult it was for Mama to maintain her sanity under such torture.

I, at least, was fortunate enough to have a summer job that gave me a daily escape from Stank's dangerous brooding. Mr. Isler helped me fill out an application for the government program called CETA, the Comprehensive Employment and Training Act for "disadvantaged" young people.

It appeared that people could not determine what name to give to the young people who would benefit from the program. It always depended on who was talking. Some people called us "underprivileged" while others called us "disadvantaged." The words never mattered to me. It was just a stupid battle of empty words—people trying to dress up with pretty language something I lived with every day of my life. Underprivileged? Disadvantaged? What difference did it make? We were poor. I left it up to others to debate about semantics. I was just happy to have a job where I could make a little bit of money to help me get ready for high school.

The program proved to be a double blessing. I did not have to spend my days looking at a sulking burned man and hearing him verbally abuse my mama, and I had my first government job.

We were told to report to the Scotland High School library for orientation. It was like we were joining the FBI or something with the way they lectured us and made us sign all those forms. It looked like we were going to be signing away our lives or something when the program director gave us all the forms.

"It is important that each of you fill out your tax papers correctly. We have to make sure everything is done right so we won't get into trouble with the federal government," it was explained to us.

"I wonder what he means about all that taxes stuff. I don't know nothing about no taxes," I whispered to Glenn.

Glenn's response put the fear of God in me. "Why don't you ask Mr. Alford? You don't want to make no mistake. If you mess up now they might not hire you."

"I ain't asking. Why don't you?" I said, attempting to convince Glenn to ask for me.

Glenn gave the answer I knew was coming. "I ain't going to look like no fool in front of this big crowd just because you don't know what taxes are."

I had never learned about taxes or any other economic survival skills. Why did I ever need to know about taxes? I didn't have anything the government could want. I never gave thought to finance; it was the last thing on my mind. I spent every day struggling just to make it from day to day. I knew street economics, and taxes were not a part of the equation.

I whispered to Glenn, "I'm just going to sign this line that says I don't have any dependents. I ain't got no children and I have to take care of myself. I've been doing that all my life."

Mr. Alford started his next round of instruction. "This next form is about health insurance. The job will take out insurance on y'all so that if anything happens you can at least go to the doctor or hospital."

"Mr. Alford might as well be speaking a foreign language," I whispered under my breath. "I ain't never had to go to no doctor before. When I got sick, Mama or Grandma took care of me. Man, he don't have to worry about me getting sick. I can't afford to get sick. I know I'm going to have help out at home now that Stank ain't working," I told Fred.

I got up the nerve to speak to Mr. Alford. "Mr. Alford, I don't need insurance. I ain't never had insurance before and I made it just fine."

"Leonard, you have to sign up for insurance. The government won't let you work without health insurance."

"I wish somebody had told me something about insurance before. If I'd known then what I know now maybe I wouldn't have taken all those stupid home remedies my Mama and Grandma made me take."

Mr. Alford tried to keep from laughing but he could not help himself. His face seemed to be calling forth his own memories.

"Leonard, stop acting like you just been let out of a cave or something. You letting everybody know your ignorance," Fred said.

"Fred, why don't you stop trying to be so sophisticated—like you know what taxes and insurance are all about. I don't want you to forget that you come from the same place I do."

As I said this, Fred started sliding slowly away from me. I guess he did not want anybody to know he was from Newtown.

After, I said, "I'm glad we're through with all that crazy paperwork. Now maybe they will tell us where we're going to be working."

The list of possibilities was enormous. The job descriptions caused us to daydream about which would be the most glamorous place to be hired.

"Man, I bet I could do this Summer Day Program job with my eyes closed. I already got all the experience they could be looking for," Calvin said.

"Calvin, what kind of experience do you have that makes you think somebody will trust you with their children? I don't think they will give you a job like that. Ain't you the same nut that almost caused us to get drowned?" I said, reminding Calvin of his almost reckless thirst for life-defying stunts.

"That ain't nothing but a pie job, anyway. I need something that will make a man out of me," Fred said.

"I don't think there's a job on this list that can make a man out of you. I bet you'll be the first person to get fired," Sylvester teased.

We decided to make a covenant between us that would constantly remind us of the potential good fortune that awaited us. We realized employment was a privilege, and we did not intend to take it for granted: "Whatever job we get, let's make a promise right now to work and save as much money as we can. We can see who will save enough money to buy all the latest clothes before school starts."

The usual hands stacked in the center, and the chanting of the Pine Street Patriots' motto was all that was needed to seal our covenant.

The CETA job would do a number of things for me as a rising high school freshman. It would, as our covenant made clear, provide me with the necessary funds to purchase the latest fashions. Mable was gone, and I would be a freshman looking for a new girlfriend. I was not about to leave it to chance that someone else would come along. I intended to show my colors like a male peacock. High school would be a much tougher playing field when it came to finding a girl to swing on your arm, and being a freshman made it even tougher.

The CETA job would also give me a much-needed break from Stank. The excitement of having a "real job" outweighed the mystery of not knowing where I would be working. One could end up doing anything, from working with the county parks and recreation department to working with underprivileged children from the city projects. What a strange concept—the underprivileged working with the underprivileged. I thought at the time that it was a wonderful idea. What better person could you find to work with the poor than somebody who had been in their shoes? However, with my luck, I would probably end up working in somebody's cornfield.

We watched our mailboxes like hawks waiting for the letters that would tell us where we would be working for the summer.

Almost on cue, all our letters arrived on the same day, and we gathered where we had always gathered to discuss this important news.

The shouts echoed throughout the community: "I got my letter! Now I'm going to make me some money!" The porch of the barn was the perfect place to open our letters and celebrate.

"Robert, where are you going to be working?"

"Give me time to open the doggone thing first. Can't you see I'm trying to get it open as fast as I can?" Robert's tongue hung from the side of his mouth as he struggled to tear the white envelope without damaging the contents. "Why y'all standing around waiting on me to open my letter first? Why don't y'all open yours, too? I know y'all just waiting to see if I'm the one who will end up with that job working in somebody's cornfield."

Robert's fingers immediately stopped ripping the seal of his letter, and his tongue now became a warning that he was not going to open his letter until each of us opened ours.

"Okay, let's count to five and open our letters together. Who's going to do the counting?" Curtis asked, knowing that the one counting could cheat.

It was a known fact that the counter would cause everybody to open their letters first while he waited in triumph.

"Don't let Fred do it; he'll cheat for real and then laugh at us. Leonard, why don't you count? We trust you," Curtis said.

So I counted. "One, two, three, four, ready set go."

The sound of paper being torn rippled through the morning air. It was like a sound of freedom, joy, and celebration. These letters held the first full-time summer jobs with any substance for each of us. We would be real, tax-paying citizens now, and that would help build our self-esteem.

The new jobs would make us somebody, at least in the eyes of the government.

Our eyes became glued to the black and white words on these official-looking pieces of correspondence, and in the few seconds of silence we drank in the historic meaning of this step into adulthood. And it was literally seconds before adulthood was forgotten and we started ranting about who got what job.

"Leonard, where you going to be working?"

"I'm going to be working on some painting job, and I don't know the first thing about painting. Who in the world made these stupid assignments?"

Calvin's eyes darted back and forth wildly in apparent disappointment as his letter revealed he'd be working at a day camp for children.

"I know they made a mistake now if they let Calvin work with somebody's children. He's apt to have them all jumping across somebody's creek before the summer is through. I'm the one who needs that job; I'd show them how to run a day camp," I said.

"Well, it don't look like we're going to be able to change these assignments, so we might as well give them a try. I ain't about to pass up this opportunity," Robert said.

The letters revealed where we were to report for the first day of work, which would be the following week.

My jaw about hit the floor when I reported for my first day. I certainly did not expect to see Mr. Isler standing in the office of the Scotland County bus garage. The summer teenage employment gods were smiling down on me. *This ought to be a piece of cake*, I said to myself as the smile spread from the inside out.

"Mr. Isler, are you going to be my boss?" the words spilled out before I could stop them.

Mr. Isler's response was like music to my ears.

"I saw your name on the list as a qualifier for this program and took the liberty of signing you up to work with me painting classrooms in the county schools. I hope you don't mind."

"I don't mind. As a matter of fact, I'm thrilled. I have to warn you, though. I don't know the first thing about painting."

"You didn't know the first thing about fixing a fence either, did you?" Mr. Isler reminded me. "I wouldn't worry about it. If you work hard, you'll learn all you need to know."

Mr. Isler always had a way of countering my lack of confidence, and that would be the thing that would help me become the best painter on the crew.

Sure enough, as the summer quickly flew by I had gotten so good at painting that Mr. Isler gave me the job of training new crew members. Eventually, I was moved from just painting walls and started doing trim work, which was tougher.

"Leonard, now you'll have a trade that you can make money at for the rest of your life," Mr. Isler asserted. "I'm going to put you on the truck with me so you can learn about inventory and other details about the business side of this job. I think you're ready for the next step."

It was becoming apparent to me that I could accomplish things that would carry me forward in life. I certainly did not want to end up like Stank, almost losing my life in a dead-end job. I eagerly consumed every lesson Mr. Isler was willing to teach me. The lessons helped take my mind off the increasingly volatile situation at home.

I became so consumed by work and the new things I was learning daily that I did not realize Mama was about to reach her breaking point.

"I don't want to do it, but I think it might be the best thing to do," Mama started.

I did not have a clue about what she was talking about.

"The best thing to do about what? What are you talking about, Mama?"

"You so wrapped up in that job," Mama said. "You don't have to stay here and put up with being cursed out every single day. I have to sit here every day and get cursed out and pushed around no matter how hard I try to do what's right. Yesterday I thought for sure Stank was going to hurt me. He's been getting upset over little things. I'm just waiting for the doctor to turn him loose and finish his treatment, and then I'm thinking about moving out of this hell."

"But Mama, we can't move in the middle of my job. I also want to finish my first year of high school before we move," I said as Mama's words sank into my head.

"I think it will take about a year for the doctors to finish treating Stank's burns, and you'll be able to finish your freshman year at Scotland High School," Mama said.

"I hope Stank will change by then," I told Mama.

"We'll see, but I don't think he'll change. If anything, I think he'll get worse."

So I finished my first summer working with Mr. Isler in the CETA program under the threatening cloud of being uprooted again. I was beginning to feel like one of the children of Israel wandering through the Sinai desert trying to make it to the Promised Land. I knew that even in the wilderness some manna falls, and life becomes at least bearable. Therefore, my anxiety never dimmed the teenage drive of one day becoming popular enough to win another cutie like Mable.

If that was going to happen, I needed to shop for some decent clothes. I could not let money be a matter of concern, and fortunately the one place to buy the latest fashion was located in downtown on Main Street. Summer weekends were spent gazing through the windows at the sharply dressed store mannequins in Laurinburg Department Store and Barron Mills, a men's clothing store.

We would spend the better part of our nonworking lives that summer window shopping and praying that we would one day be able to afford something other than the overalls and brogan work boots we got every year before school started. I was always ashamed to wear clothes that immediately revealed my social class. The only way we even afforded these clothes was through the dreaded layaway plan. Months before the first day of school, Mama would take us shopping and put down a small amount of money to keep clothes on layaway for us. The clothes stayed in layaway until Mama was able to finally get them out, which often meant never.

A store called Hot Fashions became our redemption; it was the store with all the latest fashions for a Black teenager coming of age in the 1970s. Hot Fashions was owned and operated by an Asian family, the first foreigners to own a shop on Main Street. In its advertisement, Hot Fashions boasted of being the only store to carry the latest fashions straight from New York City, the fashion capital of the world.

"Look at that silk shirt and those polyester plaid pants. I know I'll look good in that outfit, and I can already feel the wind blowing those cuffed bell-bottoms around my ankles," I said to the others.

It did not matter that these expensive clothes were of poor quality; all that mattered was that they looked good enough to impress.

"I don't know why y'all spending all that money on those cheap clothes that don't last no time. What y'all need to do is buy you some overalls and brogan boots," Mama would say.

"Yeah, so we can be the laughing stock of Scotland High School for showing up at school in those old-fashioned clothes," was the response we made to Mama's call for practicality.

"I'm so glad you don't buy my clothes, Mama. If I still depended on you to buy my clothes, I'd get into a fight everyday trying to protect myself from all the teenagers who wouldn't let me have a moment's peace," I said.

Even in junior high school, I had witnessed what happened to teenagers when they failed to wear the right style of clothes. I had been on the receiving end of too many taunts as a child because of the clothes I wore.

"Look at those hot boxes Leonard got," were the only words necessary for everybody in my math class to point at my feet and joke about my shoes.

Converse All Stars were the shoes worn by the cool people, and ours was a choice of being popular or starving to death. There was no way Mama could afford to buy five pairs of Converse All Stars. Her words were repeated so often that they were imprinted on my brain: "If you want those high-price shoes, get a job."

When I get rich and make me some money, I ain't going to be wearing no high-water overalls. Lord knows I ain't wearing no more hot boxes—those reject sneakers for geeks, I promised myself.

I knew I would probably get one or two good wears out of the flashy clothes from Hot Fashions, but that was of no concern to a working man with every intention of attending high school in style.

The owners of Hot Fashions made a fortune off of us. It was becoming quite evident that these Asians deliberately located their store within walking distance of our neighborhood. It was as if they preyed on our desire to at least look like somebody important even if we could not live the lifestyle of the rich and famous.

Hot Fashions, unlike other stores on Main Street, catered to the hunger of Black teenagers searching for self-esteem. The interior of the stores reeked of "Blackness" from the minute you walked in. It was not unusual to walk into the store and hear Curtis Mayfield soulfully belting out the words of "Superfly" over the intercom rather than the somber sounds of elevator music heard in many clothing stores.

These Asian owners had it down to a science, and you could not help but buy something from them. They stocked all the latest Black fashions, including platform stack shoes. Stack shoes were platform shoes for men, and they were so high off the ground that you thought you were walking on stilts. It took at least a week to learn how to walk properly in these shoes without falling and breaking your neck. It was difficult to tell which was stranger, walking in platform shoes or witnessing a Black ghetto teenager trying to buy clothes from an Asian who could barely speak English. I am sure it was a sight to see them trying to pick up the unique slang of Black language. I am sure they got lots of grief from other store owners about their choice of customers, but the Asians monopolized the market on poverty-stricken teenagers that other store owners refused to serve.

But it took more than fine clothes to make you popular. The clothes and shoes were only a part of it. One had to wear the right hairstyle as well. Therefore, gone were the days of walking up to Veteran's Barber Shop for what we called the "schoolboy" haircut. Mr. Ed would cut your hair so close that the sun glistened off your head whenever you walked out into the sunshine.

"Mama, we don't want no more baldheads," we protested one by one without luck. It was a baldhead or nothing at all.

"Now, Curtis, you take this money and make sure you tell Mr. Ed to cut y'all hair as close as he can get it because you know how quick y'all nappy hair grows back. I ain't got no money to be getting y'all hair cut every week. It's going to be a long time before you get another haircut," Mama would demand.

"I don't want to go to the barbershop with Curtis. He's always slapping us on our baldheads while we walking home," I whimpered.

Darryl joined the chorus of dissent. "Yeah, our heads are already stinging after Mr. Ed gets through raking those clippers across it. We don't need Curtis slapping our heads after that."

If I could help it, trips to Mr. Ed's would become a distant memory. I just needed to get my hands on a blowout kit and some Afro sheen. I was not about to enter high school with a baldhead.

Once all my shopping for the right clothes concluded, I purchased the blowout kit that would make my transformation complete.

Shirley, my oldest sister, spent her childhood in Chicago with her daddy, but teenage pregnancy caused her daddy to send her packing back to Laurinburg. Shirley could do wonders with hair. She became the one beautician in Newtown who could transform the nappiest and most unruly hair into a work of art. Shirley had already changed the lives of countless teenagers with her magic fingers. I think most of the teenage boys in Newtown owed their dazzling Afros to Shirley's hard work.

"Shirley, can you put this kit in my head?" I asked after I got my blowout kit.

"I'm tired of fixing hair. I've been doing hair all summer. Why don't you just go get your haircut like you always do?" Shirley complained.

"Come on, Shirley, you know I can't go to school looking like this. Don't you know I'll be in high school? I'll pay you," I said, pulling a five-dollar bill from my pocket.

Shirley relented under the pressure of money. "All right. I'll do it later on today."

I did not realize how difficult and painful the process would be to put a blowout kit on somebody's head.

"Ouch, Shirley you're hurting my head! Don't pull so hard!"

"Well, you said you wanted me to put this mess in your head. I've got to get all these naps straightened out of your hair before I put these chemicals on."

"Chemicals? What do you mean, chemicals?" My question briefly gave me respite from Shirley's rough handling of my hair.

"Turn your big head around this way," Shirley said.

"You don't have to break my head off," I said as Shirley jerked my head forward.

"Why do you think they call them blowout kits? It takes chemicals to straighten out this nappy stuff."

"What are those gloves for?" I asked as Shirley slipped the latex gloves over her long fingers.

"I have to wear these so the chemicals won't get into my skin," Shirley explained, much to my horror.

"If those chemicals can hurt your skin, what are they going to my skull?"

Shirley answered my frightful plea for assurance.

"I don't think there's a chemical in the world that can penetrate your thick skull through all these naps. I've done this a thousand times, and ain't nobody's skull got burned yet. You ought to know ain't no company going to put out a kit that will hurt somebody. If a company put out a product that'll burn somebody's head, they'd have lawsuits coming out their ears."

I allowed Shirley to move the arm that I had been using to protect my head from her gloved hand filled with the first application of white treatment cream.

"It don't feel so bad but it smells terrible," I said as my sister rubbed the cream into my hair.

"Now you got to let in sit in there for a little while." Shirley grinned in my direction.

"Why you grinning like that?" I asked.

In a few seconds, I knew why.

"Shirley, this stuff is starting to burn my head! Take it out!" I screamed.

"If you want your hair to look right, you've got to let it stay in there a little bit longer. If you take it out now, you're going to wish you had a baldhead," Shirley warned.

I had never thought water could feel so good on a person's head as Shirley rinsed the burning cream from my hair.

I ran my hand across my wet hair. "It feels so slick and greasy. What did that stuff do to my hair?"

"Boy, your hair just wet! Wait until I dry it and I'll let you see it in the mirror," Shirley answered.

I was almost afraid to look into the mirror. If my head felt this weird, I was frightened to think what it looked like. It felt like somebody had air-dried my head. I felt like a cat that had been placed in a dryer.

"Look at my hair!" I yelled when I saw myself. "It looks like a puffball. Shirley, I know you don't expect me to walk around looking like this."

"I ain't finished yet. Sit your butt back in the chair, and let me put this gel on your head."

"I hope that ain't some more junk that will burn my head," I said.

"This ain't going to burn. I just have to use it while I cornrow your hair."

"Shirley, you didn't tell me you were going to plait my hair. I don't want to walk around looking like a girl!"

"Just sit still, boy, and let me finish. Cornrows ain't going to hurt you. Don't you know it's the style now?"

"Yeah, I think I remember seeing a lot of boys with their hair cornrowed," I said.

"You got to wear your hair like this for the rest of the day and sleep on it tonight. When I take it all loose in the morning, you'll see the difference," Shirley spoke as she plaited the last strand of hair.

"It does look kind of cool. Thank you, Shirley, and here's your money," I said as I hopped joyfully from the chair.

"I can't wait until morning so I can see what my hair looks like."

I know one thing; it better look good after all the suffering I've gone through to get it done, I said to myself as I climbed into the top bunk beside Curtis.

"Leonard, your head stinks; you're going to have to sleep at the bottom of the bed tonight because I ain't smelling that stuff all night long."

"It might stink now, but wait until you see it in the morning when I take it all loose," I answered.

In order to stop his complaining, I crawled to the foot of the bed we shared.

I must have been the first person awake in the entire house.

"Come on, Shirley, it's time for you to take these cornrows out my head."

"Can't you wait a little while longer? Go back to sleep and be patient," Shirley groaned, turning over and once again falling asleep.

"I'll just take them out myself. It can't be that hard. I'll just read the instructions about how to comb my hair with this Afro pick," I conversed with myself on my way toward the nearest mirror.

I had no idea that removing each cornrow would be so difficult, but I was determined to get every one of them out.

I could not believe what I saw in the mirror. My hair was longer and easy to comb. The comb slid with ease through my hair, and the Afro pick proved essential to shaping my Afro into its proper shape. It looked like a different person staring back at me from the mirror.

"Curtis, Shirley, y'all come here quick! Look at my hair!"

"Boy, have you lost your mind waking everybody up this early on a Saturday morning?" Curtis said.

I did not care how early it was. I wanted the world to see the new me.

Summer became a time of preparation for high school. Therefore, I spent days taking care of my Afro and buying all the right clothes.

I'd become so preoccupied with my new job and self-image that I'd all but forgotten my mama's trials with Stank. There was nothing that could snap Stank out of his depression. Not even a short-lived renewed interest in his egg-selling business proved strong enough to break the grip. The chickens would have died out if Mr. Leo had not convinced Stank to let him add the remaining chickens to his chicken coop.

The crying spells and verbal tirades increased with each passing day. Stank would talk for hours on end about the fire.

"Leonard, I was sitting right there by those tanks when that fool placed that hot torch on top of them."

The conversation always began like that, and then you would see the tears begin to silently flow down the sides of Stank's face.

"The first explosion blew me out of the bag room and out into the middle of the floor. There was no escaping the fire when it came. All the walls were gone, and there was only a narrow strip of the floor left. I ain't never prayed so hard in my life. It was like I heard this voice saying, 'Crawl on the strip toward the light,' and so I just starting crawling for the nearest section of the blown-out wall. I didn't know what I was going to do when I got there. I just crawled as fast as I could."

It always happened at this point in the recounting of the horror he suffered in the fire—Stank became a basket case, crying with reckless abandon.

"When I reached the edge of the remaining part of the floor, I just hung on for as long as I could. I couldn't hold on forever, and so I just let go as the rest of the floor started collapsing. I had no other choice. I let go and started falling to the ground in the middle of all the dust and brick that came tumbling down with me."

It was a mistake of the highest order if you attempted to interrupt or leave prematurely while Stank was telling his story. If you tried leaving, you would get cursed out and maybe even struck with the closest object he could get his hands on. Therefore, it was safer just to sit and let Stank talk for as long as it took.

"The pain was so bad that I just wanted to die. The skin was dropping off me like wax off a hot candle. It was not the closest thing to hell; it was hell."

It was hard, listening to this story over and over again, but the most devastating part came when Stank started talking about his friends.

"Why did they have to die like that? Why did I live but they died?"

This was especially hard for me to listen to because I had asked the same kinds of questions about my living through premature birth. Stank would look at you with tears in his eyes, grasping for an answer that no one could give. The more he told the story, the madder he became, and with no answer to his question, he would turn vicious on whoever was unfortunate enough to be the listener at the time.

It was a chilling thought to know Mama went through this every night and almost every day.

There would be no counselor to help either Stank or my mother to get through this ordeal. They did the best they could on their own. It was becoming increasingly apparently that their relationship would not last through this midnight. The signs were present every day pointing to the fact that we were living on borrowed time.

Soon we would be called upon to take drastic steps. I just did not know the steps would take us to Scotland Acres Mobile Home Park.

Chapter 14

Trailer Park Trash

I thought for sure I had left the vanity of material things behind me. I would soon learn this was far from the truth.

What was happening to me? I had always heard teenagers could be self-centered, but I never thought it would happen to me. I was the one who was always sensitive about how others were treated. It would not take long to for me to discover there is something about the self-centered ego bug that bites every person born into human existence.

The last thing on my mind was Stank's mental condition. I was focused on only one thing, and that was making sure I would start high school in style. I must have looked at those clothes a million times. I thought nothing could be so perfect.

It was the first time in my life that I was given a choice about what I was going to wear on the first day of school.

I was basking in the glow of being able to buy my own clothes. I could not shake the idea that all my elementary and junior high school days had been spent waiting to see what clothes my mama would put on layaway. I hated the layaway plan about as much as I hated what Mama put on layaway. I knew better than to complain, because complaining only meant the lecture: "As long as I am raking and scraping to put clothes on your back, you'll wear what I buy or you'll go to school naked." Therefore, I learned to complain in silence beneath my breath. *I wonder how she'd feel if she had to go to school with hand-me-down looking clothes.* Thank God those days were dead and gone.

I looked with pride at my new wardrobe of the latest fashions and asked Curtis for fashion advice.

"Curtis, which pair of these pants should I wear? Do they match? I like these brown bell bottoms with the cuffs in them, but I don't think they'll match my dashiki."

"Leonard, you can go to school naked for all I care. I ain't your fashion designer."

I could understand Curtis's lack of interest in what I chose to wear to school. I was sure he was just jealous. I was too vain to think he had grown tired of my bragging about my new clothes all summer long. The bathroom mirror became my modeling runway as I spent almost every day in front of it, holding up pair after pair of pants to my waist, trying to visualize which pair looked right for the first day of high school. I spent even more time in front of the mirror admiring my glorious Afro. Pleased with my new look, I was certain I would no longer be the laughing stock of school classmates.

The summer job afforded me this new indulgence and sense of pride. If a teenager did not show some pride in their appearance, who would? The stakes were high, and I was not about to start off the school year on the wrong foot or in the wrong style of clothes. I wanted to make sure I gave myself every opportunity possible to try to fill the void of Mable's absence with a new girlfriend.

The first day of school could not arrive quickly enough for me, and as the day drew closer, I found myself having trouble sleeping. What sleep I did get was disturbed by weird nightmares. The last nightmare I could remember had occurred years before when we lived in Evans' Quarter. I'm not sure one would categorize the dream I experienced two days before the start of school as a nightmare, but it seemed like one at the time.

The dream started before I had even closed my eyes. I was standing over a huge mountain of candy of every imaginable sort. I stood guarding the candy with pride, protecting it from would-be thieves. Every inch of muscle in my body suddenly tensed when Fred appeared in my dream. I somehow knew Fred was there to steal my candy, and sure enough, he reached his hands toward the pile. I then knew how a cat felt when its body arches into a fighting stance. The dream came to a climax when Fred reached over into the mountain of candy. I grabbed his arm and proceeded to bite down with all the force I could muster.

"Ouch!" The panic-ridden scream of human vocal cords rang out.

In an instant, Willie was punching me in the stomach.

"Leonard, what in the world is wrong with you? Have you gone crazy or something?"

Willie's stunned and bewildered face stared at me in disbelief. Willie held out his arm and shouted into my equally disbelieving face.

"Why did you bite me like a mad dog? You almost bit my arm off!"

"I didn't bite you, boy! You had no right hitting me in the stomach for something I didn't do."

"Well, if you didn't bite me, where do you think these teeth marks came from?" Willie held up his damaged arm as proof of my assault.

"I must have thought you were Fred."

Willie furiously countered my weak attempt at justification. "Don't try blaming Fred for your crime. You know Fred don't sleep with us."

"I must have dreamed Fred was trying to steal my candy," I answered, still trying to find some explanation for my attempt at trying to bite Willie's arm off.

"I don't care who or what you were dreaming about. Nothing gives you the right to go around biting the stew out of people! Mama just told you yesterday that if you kept treating people like dirt and bragging about them stupid clothes, something like this was going to happen. I ain't never seen nobody lose their mind about going to high school."

Willie finally stopped yelling in my face, but he was still rubbing his arm.

Willie's reminder of Mama's warning burned its effect into my mind. I had heard those same words from Grandma Gladys, but Grandma's usually came with a biblical anecdote. She often said, "The Bible says don't let the sun set on your anger." It was not exactly anger that I was letting the sun set on. However, my arrogance and pride produced the same effect—weird nightmares.

It must have been the combination of nightmares and waking up with a fist in my midsection that caused me to brag less. Yet nothing could diminish my excitement about attending high school; not even the constant arguments between Mama and Stank could dim that joy.

I woke at the crack of dawn on the first day of school. I had to be the first one in the bathroom in order to make certain that every inch of my body was immaculate. I'd never taken this much time getting dressed in all my life. It usually took me just a matter of seconds to get ready for school. But today, the painstaking and tedious task of undoing the corn rows in my hair took nearly an hour, and then I needed another twenty minutes more to pick the Afro into perfect shape. I did not intend to go to school with a warped-sided 'fro.

"Leonard, what are you doing up so early?"

"I just thought I'd get an early start so that I wouldn't miss the bus. Mama, you know how early the bus comes around here."

"It looks to me like you dressing for some kind of fashion show," Mama answered. "It shouldn't take that long for a boy to get dressed. You ain't never taken that long before."

"Well, I just want to look my best on my first day at a new school. Is there anything wrong with that?" I responded to Mama's observation.

I walked to the bus stop with staring eyes burning through my back. I could feel all eyes on me. It was as if people could not believe I could dress so sharply.

I do not think they were ready for the change. Everybody had grown accustomed to me walking the streets of Newtown barefoot and nappy headed.

Sylvester took the first potshot. "Leonard, man, you look like Superfly."

"No, I'll tell you who he looks like," Robert said, joining the fray. "He looks like one of the Jackson Five."

"Y'all just jealous. I know y'all wish y'all can look like this," I said, prancing through the crowd of staring eyes like a fashion model on an asphalt walkway.

There was no doubt about it. I was looking sharp. Why else would everybody be paying so much attention? It was a good thing I had decided to dress so smartly for the first day of school. It was the day of the dreaded high school photo identification. I had seen those horrible pictures before in high school photo annuals. The camera had a mind of its own, and that mind often seemed determined to make you look like a convict. The black and white photos always made Black people look even darker.

The high school annual camera even found a way to make Mable look terrible. I still remembered the day Mable took out her annual. I would have never known it was Mable if her name had not accompanied that unforgettable mugshot.

"Mable, that ain't you, is it?" I'd asked in disgust as we sat on the front porch looking through her class pictures in the 1974 edition of the Scotsman, Scotland High School's annual. "Why did they make you look so dark? And look at the way they made you turn your head."

Mable just threw up both hands wearily and said, "I don't know why they make Black people look so dark; maybe it's the kind of film they use."

I made up my mind right there on the spot that I was not going to be the victim of a wayward camera. I did not want to look like I just stepped out of a jailhouse lineup.

It has been said that "the clothes make the person," and truer words could not have been spoken especially to a peer-pressure-driven teenager just starting high school. If I had known that the clothes you wore could not change how people looked at you if you were from Newtown, I would not have spent so much money on clothes. Clothes could not change the fact that I was still living in a rural ghetto, and high school would soon teach me the difficult lesson that everything depended on which side of the tracks you were from.

Scotland High School was like a melting pot populated by students from all the county junior high schools. It was the only high school in the whole county, and junior high schools from across the county fed their rising tenth graders into Scotland High School. I could not imagine what it would be like attending high school with archrivals from Carver, I. Ellis Johnson, and Shaw. It would be like putting rival gangs such as the Sharks and Jets from *West Side Story* together for a World Wrestling Federation cage match.

We had all grown up reading newspaper accounts of the racial tension at Scotland High School during those early years. Scotland was built in 1967 to comply with the *Brown v. Board of Education* ruling by the Supreme Court. The all-Black schools that had previously housed all grades, kindergarten through twelfth, became junior high schools. The tenth through twelfth graders were bused to Scotland High School. The racial tensions had lasted into the early 1970s. It was a true testament to the courage and strength of the county leaders and students that things went as smoothly as they did. It was not an easy transition, but it did transform Scotland County.

The junior high rivalries continued, but their nature changed once the junior high schools were integrated. These rivalries took at least a year to die down, and then everybody became "Fighting Scots," leaving behind old junior high loyalties.

It was of some comfort knowing I would be lost in a sea of freshmen. I would at least have that time to collect myself without worrying about standing out. The upperclassmen could never humiliate all of us. With a student body of well more than one thousand teenagers, my first year of high school was nothing to brag about. However, I was determined to find my place among the crowd.

One way to do that was by getting involved in extracurricular activities. Students were encouraged to choose at least two clubs to become actively involved in, and fortunately the clubs met during schools hours.

I naturally gravitated toward the Bible and poetry clubs. I joined the Bible Club as a corrective measure for not attending church. Grandma Gladys was gone, and I needed some religion in my life. I think I joined the Poetry Club because I thought girls would go crazy over a man who was poetic. I had grown tired of copying lines from romantic love songs on the radio to try to impress girls. I hoped that maybe the Poetry Club could teach me some skills and I could write my own lines. That club didn't really help me, but the Bible Club would become my sanctuary in the near future as unforeseen storm clouds began brewing in the distance.

The first quarter of high school seemed to go by quickly and without much fanfare. However, things at home were rapidly going downhill. Stank's behavior steadily grew worse. The doctors had done all they could to help heal his physical body, so he was released from care.

I always wondered why they did such a thing. Certainly, these professionals must have recognized Stank's mental depression. Why did they release a man who clearly needed much more help? Why didn't they recommend a psychologist to treat his spirit? Stank was released half-healed. The rest of his healing would be placed in the hands of a family with no psychological expertise. We had no clue what to do for a man constantly reliving the torment of a living hell.

It became hell for us trying to keep Stank out of the streets on weekends. Mama tried to make him stay home.

"Stank, why you want to throw away your unemployment check at those no good bootleggers' houses? You know them people don't mean you a bit of good. Can't you see you're just killing yourself drinking liquor from God-knows-who? Bootleggers are apt to do anything to that liquor. Ain't you scared somebody might put something dangerous in your whiskey?"

I watched and listened to my mama struggle every weekend trying to reason with a man who really didn't care if he lived or died. I guess when you've been as close to death as Stank had been, the threat of death does not frighten you anymore.

"Doretha, I don't know why you worried about me anyway. I should be dead and you know it. I should be six feet under like all the other men who died trapped in that hellhole with fire all around us," Stank would argue. "I'm going to die of something, and don't tell me no stories about hell. I've already been there."

It was a waste of time trying to convince Stank he had something to live for. The routine of going over the same thing over and over again became a burden. Maybe it was best to let him go into the night and just pray he would make it back home before somebody killed him.

The blood from the deep gash splattered across the floor as Stank stumbled drunk onto the kitchen floor.

Stank's left hand was almost unrecognizable. The hand was so deeply slashed across the muscle of the palm that it looked like somebody had gutted a fish and cut it in half. The blood ran hot and quick, like a spring of red water.

"Mama, is he going to bleed to death?" Curtis asked.

"Curtis, you just do like I tell you and don't worry about him bleeding to death. I'll stop the bleeding. The cut ain't that big, but it's deep," Mama responded.

"Why is he bleeding so bad if it ain't that big?"

"It's bleeding fast because his blood is hot from all that liquor he's been drinking."

I don't know if Mama's words were true, but they sounded right to us as we stood staring in wide-eyed amazement at Stank seemingly bleeding to death right before our eyes.

"I bet he kept falling down all the way home," Mama said through nervous energy. "He's so drunk, he can't even stand up."

She kept talking in order to keep her nerves from snapping. As long as she was talking, she felt in control.

"I bet you went somewhere and got in a fight with somebody. I know how your mouth gets loose when you've had something to drink. I know how you like to run off at the mouth ever since that fire, and you must have said the wrong thing to the wrong person."

Mama continued trying to stop the steady stream of bright red blood still flowing from the cut.

Stank might have been injured and drunk, but he still kept talking, too.

"Doretha, I'll kill that nigger who cut me. You just fix this cut and stop trying to tell me what to do. Leonard, go get my gun, and make sure you bring some bullets to go in it. I might be hurt and might have had a little bit to drink, but I ain't too drunk to kill that nigger."

"Stank, who you talking 'bout killing? I know you ain't talking 'bout shooting nobody when you can't even get up off the floor."

"Leonard, don't listen to Doretha. She ain't got no sense," Stank grunted. "Stop standing around like you lost your mind! Do like I ask you! I'm going to kill that nigger Jelly Bean, and then we'll see how bad he is."

"Stank, have you lost your mind? You know Jelly Bean ain't nobody to be messing around with."

"Ain't Jelly Bean the man who killed them people and burned them up in their house?" Darryl whispered into my ear as I turned to go get Stank's gun.

"I think he had something to do with it," Curtis answered.

Jelly Bean was notorious and would cut anybody who got in his way. The stories of his exploits were known all over the Black neighborhoods, especially in bootleggers' houses.

"Leonard, bring me my gun like I told you!" Stank yelled.

"Why don't you leave that gun alone? You're going to hurt somebody!" Mama cried.

"I plan on hurting somebody, all right. If Jelly Bean is crazy enough to follow me home like I dared him. I'm going to kill him right here in the backyard," Stank promised.

Stank gained enough control to stand and stumble to the drawer where he kept his pistol and bullets. Somehow he was also able to load it and turn the cylinder.

We all knew Jelly Bean would show up; after all, he had a reputation to uphold.

The squeak of Jelly Bean's old rusty bicycle, his only means of transportation, could be heard over Stank's spinning of the pistol's chamber.

"Stank, don't go out there causing no trouble with that man. Y'all don't need to be fighting in front of these children," Mama pleaded.

Stank began stumbling toward the front door, waving the gun back and forth and aiming it at the opened screen door.

"I'm going to kill him! He can't cut me and get away with it."

Stank's words became increasingly hostile as he got closer to the threshold of the door.

He lost what little bit of control he had when Jelly Bean came into sight, still sitting astraddle his bicycle.

"I'm going to blow your head off!" Stank yelled at Jelly Bean.

I don't know if was the liquor or anger that caused Stank to miss seeing the threshold in front of his feet, but suddenly he stumbled over it, falling to the floor in a tirade of profanity. The gun immediately fired, sending everybody scattering in all directions for cover. Jelly Bean disappeared without a trace, followed by Stank's words echoing into the darkness behind him.

After making sure everyone was safe, the only thing I could think of was the vision of the infamous Jelly Bean flying down the road on his bike at full speed, like the witch in *The Wizard of Oz*.

"Stank, don't you know you could've killed one of these children!" Mama shouted through her tears.

Stank disregarded the danger he had put us in. "That nigger better be glad I couldn't get my gun right or he'd be dead."

"Look at the hole he shot in the floor!" I cried in disbelief.

I knew it would only be a matter of time before Mama would be forced to make a drastic decision about what course of action needed to be taken in order to ensure our safety. However, Mama remained true to her word that she would allow me to complete my first year of high school before making her decision.

I never took the gift Mama gave me for granted, and I lived each moment of high school to its fullest. I studied my butt off. The study produced excellent grades, and because the high school provided a whole class period once a week for club activity, I was able to take advantage of time in the Bible Club.

I lost myself in books. I literally devoured any book I got my hands on. It didn't bother me when classmates started calling me a bookworm. Books could take me to places I had never experienced in reality. Books offered me the opportunity to leave behind the turmoil of home for a little while, at least. I discovered the ability to tune out everything by getting lost in the hopes and dreams offered by books.

Unfortunately, this new passion came with its own unpleasant side effects. I soon lost my interest in clothes. It was no longer a matter of life and death if my clothes did not match. The only thing that still held importance was my hair. There was no way I was going to school with a nappy head. I did not want to be singled out for the taunts that came with the curse of nappy hair. These taunts came in the form of songs like, "Ha, ha, what's the matter with your Afro; it won't grow into a natural 'fro; go and get your comb," or the all-time classic, "Your hair's so nappy Wilson can't pick it."

I could take the taunts about being called a nerd, but a nappy-headed nerd would be absolutely too much to handle.

Being called smart in high school was altogether different. It didn't seem to bother me or other people that I was smart in junior high school, but there appeared to be some kind of stigma attached to being smart in high school. It was not cool. It was especially difficult to be labeled smart if you were from Newtown. I guess it must have had something to do with Newtown kids' reputation for being tough on the streets.

It was indeed a death warrant for a Black male on the streets of Newtown to be book smart. Book smarts were a liability instead of a badge of honor. Therefore, one had to be willing to pay the price for being smart.

The risk included being an outcast among outcasts. I knew the risk of not fitting in anywhere. I would not fit into the White world of intelligence simply because I was Black and from the wrong side of the tracks. I would not fit in among the teenagers in my community because I would have been accused of trying to be White. I learned in my first year of high school what it meant to caught between a rock and a hard place. I was learning what it meant to be "damned if you do and damned if you don't."

I tried extremely hard not to let my book smarts interfere with my conversations and friendship with the Pine Street Patriots. I had already broken the covenant not to allow anything to come between us when I met Mable. Therefore, I was determined to keep my smarts under wraps as much as possible.

It first leaked out one day after school as we stood skipping rocks across the Kenny Pool.

"This is a piece of granite. It has quartz, mica, and feldspar in it," I observed.

"Leonard, what in the world are you talking about? That ain't nothing but a stupid rock," Sylvester said in total confusion.

"Sylvester, can't you see this brown and white stuff in this rock?"

I held the rock to Sylvester's face and pointed out each mineral before launching the rock across the Kenny Pool.

"I don't care what's in it. It's just a stupid rock, and yours didn't skip that many times. It don't matter what you know about it if you can't make it skip across the water at least five times," Sylvester added.

"Where did you learn such nonsense anyway?" Calvin asked me.

"I learned about rocks and minerals in Mrs. McLaurin's earth science class," I explained.

The cat was out of the bag now, and not even the Pine Street Patriots would be spared my Mr. Spock-like fascination. I was lucky they were friends. I would have to watch myself so I would not make the same mistake with anybody else in Newtown.

I enjoyed school and hated missing one day. I probably would have gone on weekends if it was possible. It became my new purpose in life to try to learn all I could just for the joy of learning. I never thought it would get me anywhere. Education never came up in conversations around our house. I was never told that education could be a way out of poverty. I guess my mama was too busy trying to cope with Stank, and he was too busy feeling sorry for himself. Education took a back seat, because every ounce of brainpower went to just struggling to live day to day.

I don't think Mama realized how important school had become for me until the day my books came flying into the house ahead of me.

"Who just threw these books into this house?"

I had slung the books with all my might into the opened back door, and they had landed in the kitchen sink. I was upset because I had gotten my grade report for the first six weeks of school and had made a C in science. Science was my favorite subject; the C made me furious.

"I'm going to ask one more time. Who threw these books in this kitchen sink?"

Mama was highly upset by the time I finally followed my books into the kitchen. I was still sulking from the effect of a report card with all As and one C.

"Leonard, have you lost your mind? You ought to know better than to be throwing school property like that. If those books get damaged, who do you think is going to pay for them?" Mama asked.

I was so furious that I did the unthinkable. I raised my voice with a smart remark to my mama.

"I'll pay for them! I worked this summer, didn't I?"

"I'll tell you what—if you don't straighten out your attitude right this minute you're going to find those books hitting you upside the head. Don't make me have to knock some sense into that head of yours. I get enough verbal abuse from Stank, and I ain't about to take no lip off a child," she replied, waving her warning finger about an inch from my face.

I immediately came to my senses before Mama made real on her threat.

"I worked hard in that class, and the teacher gave me a bad grade."

I dejectedly held out the report card with trembling hands while Mama wiped flour from her hands.

"I don't see why you're so upset. This is a good report card."

"Mama, you don't understand. It's not fair. I deserve better than that," I cried.

"Leonard, you've got to learn that life is not always fair. We don't always get what we deserve. I hope you don't think we deserve to be living back here behind the feed mill in this hellhole. I hope you don't think Stank deserved what happened to him in the fire."

"But Mama, I worked hard. I thought you got rewarded for working hard."

"Leonard, let me tell you something you need to learn that them books won't teach you. There are people in this neighborhood who've been working hard all their lives trying to make it out of here, but the harder they try to dig themselves out, the deeper they get in the hole. If I were you, I'd be happy with that report card."

Mama was teaching me the lesson she'd been taught from years of experience of having door after door closed in her face.

I pulled the books from the kitchen sink and dried the dishwater from them. I never told Mama how empty her conversation left me.

However, there was one good thing that came from Mama's advice. I became convinced I would do everything in my power to show the world that people in Newtown worked hard and deserved better. If it meant getting an education was my ticket out, I would pay that price against all the odds. I vowed to use the gift of that kitchen conversation as a tool to temper my book smarts with a healthy dose of reality.

Regardless of where life ended up taking me, I would never forget where I had come from. I made up my mind that education would never cause me to distance myself from the community that nurtured me. It would not be easy to forge an identity that held both those tensions in balance. I knew I would still be viewed as Newtown trash no matter how much I learned. I would just be a smart exception. I did not want to be the world's exception or the token poor Black kid who slipped through the bondage of poverty. I wanted the world to know that every child from Newtown deserved a chance.

The first year of high school appeared to be slipping away so quickly, and I had learned so much. The year began with just wanting to follow the usual unspoken journey to nothingness that all African-American male teenagers living in Newtown were expected to follow. High school was supposed to be the place where I hit the brick wall and began my slide into the dark pit of jail, drugs, or fathering children. But Grandma Gladys said I was different, and my first year of high school proved her words once again to be prophetic.

Somehow, I knew in my heart that the journey was just beginning, and I would have to search long and hard for each silver lining. I would need those silver linings as I kept pushing toward some unknown destiny. There was some force that would not let me quit.

The temptation to give up certainly became a possibility with each new obstacle. I was unaware that a major obstacle was just around the corner.

"Why y'all want to leave a man who has gone through so much hell already?" I asked, jumping into the middle of the family conversation that would determine if we were staying or leaving.

"I don't know what planet you been living on lately," Curtis said to me. "I know you don't think we should stay here with Stank after all he's put us through."

I continued to be the voice of reason and compassion.

"I'm not blind, and I know that Stank ain't been the most pleasant person to be around, especially after the fire. I just don't think it's right to leave him now. It's no telling what he'll do if we leave him like this."

Calvin jumped in to add his two cents' worth. "Leonard, all that sounds nice and lovely, but what are you going to say if Stank goes off and kills every last one of us? You know as well as the rest of us that he ain't been right in the head lately. One of these days he's going to come in here drunk, set the furniture on fire, and burn us all up in here."

Indeed, Stank had on more than one occasion come home upset about something and begun pushing furniture outside and lighting fire to it.

"And I know you ain't forgot that big hole he shot in the floor trying to kill Jelly Bean," Calvin added.

"I ain't forgot about none of that, but I still don't think it's right to be leaving him like this. Where we going to go anyway? We ain't got no money," I said.

Mama simply listened to us as we went back and forth with our reasons for staying or leaving. I could read the decision in her weary eyes. Her eyes told the story of a woman who had been drained of everything she could give. There was nothing left in her eyes. They were empty and dull; all the light had slipped out of them.

It was another one of those moments when a teenager was called upon to make sense of something that did not make sense. How were we to decide when both adults lived in a darkness that stripped what little light penetrated their otherwise-dismal existence? Life truly had been unfair to both of them. Life did not leave them many options to save their relationship. It appeared to be doomed from the start.

It became a clear-cut choice of the lesser of two evils. It was a definitely a poor person's choice.

I had learned through experience that a poor person's choices were quite different from the options and choices of people with money. If you were poor and got into trouble, you could not buy some fancy lawyer to get you out of trouble like rich people, and that was the reason why the jailhouse was full of Black folk, especially men.

If a Black teenage girl got pregnant, there were only a few options for survival. She could sign up for welfare or let Grandma raise the child. She could put the child up for adoption, realizing that Black children are most likely the last to be adopted.

If you needed counseling, you simply got advice from whatever source sounded credible, even if it came—like it often did in Stank's case—from a bootlegger's house.

It would have been an easy decision if Stank could have afforded counseling to help him deal with the trauma and anxiety of being so close to death. He would have learned how to cope with the agony of losing friends and being the lone survivor. If the professional help were available and affordable, we may not have needed to have this family conversation.

However, I could not help but wonder if Stank would have accepted the help. It was a valid observation. How could somebody who had grown up learning not to trust professionals or society suddenly be willing to share pain? No one in the past seemed concerned about how badly a person suffered. Stank probably would have said the same thing I would say: Why you so worried about me all of a sudden? Why now, when in the past I've been just another nigger swallowed up by a system that don't care whether I lived or died? My mental health was never a concern of yours when I lived in a shack. My mental health was never a concern when my family had to beg for food and my wife had to cook meals on a wood-burning stove. Now that I've been almost burned to death in one of your factories, you want to help me.

Trusting anybody bearing gifts was almost always looked upon with suspicion. It would have taken months for Stank to trust anybody, and we did not have that kind of time.

However, I was grateful that the move would not take place until well after school was over. There is never a good time to move away from friends. We had gone through so much together and overcome all kinds of odds. It was a major accomplishment to have still been alive and in our right minds. I did not want to have to face the Pine Street Patriots and tell them we were moving.

Therefore, I never allowed it to be a part of our conversation during our last weeks together. There was really nothing to talk about. None of us had any idea when the day would come. All we knew was that the decision was already made.

There was not a snowball's chance in hell that Mama would endanger us much longer. The atmosphere around our house was filled with the combustible danger of gasoline under a sunlit magnifying glass. The burning rays of Stank's unstable condition were focusing and narrowing and burning hotter and hotter, rapidly threatening to destroy us all.

Instinctively, I knew the time would not be long; that is the only way I can explain my frantic attempt to reclaim the magic I had grown up with in Newtown.

It must have sounded childish when I asked the Pine Street Patriots to sell bottles for a cookout.

Fred was the first to disagree with my proposal.

"Leonard, what we going to look like—half-grown men picking up bottles? I ain't helping y'all. I don't want nobody seeing me doing such a stupid thing. I want to be able to hold my head up next year. I can hear people laughing at me now. 'Y'all, guess who I saw picking up bottles on the road?'"

Fred's reminder of the kind of high school ribbing we would all be subjected to if any classmates saw us picking up bottles seemed to make everyone shy away from my idea.

"Well, I just thought it'd be a good idea for the summer," I answered. "If y'all don't want to do that, then somebody come up with a better idea. I know one thing—I don't have any money left from last summer's job."

"Yeah, because you spent all your money on those stupid clothes," Curtis reminded me.

"It ain't just the money or the cookout that's important. I just thought it be good to do some of the things we use to do back then," I responded.

I could not tell everybody that we would soon be moving, and that was the reason I wanted to recapture our adventurous spirit.

I understood that high school had changed us and that it would be an exercise in futility to try to convince the Pine Street Patriots to do any of the stuff we enjoyed as younger boys. Everybody wanted to be a grown-up now.

Therefore, I made the decision to go it alone. I spent my remaining days in Newtown visiting all the places that had shaped the person I was becoming. I even walked back to Evans' Quarter to visit Deadman's Creek.

I let the fishing line from my pole just dangle over the black waters of the Kenny Pool. I was not interested in catching any fish. I had seen movies where people would stare into a pool of water and see all kinds of reflections. I was kind of hoping I would see something in the mirror of this black water that would ease my anxiety about leaving the one place that held any meaning for me.

Unfortunately, all I saw was the occasional ripple caused by a fish attempting to capture some bug floating on top of the water. The water that had once been a source of joy for me was now just a reminder of days that had slipped by all too quickly.

I tried avoiding the most painful memory of all by staying clear of Mable's house, but that was next to impossible. When I woke each morning, framed in the window of my bedroom were the red bricks and black shutters of the house where my first love had once lived. The move looming in the distance made it almost intolerable for me to walk by the house.

What other place in the world could satisfy my body and soul like Newtown? I felt secure in its environment. Yes, it was crime-infested and poverty-filled, but there was something wonderful about it as well. I cannot describe what it was, but its surroundings became the crucible for my hopes and dreams. Newtown was the place where I had learned to love unconditionally. It was the place that taught me to treasure all human life. It was the place I had first learned that love could be shared even with girls. It would be so hard to move away, but I knew it was coming and tried to prepare myself as best as possible.

The dreaded news came in the hottest part of the summer. The heat probably increased my feeling of being in hell when Mama announced we would be moving to a place called Scotland Acres Trailer Park, about fifteen miles from the city limits of Laurinburg.

"We'll be moving while Stank is at work, so I don't want none of y'all to be telling people. If Stank finds out, y'all know he might go crazy and hurt all of us," Mama warned.

I wanted to just get out of the room as fast as I could. It felt as though the walls were closing in around me.

I tore through the screen door and immediately stopped when Mable's house came into view. I was overcome with sadness, and I just stood there and repeated the ritual of tears, feeling them wash over me just as they had when Mable first moved away. I was hoping the tears would somehow help me. I was at least hoping they would wash away the pain, but it did not matter how much I cried. The hurt, pain, and sadness just got worse.

Again I walked to the Kenny Pool, slipped off my shoes, and let the water run across my feet. Before I knew what happened, I jumped in, allowing my tears to mix with the water of the Kenny Pool. I was now a part of its water, and nothing could change that, not even this terrible move. I was now a permanent part of Newtown.

I did not think it would hurt anything to whisper one last prayer.

"Lord, if you are really up there, please don't let us have to move."

I did not think such a prayer was selfish; after all, hadn't that little girl in the movie *Miracle on 34th Street* asked Santa Claus the same thing? I was not asking Santa; I was asking God. If Santa could deliver the goods, certainly God could.

It appeared that things did not work that way in heaven, or was poverty an evil that God could not defeat? The grip of poverty had already cost me so much. It was always there to close some door or steal my dreams. Poverty was beginning to seem like a permanent part of life for us. It was becoming a cycle with no break in the chain.

Once again, some manifestation of poverty's evil was consigning us to the nomadic life.

When Stank was working at the mill, we had learned he was the only person who sweated in his mouth. It had become a standard refrain when he got off work during the week: "Who drank all my Kool-Aid? I leave this house and work like a dog in that feed mill, sweating all in my mouth, and y'all crazy children drink up my stuff."

After the accident, it didn't matter that Stank was out of work because of his injuries sustained in the fire. He always found something to yell about.

Stank had begun making it a habit to stop at the Laurinburg Milling Company on Fridays just to talk to the men who'd gone back to work. I guess that was what caused him to drink so heavily on the weekends; going to the milling company brought back too many painful memories.

Unfortunately, this day would create another terrible memory for Stank.

The truck backed up to our door was an all-too-familiar scene. The orange disk that had once been the bright yellow glow of the sun was sinking over the apex of the surviving grain silos of the milling company. Stank would be home in about an hour. He would come home to a house without the loud chatter of children running in and out of the screen door. He would not have to scream at us anymore about letting flies in or tearing holes in the screen. There would be no more shouting about who drank the last little bit of Kool-Aid.

Stank would no longer have anybody to talk to about how he was dealing with the effects of the fire. I hated trying to talk to him about the fire. I always tried to stay clear of him, especially when he got into one those moods that caused him to cry when he would get started.

The truck backed up to the door would take all that away from him.

"Mama, why we leaving all this stuff in here? We might need this refrigerator, and I know you ain't going to leave your favorite stove behind," I questioned.

"I thought I told you we wouldn't need those things because the trailer already has them in it and everything is totally electric," Mama answered. "Now, I want you stop asking all those stupid questions. We got to get the rest of this stuff on the truck."

History has a way of repeating itself, and in our case it was becoming routine. The scene of a truck backed up to our door was all too familiar. Unfortunately, it is the price one pays when poverty is the creditor.

The destination this time was a trailer park. Our home would come with wheels attached. Therefore, if we ever moved again, we could just hitch the trailer behind a truck. It was to be a different experience for me. I had never lived in a mobile home before. However, I had heard all kinds of negative things about them.

The one rumor that frightened me most was that a trailer burned up in seven minutes. I had already been displaced by fire, and now we were moving to another tinderbox.

The questions raced out of my mouth.

"Why we moving into a trailer? What if it catches on fire, and what if a storm comes and blows it down? I hear that trailers are made of tin and insulation, and summer feels like Dante's Inferno."

It took all of my mama's effort to try to answer each question and calm my fears.

"Leonard, a trailer is better than anything we've ever lived in. There will be air conditioning to keep it cool in the summer."

"But what about the winter when that tin gets cold? We're going to freeze to death, and we can't build a fire in a trailer, can we?"

"Leonard, why don't you stop worrying so much? The trailer will have gas heat."

The thought of gas heat did appear to give me some consolation. We wouldn't have to chop wood anymore. Maybe moving to a trailer was not such a bad thing after all.

"Why are we leaving all this furniture here?" I asked again.

I know Mama was growing tired of me asking the same things over and over again.

"Leonard, you don't know nothing," Curtis said. "Don't you know that mobile homes come with their own furniture?"

"But can't we take something to remind us of the good times we had living here?"

"Leonard, I thought I told you I didn't want to carry anything from this house but our clothes, beds, and kitchen utensils. I ain't dragging the memories of this place with me," Mama defiantly said.

I could never bring myself to repeat such words. Memories were what I was counting on to make this new move tolerable.

I vowed to never forget those places that had shaped my view of the world, even though that view was from the bottom rung of the social and economic ladder. I had survived our lifestyle simply because I was forced to dream of a different, more just world. I had survived poverty because I learned to give thanks for the simple things in life. It did not take a whole lot to satisfy me.

Disappointment usually did not last very long for us. We did not have that luxury because we lived life on the edge of starvation. Therefore, sitting around moping about things we did not have any control over was a waste of time. We were too busy trying to get through the day, dreaming that tomorrow would be different.

Although I was very disappointed about leaving my beloved Newtown, I would do what I had always done, which was to roll with it. We did not have much of a choice—either we moved now or risked getting killed.

I understood why we were moving while Stank was out somewhere getting drunk as usual. It was his routine after stopping by the milling company. I guess any visit to a place where your life was almost taken away from you would make you attempt to drown the memory.

If he had known that we were moving, there would have been hell to pay.

Therefore, when Mama yelled, "It's time to go," we wasted no time climbing on the back of the truck and into T.C.'s car.

As we drove into Scotland Acres, it didn't take a genius to realize that we were in a trailer park. I had never seen so many trailers in all my life. It appeared that they had been planted by some trailer park farmer and had sprouted up into neat rows.

The uniformity was especially sickening to someone who had grown up playing in the streets of Newtown. There had been nothing uniform about the assorted jumble of shacks that lined our streets.

"It's going to take me a long time to get used to looking at all these trailers."

"Leonard, you better get used to it because this is going to be home for a long time," Mama said.

The comment didn't bother me, because I knew the odds were against us staying in one place for very long.

Calvin asked the question that all of us wanted answered. "What is there to do out here in this field of trailers?"

"I'm sure y'all will figure out some kind of devilment to get into," Mama said knowingly.

That might have been an easy task when we were in elementary school, but now I was a teenager. I needed more than the usual childish adventure now that I was a young man. I had changed a great deal, and now the questions of life were screaming in my ears. I needed concrete answers to the questions that had haunted me as a child.

However, the more things changed, the more they stayed the same.

We were still forced to purchase food out of a storefront grocery store on credit. Little Jim's was nothing like Mr. Nunny's. The proprietor of Little Jim's was a ruthless businessman. He added extra charges to a person's end-of-the-month grocery tab until one could easily owe almost a whole monthly welfare check at his store. I hated shopping at his store. It was always dark in the store, as if some evil lurked between the dusty shelves. Mr. Nunny's store had always been bright and full of cheer. I never hesitated to strike up a conversation with Mr. Nunny, but I was scared to death of Mr. Jim.

"Mama, please don't send me to that store," I pleaded every time I was asked to go pick up something from Little Jim's.

"I know Little Jim's ain't the best place to get food, but he's the only one who will give us credit. If it wasn't for his store, we'd starve to death."

There were no longer many storefront community grocers who would allow people to get food on credit. Mr. Nunny had been tragically shot to death during a robbery attempt, and even if he were alive, there was no transportation to get to his store from Scotland Acres.

How long would we have to live like this? I would spend hours contemplating that and many more questions concerning the social injustices that were becoming more evident the older I became. Was there anything that could break this vicious cycle, or were we destined to live out our lives in poverty? For the first time in my life, I started doubting the words of Grandma Gladys about silver linings. I was a young man now and felt like I needed something more concrete to hold on to. I had shown the resilient spirit that all children seemed equipped with at birth, but now that spirit was waning.

"Doretha, there's a battle for that child's soul."

Grandma Gladys's voice from the past echoed through my mind during many of my now frequent moments of questioning. She had spoken those words to help me sleep through nightmares. Could these same words be true about the living nightmare that we lived each day? This was indeed the transition that would determine if bitterness would cause me to become an angry Black male. How would I handle knowing that my living in poverty was not normal?

Looking at the huge field of trailers that appeared to stretch for miles brought back to mind the piercing reality of Mrs. Ruth Monroe's prophecy: "There ain't no use in getting a birth certificate for this child. He ain't going to live through the night."

The thought of living in Scotland Acres seemed to be hastening her prophecy. It was the closest thing to death I could think of at the moment. Something about the sight of these houses on wheels appeared to be sucking the very life out of my spirit. Little by little, the fight to make it from day to day was taking its toll.

Suddenly I was old enough to feel the damage being done. This was the moment of major conversion for me. The bitterness, anger, and, yes, even hatred were threatening to overtake me. I had no one person to direct my anger or hatred toward, so I decided the whole world would have to do. Somebody had to take responsibility for the gross injustices in my life.

It was already taking every ounce of my ego's strength to trust anybody, and the more I understood about my condition caused me to become even more withdrawn.

"What's the use of dreaming?" I whispered into the silence.

I was born a nobody. It certainly was beginning to look like I would die a nobody. There was nothing about Scotland Acres that could make me feel any different.

"Come and go with us," Calvin called through the wafer-thin door that entombed me and all my thoughts.

"I don't want to go with y'all. There's nothing out in this godforsaken place I want to see," I answered to the voice penetrating the closed and locked door.

Curtis joined Calvin's attempts to get me out of the room.

"You can't stay in there forever. Mama said you might as well get used to living out here, because she's not moving back to Newtown."

"I don't care what y'all say. I don't like this place and I never will."

Curtis suddenly became the voice of reason. "Leonard, you've got to give it a chance. I don't like it either, but we've been through this a thousand times."

Curtis was right; we had hated to move from Evans' Quarter but had learned to make the best out of our circumstances. But we were so much younger then. I was reminded with each glimpse out the trailer's window that I was getting too old to be climbing trees and making straw huts like we did back then. What possible silver lining could be found in a wilderness that might as well have been the Sinai Desert as far as I was concerned?

It seemed as if I was destined to spend my days moping around in a fog of discontent. The trailer we lived in was too cramped, and I wasn't about to dare to try to make any friends.

My brothers tried everything humanly possible to break the melancholy spell that gripped me.

"Leonard, did you see that girl who lives across the road from us?" Curtis asked.

"I ain't interested in nothing in this trailer park," I answered. "If she lives out here, I know she can't be hitting on much."

I had begun to view anything from Scotland Acres, including people, with utter disdain.

"Leonard, she looks better than Mable," Curtis replied, continuing to try to spark my interest.

"Why don't you stop lying? You know ain't no girl on this planet that can replace Mable."

I rose from my secluded spot behind the closed door with all intention of knocking Curtis into next week for dishonoring the memory of Mable with some trailer park trash of a girl.

"Let me tell you one thing, Curtis," I screamed into my brother's astonished face. "It's bad enough that Mama drug us way out here in this wasteland; don't go making it worse with your stupid attempts to get me to like it. But just to prove to you that nothing good can come out of this hellhole, I want you to show me this beauty you're all excited about."

Curtis pointed and my eyes followed his finger. "She's sitting right out there on that tree stump."

Now I knew she was nothing to fuss over—living in a trailer park and sitting on a tree stump.

Geraldine was indeed sitting on a tree stump. And for the moment, at least, I had to agree with Curtis—she did look kind-of good from a distance.

"Let's go over there and talk to her," Curtis suggested.

"Boy, you must be crazy. You don't know that girl and you can't just walk up to a stranger and start a conversation," I said.

However, Curtis was already out the door before I could finish my statement. I was forced to go after him before he made a fool of himself.

The closer we got to the girl, the more clearly I could see that Curtis had spoken the truth. She was a beautiful girl, but she was no Mable.

I could also see the wide-eyed look of shock on Curtis's face. He looked like he'd seen a ghost or worse—maybe that the girl had suddenly grown a third eye in the middle of her forehead.

"I knew it," I whispered to myself. "There's something wrong with her. She's got some kind of handicap."

The thoughts of what could have caused Curtis to look so shocked continued to run through my head. My steps became deliberately slower. *I'll let Curtis break the ice so I won't look like a fool if there is something wrong with her,* I thought to myself. He was the one who was so fired up about us meeting her.

"Hi, my name is Leonard," I said as I approached Curtis from the rear.

It would later turn out to be a good thing that I could not see Geraldine's entire body, but what I saw took a few seconds to comprehend. There on this pine stump sat a beautiful girl who couldn't have been over sixteen years old.

"My name is Geraldine." She spoke in a whisper. "I saw y'all moving in the other day. We don't get that many people moving out here."

If I hadn't been trying to get a look at what was causing Curtis to stare in disbelief, I would have probably answered back with some smart remark like, "Yeah, I can see why nobody wants to move out here in these sticks."

Now that the introductions were over, I moved closer to Geraldine, who appeared to be trying to hide her stomach. But pregnancy is something that after a certain point becomes hard to conceal.

I immediately began to ask God's forgiveness for the random thoughts about Geraldine having a handicap. I felt like my heart would burst wide open. My feelings soon changed to pity.

Geraldine, realizing we knew she was pregnant, became surprisingly willing to talk to us.

"What is there to do out here?" I asked.

Geraldine seemed to answer by looking down at her almost perfectly round stomach. I could see in her eyes that her unspoken answer was, "Nothing but get into trouble, like getting pregnant."

I tried to change the subject, but Geraldine had already recovered from her momentary embarrassment.

"Lots of people go swimming at Skeeter Lake," she answered.

"Why do they call it Skeeter Lake?" I asked.

I was now slowly overcoming my own sense of pity and embarrassment. It was becoming increasingly clear that Geraldine was not some trailer park trash but a person with hopes and dreams just like me.

"They call it Skeeter Lake because the mosquitoes are the size of small birds and will suck all your blood out of you."

"If the mosquitoes are so bad, why do people go out there?" Curtis asked Geraldine.

"It's the only place to have fun during the summer. People go out there and have cookouts and swim parties."

"What grade are you in?" I boldly asked.

"I'm going into the tenth grade," Geraldine answered with pride.

Curtis could no longer contain his curiosity, and the words came gushing out of his mouth.

"But they won't let you come to school like that, will they?"

"He didn't mean nothing," I apologetically spoke in defense of

Curtis for asking a question that I wanted answered as well but was too chicken to ask.

"You don't have to apologize," Geraldine said without a hint of hesitation. "I've had a homebound teacher during the school year, and my baby is due before school starts back. I'm going to get my education and go to college."

I was suddenly ashamed of myself. I was complaining about living in a trailer park, and here on a tree stump sat a young girl who should have lost all hope but was unwilling to let go of her dream. This girl who I thought had a handicap was teaching me once again about silver linings. What right did I have to discount the dreams of the people of Scotland Acres because I couldn't get the words "trailer park trash" out of my head?

I wanted to reach out and hug Geraldine for the gift she had given me from her stump. Geraldine was no Mable, but she had a beautiful spirit.

"Come on, Leonard. It's time to go now," Curtis begged.

But Geraldine's spirit had given me hope, and I didn't want to leave. "Okay, Curtis," I said.

Before I knew what was happening, I had thrown my arms around Geraldine and was hugging her. The spontaneous hug was not of pity but of thanksgiving.

I should not have been surprised when she hugged me back.

I stopped hiding behind the door of my tiny room and started looking once again for the silver linings that were all around me. Conversations with Geraldine made life in Scotland Acres Trailer Park at least tolerable. There was nothing I could not talk to her about, including how she got pregnant at such a young age. Geraldine never sounded bitter or angry.

"I know people talk about me like I'm a dog, and I can see the looks I get around the trailer park. Most people try to avoid me. That's why I was so surprised when you came over here to talk to me," Geraldine shared. "When I got pregnant, people started treating me like Hester Prynne in *The Scarlet Letter*."

"You mean you've read *The Scarlet Letter* by Hawthorne?" I asked in delight.

"Yeah, I like to read, and I write poetry as well."

"I didn't think anybody out here liked reading much less writing," I responded to Geraldine's unbelievable revelation.

"Sometimes when I get tired of people staring and whispering behind by back, I come out here and sit on this tree stump to read or write my feelings on paper," Geraldine replied.

"I used to have a favorite tree, too. I called it the Vision Tree." I felt comfortable sharing things about myself with Geraldine.

"That's a wonderful name for a tree. You know people always say 'if walls could talk,' but I think trees would have much more to say. They've been around for so long. Just think about all these trees around here. I bet they have a million tales to tell."

Once again, with a quiet wisdom, Geraldine was teaching about the silver linings that could be found even in trees.

"I know this stump I'm sitting on could tell you all my thoughts. It could tell you the countless times I've been hurt by insensitive people. It could tell you the exact number of tears I've cried since I've been pregnant. This tree could tell you every conversation I've had with my baby."

I could hear in Geraldine's voice that she was determined to make something out of her life. She was not going to let her present situation destroy her dreams.

"What college are you planning to attend?" I asked.

"I'd like to go to Duke or UNC," Geraldine answered with all the self-confidence in the world.

"Those schools are hard to get into," I said.

"Yeah, I know. I've had the guidance counselors tell me a million times that I might as well go to a community college. I don't know where they get off trying to tell a person what's in their heart. I have excellent grades that could get me into any school I want to attend."

I had no doubt that this young girl would make it. Just listening to her made me start thinking about college.

Unfortunately, it never failed. Every time I would find a kindred spirit, something happened to destroy it. I should have known Stank would find us, and it did not take a rocket scientist to figure out how he had done it.

Scotland Acres was not the only trailer park in this godforsaken part of the county. Brown's Trailer Park was less than a quarter of a mile down the road from us. We had already been there visiting my mama's youngest sister, Viola, who'd moved there with her husband and daughter. It was obvious that Stank had gotten this information and had been visiting Viola as well.

"Mama, why you always going to Brown's Trailer Park?" I asked out of curiosity.

"Leonard, that ain't none of your business, and you need to stay out of it."

Whenever Mama gave such an evasive answer, we knew something out of the ordinary was about to happen, and if her words didn't give it away, her actions always revealed the truth.

The riddles were the last straw for me; something was definitely up.

"Leonard, what's round and packed with new furniture?" Mama asked.

I would not dare say it out loud, but I am sure the expression on my face left no doubt that I thought my mama had lost her mind.

"I don't know," I answered with a shrug.

"I'll show you tomorrow," Mama replied to my blank stare.

Sleep never came as I tried unsuccessfully to figure out Mama's riddle. I would just have to wait until morning to find what was causing my mama to act and talk so weird.

The morning arrived all too quickly, and my bloodshot eyes had difficulty adjusting to the sun's bright glare. I stumbled to the bathroom and splashed cold water onto my sleep-deprived face. The water had the desired effect of helping me wake up, but nothing could help me with the lingering doubt about my mama's riddle.

"Curtis, did Mama say anything to you about a riddle?" I asked Curtis, just as I had asked every other person in the house, but Curtis knew nothing about it either.

Why was I the only one to have been told about this mystery? Well, I guess I'll just have to wait on Mama to reveal her secret, I told myself.

Before I could finish knocking on her door, Mama flung it open. Another second later and I would have been knocking on her forehead.

"I guess you're ready to find out what's round and full of furniture," Mama spoke into my semi-awake face. "Well, give me a few minutes to find my shoes and put them on, and I'll show you what I'm talking about."

"Why we going to Brown's Trailer Park?" I asked Mama as we turned into the gray sandy driveway of the trailer park.

If Scotland Acres was the red clay trailer park dump, Brown's Trailer Park had to be the gray sandy trailer park dump. I could understand now why they called this part of Scotland County the Sandhills.

"We've got to stop by Viola's first," Mama said.

What does Viola have to do with this? I asked myself. *If she's mixed up in this riddle, it's got to be something crazy.*

"I'll go in first," Mama commanded as she knocked on Viola's trailer door.

I obediently stood behind her as Viola's door opened and we prepared to walk inside.

I couldn't believe my eyes as they flew wide open at the sight of Stank sitting on Viola's couch. The face peering at me through the glass door of Viola's trailer still bore the marks of the fire. The two-tone colored face had the look of a wrinkled brown paper bag. I never thought I'd be staring at this face again, and yet there he sat with an expectant grin smeared all across his grayish-pink lips. There was nothing on earth that could have prepared me for this moment.

I wondered why my mother had chosen me for such a shock. Could it be that she felt I would be more sympathetic to her desire to invite Stank back into our lives?

She would soon find out I wanted no part in such a turn of events.

Although I hated living in Scotland Acres Trailer Park, I still could not bring myself to forgive Stank for causing us to move in the first place.

Stank's first word, "Hi," rolled from his charcoal lips.

I didn't stay around to hear the second word. I turned and walked out the door, hoping that Mama would follow me and never turn back.

That may have been my hope, but it certainly was not in Mama's plan. She stayed right where she was, watching me run across the field that separated the two trailer parks. She did not even yell for me to come back; she just let me keep running.

What self-respecting mother would allow her child to face such a traumatic experience without some kind of comfort? But Mama's choice was made, and it was one that drove a wedge into my already-fragile relationship with her. I was certain my other brothers and sisters would feel the same as I did. After all, they had taken the stand with my mama to leave Stank in the first place.

Without hesitation, I told each of my siblings about this horrible turn of events.

However, to my dismay, nobody appeared to care one way or the other. I had assumed they were fed up with eating off the credit of a storefront grocery store. They were thinking with their stomachs and not with their hearts.

Mama walked through the door as if nothing had happened. "Y'all come in this house. There's something I want to talk to y'all about."

My siblings gathered in response to Mama's rallying call. Mama started speaking without once looking over at me. If she had looked, she would have noticed the wide range of emotions that surely danced across my face.

"I know that Leonard has already told y'all that Stank is up to Viola's. I know that Stank caused us nothing but trouble in Newtown, but he's changed."

"Y'all have to got to understand the reason he was acting like that," Mama explained. "Stank was just angry in Newtown because he didn't have a job and couldn't take care of us like he wanted to."

I wondered how she'd figured all this out now and had not realized it while we were still in Newtown. With lighting speed, Mama anticipated coming questions, as she looked in my direction for the first time in this family discussion.

"Stank has reached a settlement with McNair over the fire at The Laurinburg Milling Company."

So that was it. Stank had all of a sudden come into some money, I thought to myself.

I couldn't stop the thoughts that ran through my mind as a result of this revelation. They were sinister thoughts. Mama had suddenly become a ruthless gold digger.

Stank's dream of owning his own property and home was relayed to us with excitement by a mother drunk with the possibility of finally having something to call her own in a world that had basically stripped her of all hope.

"This can't be happening," I kept whispering to myself.

I meant to whisper "I can't take this anymore!" but the anger inside me caused the whisper to become a shout.

"Leonard, don't you walk out that door. You need to sit down and listen to reason," Mama warned me as my legs turned toward the door.

This wasn't reason. It was madness, and I was sick and tired of living a life of madness. However, I had no idea that the madness was about to get worse.

"I asked Stank to come over here tomorrow, and he's going to talk to y'all about everything."

I could not keep the words bottled up inside.

"That's crazy! Why did we leave in the first place, if all we're going to do is go running back?" I asked, wondering why nobody else could see it. "What's going to be different this time? As soon as Stank starts acting up, we'll go running again, and I'm getting fed up with moving all over Scotland County. I didn't want to leave in the first place, because I knew something like this was going to happen. Why can't we just get in one place and stay?"

It was part of the nomadic curse we were under, and no words were strong enough to break it. I could see it in Mama's face. We were destined to pack up and move once again.

The only fortunate thing about this new move was that the place wasn't on the other side of the county; it was just down the road.

"I don't see what everybody is so excited about; we're just moving from one tin can to another," I observed.

"But it will be our tin can," Mama answered. "How many of y'all want to walk down and see our new trailer?" I just looked on in disgust as my family started marching out of the door.

"Leonard, ain't you coming with us?" called my sister Shelia in a pleading voice.

"I ain't moving from this spot," I defiantly answered.

"Well, suit yourself," Mama responded.

I could not understand why anybody in his or her right mind would want to move again after living such a nomadic life. Another move meant enduring yet again the agonizing task of leaving old friends and trying to find new ones. It was a task that I, for one, was not looking forward to, but I knew nothing could stop my mama once she got something in her head. My display of dissatisfaction would do nothing to stop the rolling wheels of this inevitable move to the trailer park down the street.

Mama wanted this reconciliation with Stank to work more than anything on earth. Having a stable family was the one thing that always slipped through her fingers. It didn't seem to matter what it cost; Mama went after this dream with all her might.

"This is our final chance to have something to call our own," Mama explained to us after they returned from the inspection of the new trailer. "It might be a trailer, but it's ours."

Her words found their mark, and the guilt of selfishness began burning its way deep into my heart. *Who was I to stand in the way of my mama's dreams? Had my mama not suffered enough? Why not allow her to hold on to one final hope?*

I don't think anybody was too concerned about the distant future; what mattered now was the immediate future, which seemed full of promise, at least for the moment.

Though I finally made my peace with this new move, it would not make the move any less difficult. However, for the sake of my mama's hopes and dreams, I resolved in my mind that I would give it a shot.

The broad grin of acceptance on my face let Mama know that I was now ready for the move.

The dirt was the same color; the trees were the same. The only difference in Brown's Trailer Park and the one we'd just moved from was the race of the people. Scotland Acres was a mixed population consisting of mainly African Americans and what society classified as "poor white trash." I never understood why race invaded everything. I never thought color barriers were all that important if you spent each day simply trying to survive. It was not a very logical thing. Poverty was poverty, whatever color it happened to come in. But I guess it made greater sense to have poverty grip one race, especially if that race happened to be Black.

Brown's Trailer Park was such a place, and the world was right again. Our poor Black family was once more in its proper place.

Brown's Trailer Park's infamous landlord was Mr. Brown. I remember Mr. Brown being a quiet, unassuming man who raised hogs with a passion. He was another Black man who had become successful; at least that was the way the jet set of Laurinburg viewed it. However, from where we were living, there was nothing successful about a Black man who took advantage of his own race.

The new two-tone blue and brown four-bedroom mobile home stood out like a sore spot in a vast sea of rundown trailer homes in Brown's Trailer Park. Our new home was placed on lot number forty-two, and by some luck of the draw, it was located near one of the two dirt road entrances to the mobile home park. The wheels on the mobile home were still visible from the obvious lack of underpinning, and the only thing keeping it from blowing away with the first strong wind was the metal strips driven by stakes into the soft sandy loam prominent in that area.

Nevertheless, this was home now, and the appearance of injustice or flaws in the house had to wait until we had made the run of every nook and corner of the mobile home.

One of the amazing discoveries we made was the new appliances. Unlike the rented mobile home in Scotland Acres, this one had new appliances in it, including the major luxury of a washer and dryer hookup, which we would never see used since there was no money to purchase the machines. But at least the stove was new and electric, and there was a new gas furnace for heat and a window unit for air conditioning. The mobile home also came equipped with window treatments and a few wall paintings and decorations for good measure.

"Why don't y'all girls take the room on this end?" Mama said.

The fresh arguments broke out after the necessary sibling inspection.

"Y'all boys just don't want to be down on this end because Mama and Stank's room is down here," Diane shouted, stating the truth.

"There ain't but three of y'all," Darryl retorted.

Shirley and her husband, Curt, decided to remain in the trailer in Scotland Acres, making Darryl's words true. There would be three girls, Shelia, Vanessa, and Diane to sleep in one room, and five boys to sleep in the two rooms at the rear of the trailer near the hitch used to pull it to the site. The largest room in the entire trailer happened to be Mama and Stank's, and the only thing separating their room from the girls' room was a bathroom. The other rooms in the house were so small that the only non-built-in furniture that would fit into them was bunk beds, which brought their own set of logistical nightmares, especially about who was to sleep where. Fortunately, the closets and dresser drawers where built into each room, so the need to buy other furniture was rendered unnecessary.

"If we've got to take the room down here, I'm sleeping on the top bunk," Diane said above Shelia and Vanessa's constant objections.

"Why you got to have the top bunk?"

"Yeah, what makes you so special?" Vanessa joined Shelia's protest.

"I'm the oldest, and y'all pee in the bed," Diane answered. "I ain't going to school smelling like pee. It's bad enough that we've got to share the same room." Diane wasn't through yet. "I'm bigger than y'all anyway, and y'all can sleep on the bottom together, and y'all can pee all over each other," she added for good measure.

If the girls were having this much trouble determining sleeping arrangements, I could only imagine what it was going to be like when we boys started. True to form, the arguments were fierce. Of the two rooms on this end no one wanted to sleep in the one near the living room, or what we called the "front room." The kitchen and the front room were located in the center of the mobile home and were separated only by a half chipboard vinyl partition. I knew no one wanted to sleep close to either the kitchen or the front room. There was always the danger of not getting any sleep because of late-night television watchers or late-night visitors coming in and out of the front door.

Curtis and I were fortunate enough to have witnessed with much interest how our sister Diane had pulled ranked on Shelia and Vanessa. We both made the decision that two heads were better than one. Therefore, we made a mutual deal to team up in demanding the last room in the mobile home. It was by far the best room besides the master bedroom. The last room near the hitch had a bay window that gave us a perfect view of the dirt entrance into the trailer park. We could see everybody who came into the park.

The view would prove beneficial in the future, especially when Mama and Stank were gone, freeing us to do whatever we wanted. It became the lookout post to see when they returned, giving us the clue to clean up and straighten up any mess we had created in their absence.

Curtis began our plan of action with a reasonable request.

"Darryl, why don't y'all take the room near the bathroom on this end?" The mobile home had one full bath, and the half bath located on the end was designated for the boys.

Willie was the first to voice protest. "Why do y'all think we need to be near the toilet?"

"You know how Darryl needs to get up at night to keep from wetting the bed." I answered.

"I ain't sleeping near no toilet either," Calvin responded.

"It don't make no difference what y'all say; me and Leonard are the oldest, and it's about time we had a room to ourselves," Curtis replied.

"Yeah, Curtis, that's right. I'm getting tired of sharing a room with all of us jammed up together," I added to emphasize Curtis' point. "Y'all can do the same thing Shelia, Diane, and Vanessa did."

"Calvin can sleep on the top bunk, and Willie, you and Darryl can share the bottom bunk," Curtis said with authority.

I knew from the sound of Curtis's voice that there would be no more discussion. The coup had been successful.

With the living arrangements made, we were now ready to settle into our new home. The prospects of spending my junior and senior years of high school in a trailer park were filled with little promise as far as I was concerned, but it's always amazing how life-altering things can happen in the most unlikely of places. This would prove to be a remarkable journey indeed. Brown's Trailer Park would become my valley of refinement, and I had no idea how important its testing would be.

Yes, gone were the familiar amusements and the love of Mable that were an important part of my development in Newtown. I had already been forced to live without Grandma Gladys. Her death was still grieving my spirit. I was still not ready to move on and "get over it" as everybody was trying to do. I had all but forgotten to look for silver linings anymore. What hope could there be for me now that all things dear to me had been pulled from beneath me, sometimes forcefully and violently?

I was indeed living on the edge of faith. I knew the fire of life had all but vanished as the new school year approached.

I began complaining about returning to school before summer was half over.

"The summer sure is going fast. I wish we had another way to get to school besides taking that long ride on the bus."

"Leonard, why you whining? You're the one who loves school so much," Calvin said.

I could not understand my discomfort myself, so I let Calvin's question go unanswered. It felt as if I were sinking into the gray sands of this godforsaken mobile home park, and not even the modern convenience of a house on wheels could keep me from sinking deeper.

Brown's Trailer Park was not void of other young people, but I just was not interested in getting to know any of them. Unfortunately—or fortunately, however one chose to look at it—my attitude never stopped them from visiting.

My other brothers and sisters did not seem to be affected by this new move. In fact, they appeared to be thriving. Therefore, there was no shortage of people running in and out of our home.

"Leonard, we found this neat clay hole," Willie said, trying to convince me to move from my usual place for sulking. "The hills around it are this high," he excitedly gestured. "Bo Smith and Hoggie showed us where it was. We've been jumping off the sides of the hills down into piles of clay, and then climbing back up the hills. You remember how we used to play king of the hill on the cotton piles at the gin on Evans' Quarter? Well, these hills are even taller than those."

Willie was appealing to my adventurous nature, but I was having none of it and simply remained silent until he went away.

Just when it appeared that nothing could snap me back to life, Shelia walked through the door with Sandra. I might have known it would be a girl who would break the depression.

Sandra talked a mile a minute. Her voice had an unusual quality and sounded like a cross between the squeal of a mouse and the baritone of a Baptist preacher. She had the kind of voice that made you either laugh, cringe, or wonder how such a voice could come out of such a small body.

There was no getting around it—you could not be in Sandra's presence for long without saying something.

"Where do you live?" I asked in one of Sandra's rare quiet moments.

"I live in the trailer right there," she said, pointing to the gray-white trailer parked near the paved road that ran the whole length of both Brown's and Scotland Acres.

I knew it had to be something besides her voice that drew you to Sandra as she stood there describing her family of two younger sisters. Sandra always answered a question with more information than asked. Unable to get another word in once she started talking, I could not help but notice how beautiful she was.

I was in love once again. I was beginning to wonder if this love carousel was ever going to stop. Was I destined to be a hopeless basket case of hormones gone wild?

However, it was more than just active hormones. I truly wanted a relationship based on more than just physical attraction.

I had been searching for that sense of community ever since we had moved from Newtown. I had been looking for it ever since I had lost both Grandma Gladys and Mable. I was searching for some kind of affirmation—something to live for. It was hopeless to think that I would find anything in a trailer park to fill the gigantic void left in my heart and soul.

Besides my introduction to Sandra, the high school Bible Club would become the closest thing to filling that huge empty space.

Chapter 15

Salvation

Miss Graham, the high school Bible teacher, evidently realized my desperate need for a community that would support me through this critical time of my life.

"Leonard, would you like to attend the State Bible Club Retreat in Clemmons, North Carolina?" she asked me one day.

Change, they say, is good, but the "law of limitation" soon turns that theory on its head. Barry White put it best when he sang, "Too much of a good thing ain't good for you." Moving and constant change certainly were not good things, and these changes had reached their limits for us long ago.

Miss Graham must have seen it in my eyes. I chalked up her presence in my life as another one of those silver linings that always seemed to appear every time I was uprooted. The question always cropped up when people like this became a part of my life. *Was this God putting people in my path? Was I wearing my desperation, like my feelings, on my sleeves?*

Unfortunately, it did not take a genius to look at me and know that I was hurting.

Miss Graham repeated the question again before my brain caught up with her meaning.

"I don't know, Miss Graham," I answered.

The price and dates for the retreat had been on the board for more than a week, and I had completely washed it from my mind because of the price and the fear of being surrounded by high school Bible students from all across the state of North Carolina.

Miss Graham continued to encourage me. "Leonard, I think you would love the retreat."

"Miss Graham, I don't have the money," I said, with my first of countless excuses.

"I'm sure I can find some scholarship money for you," came the unexpected answer.

"Come on, stupid, hurry up and find another excuse," the devil on my shoulder whispered.

"You know you want to go, why don't you let somebody help?" the angel on my other shoulder countered in classic cartoon fashion.

I could almost swear the angel's voice forcing me to trust somebody to help me was my Grandma Gladys's voice. I could visualize the finger that had been pointed in my face countless times to emphasize many of the values that are still rooted in my very soul.

I could almost see my grandma sitting up in the clouds yelling at me. "Boy, can't you see this is a silver lining? Boy, can't you see God is trying to bless you? You better hurry and say 'yes' before I have to come down there and pop you upside the head!"

I had no idea that angels could be so violent, but with Grandma Gladys in heaven, I am sure she had warned God about how hardheaded her grandchildren were. I am sure Grandma Gladys explained to God how she was forced to knock sense into our heads every once in a while.

"Miss Graham, what do they do for three days at this retreat?" I asked, still searching for a way out despite Grandma Gladys's voice in my head.

"There will be lectures, Bible study, skits, and games," Miss Graham replied. "However, the greatest thing will be the new friends you'll make from across the state."

I know what it must have felt like for Adam and Eve in the Garden of Eden, for at this moment I was battling the same serpent.

"You don't want to go to something like that," the serpent said. "You ain't going to have no fun. If you go to that old retreat, you're going to miss something at home. What makes you think those high school Bible students are going to accept a trailer park reject like you? You don't even have a suitcase to pack any clothes in even if you did have something worth taking."

The battle was so intense that I was on the verge of tuning out all Miss Graham was saying until she adamantly said, "Leonard, you deserve to go, and I'll do whatever is necessary in order to make sure you get there!"

Miss Graham was true to her word. A few days after our initial conversation she said, "Leonard, I need you to stay after school to help me with some things." And then, before I had a chance to make verbal the excuse that was traveling from my brain toward my now-opened mouth, she added, "I'll make sure you get home."

I couldn't understand why in the midst of this temptation, I kept visualizing Grandma Gladys. I could hear her saying, "Close your mouth, and show some respect like I taught you. Boy, don't you go looking a gift horse in the mouth. It is all right to say 'yes,' and don't you dare forget to say thank you."

I guess this was the only way I could accept what Miss Graham did on those days I stayed after school. I would help her with odds and ends after school.

One day, we traveled to Roses Department Store down on South Main Street at the new Scotland County shopping plaza.

"Leonard, I don't want you to feel embarrassed about what I am doing, but I need you to tell me what kind of things you need for your trip to the State Bible Club Retreat."

"Miss Graham, you don't have to do this," I answered in embarrassment despite her assurance.

"Leonard, don't you go looking at this as some kind of charity. You've helped me after school, and this is my way of paying you back."

I could not allow this to be happening. I had the clothes I had spent money on for high school, but I never considered them decent enough to wear to a Bible Club retreat. The clothes I had purchased were fashionable, but they were considered to be "ghetto rags."

"Don't you need a suitcase? What kind of snacks to do you like?" Miss Graham zipped through the aisles of Roses, paying no attention to my apparent desire to run out the door and walk the fifteen miles back to Brown's Trailer Park.

Miss Graham had thrown the nearest luggage bag in the buggy and was now speeding like Richard Petty down the snack aisle.

I knew this was indeed a silver lining because God worked out the details to where I couldn't say no to Miss Graham's help no matter how embarrassed I felt at the time. I would have to be crazy not to see what was happening. It was meant for me to attend the Bible Club retreat, and the sooner I accepted that fact, the better I would feel. The sooner I accepted the gift, the sooner I would lose the face of embarrassment that was certainly clear for everybody to see. The sooner I accepted the gift, the sooner I could hear what God was saying.

It is hard to hear anything clearly when you are kicking, screaming, and pouting about things beyond your control. It is extremely difficult, but necessary sometimes, to trust—especially for a person who had been given very few reasons to trust anybody.

It ain't doing me no good to try reasoning with a crazy woman, I told myself. For one thing, I couldn't catch up to her; she was moving so fast. I never knew an old person could move that rapidly in the close quarters of a department store aisle. Miss Graham was determined that I would go to this Bible Club retreat, and I finally did the only thing I could under the power of her determination to help. I yielded to her authority and decided to just roll with the punches.

"Leonard, you can get all your clothes in this bag, can't you?" Miss Graham asked, while demonstrating how I could put my clothes in the fancy duffel-bag style luggage. "You can throw the strap across your shoulder and should have no problems getting it on the bus."

"It won't be a problem, Miss Graham," I answered childishly.

With the simple childlike resignation, the weight of embarrassment and shame soon started to lift. After all, had I not worked for the things Miss Graham put in the shopping cart? If that was not enough to convince me to let go and receive the gift she had given me, the words of Grandma Gladys were more than enough. I was now in a state of mind to hear them clearly, and as usual they made sense. With the disappearance of embarrassment, I could finally come to grips with the truth that I wanted this trip more than Miss Graham could ever know. I needed something or someone to direct my path, and this was it. Somehow I had known it the first time I saw the announcement written across the blackboard in Miss Graham's classroom.

It would always be a constant battle for me to trust or seek the help I knew I needed from others. I guess poverty has a way of leaving its battle scars on a person.

Fortunately, this battle was over for now, and I was zipping down the aisles with Miss Graham, choosing the items I would need for the trip to the State Bible Club Retreat in Clemmons, North Carolina.

The thoughts in my head leading up to Friday's departure for Clemmons were the stuff of *Alice in Wonderland*. However, despite my overwhelming joy over this trip, I was almost ashamed to admit to myself that I had never spent a night away from home in my entire life. I could not count time spent camping by the roadside with the Pine Street Patriots. I had never slept in a room without my brothers and sisters.

The fear of such a thing had not crossed my mind until the night I started packing my duffel bag.

Curtis asked a question that intensified my present apprehension.

"Leonard, who's going to be sleeping in the room with you on the retreat?"

"I don't know," I replied, acknowledging this fear aloud for the first time. "I don't know, but I'm sure it will be all right," I added, trying to bury the fear underneath a brave front.

I hoped Curtis could not see my hands starting to tremble as I carefully placed my clothes neatly into the duffle bag that eagerly swallowed them.

I attempted to refocus my mind on Miss Graham's words that had assured me that I needed this trip and had somehow earned it. I am sure Miss Graham would not get me miles away from home just to embarrass me. I did not think my fear had anything to do with her; it was the old fear of trusting in myself. *Could I spend three nights away from home without anybody realizing that it was Miss Graham's charity that made it possible for a trailer park boy to be there?*

It didn't take a genius to realize neither I nor my parents could afford such a luxury.

What would happen if someone started whispering the words that I had heard a thousand times before—those whispered words that had let me know I did not belong or was not good enough?

Although I had heard these words and worse practically all my life, I had never grown accustomed to them. I had been told time and time again, "Leonard, you've got to grow thick skin and learn not to let people's words get you down." I had grown up repeating the childish refrain, "Sticks and stones may break my bones, but words will never hurt me."

Unfortunately, no matter how many times I repeated the refrain, it did nothing to stop the pain that words could and did inflict. It was those words that were now seeping into my head, threatening to steal yet another dream.

"I wish I could go," I heard a tiny voice whisper behind me.

"Vanessa, what are you doing in here?"

"I just wanted to see your new clothes," she answered.

"No, you just want to stick your nose into other people's business," I said.

"Why are your hands shaking like that?" Vanessa's keen eyes picked up my fear.

"Vanessa, get out of my room and mind your own business!" I yelled.

"You don't own this house," Vanessa shot back.

"If you don't get your little narrow butt out of here, I'm going to show you whose room this is."

"Leonard, you don't scare me," Vanessa bravely spoke. "You just scared yourself; that's why your hands are shaking like that. I don't know why you so scared. I'd be glad to get away from this trailer park for three days."

"Vanessa, you know good and well you'd be kicking and screaming to get back home the first time somebody looked at you funny. I'm telling you one last time—get out of my room and let me finish packing."

I guess baby sisters are the same no matter the social or economic setting. Vanessa stood there like the pest she was, watching me struggle through my present battle. The funny thing about it was that I really did not mind it. Vanessa's courage was something I had a great need for at the time, but I had no intention of letting her know how her presence brought me comfort. If she wasn't scared to go on such a trip, why should I be so nervous about it?

Vanessa stood there until I had put the last piece of clothing in the duffel bag. As I zipped up the bag, she stuck out her tongue and scowled.

"You lucky dog, I hope you have a good time on that ole retreat," she said, turning and disappearing just as quickly as she had appeared.

Vanessa's sudden appearance in my room renewed my courage. I can do this, I told myself as my hands stopped trembling. Once again, I was looking forward to this trip.

I walked onto the bus Friday for the long ride to Scotland High School with my duffel bag packed and ready to go. There would be no turning back now, and my soul was at peace.

We were instructed to bring our luggage to Miss Graham's classroom before the first class period. I proudly threw my duffel on the pile with the luggage of other students attending the retreat. The trip to Clemmons, North Carolina, was a journey of letting go. For once in my life, I was determined to let go of the things that would in any way keep me from remembering and living out Grandma Gladys's cradling and nurturing words: "Leonard, behind every dark cloud there is a silver lining."

I stepped off the Scotland County activity bus into the crisp clear air of early spring in Clemmons. Taking this step was a definite epiphany for me. I knew from that moment that I would find the silver lining that would truly sustain me regardless of what happened.

It was a "thin place" of revelation. In the early Celtic religion culture, there were events and places known as "thin places." These were places where one encountered the presence of God. I was just a teenager, but I knew something was different about that moment. Every one of my five senses was tingling uncontrollably. I dare say there was a sixth sense that had all of a sudden kicked in without warning.

The entire weekend was one discovery after another, from the daily skits we performed using biblical stories to the late-night conversations with total strangers from across the entire state. I was discovering for the first time in my life that other people had dreams and hopes that often went against conventional wisdom. I was not strange after all, and I certainly wasn't the only person at the retreat who came from a poor family.

I rejoiced in the privilege of eating three meals a day, even if it was with more than one hundred and fifty other people. I didn't even mind the occasional chant that came when someone was caught eating with their elbows on the table.

"Leonard, Leonard, strong and able, get your elbows off the table. This is not a horses' stable, but a first-class dinner table. Round the room you must go. You must go."

It did not matter if you were in mid-bite. You had to get up and run around the huge dining room, and if you did not, you were bombarded with the chant, "Spoil-sport! Spoil-sport!" until you got up and took your punishment.

But the real epiphany came during a session led by our leader. I do not even remember his name. However, I do remember his talk. The chosen Bible text for his talk was taken from Romans 8:1, "There is therefore now no condemnation for those who are in Christ Jesus," and Romans 8:37-39, "No, in all these things we are more than conquerors through him who loved us. For I am sure that neither death, nor life, nor angels, nor principalities, nor things present, nor things to come, nor powers, nor heights, nor depths, nor anything else in all creation, will be able to separate us from the love of God in Christ Jesus our Lord."

I sat there transfixed, wondering if these words could apply to somebody like me. I had known nothing but poverty all my life. I had experienced the trauma of being uprooted from almost every place that had meant something to me. I had lost two of the most important people in my life, and these words were telling me there was something in this world that would never be taken from me.

I sat there wondering if this was what Grandma Gladys and Mable had been trying to teach me. Is this what the Pine Street Patriots had taught me in their own unique way? It was true—at least it felt that way in my spirit as I sat listening. God had been with me all my life, and this was the "thin place" where God decided to show up, leaving no doubts.

Although I cannot remember our leader's name, when he turned and faced me with tears in his eyes, I knew in my heart that God was speaking to me. I was witnessing the one silver lining that would carry me through the rest of my days. God would be the silver lining that kept me from becoming bitter about life.

I knew from that day forward that I would spend my time living life instead of letting life live me. I went back to Brown's Trailer Park a different person. The rows upon rows of trailers were still there, but now "nothing could separate me from the love of God in Christ Jesus." Stank was still there with the discolored leathery skin covering his face. I went back to two meals a day, one at school and one at home, but in my head were the words, "No, in all these things we are more than conquerors through him who loved us."

My physical surroundings had not changed, but that did not matter now. I knew that it would not always be this way. I had gone to the retreat ashamed of where I lived and who I was, but the liberating presence of God changed all that.

I would soon find out how much it had changed me when I became president of Scotland High School's Bible Club during my senior year. I knew then that I could never give up on the dream of becoming more than trailer park trash. I threw myself gladly into my role as president of the largest club at Scotland High School.

Charles McClennahan, the past president, became a wonderful mentor and helped me in my new leadership role.

"Charles, I don't know how to do this job," I told him after he nominated me for president. "I've never done anything like this in my life."

"Leonard, you'll be okay, and Miss Graham will help you. It will be a piece of cake. You'll see."

"But Charles, I don't have a car. How will I attend the meeting and other activities after school?"

"Don't worry about that," Charles answered. "I'll give you a ride whenever you need one."

"But I live way out in the Sandhills. That's fifteen miles from here, and I know you'll need a lot of gas to get way out there."

"Leonard, I told you not to worry about that," Charles re-emphasized. "Both of us belong to the club, and it was my every intention to remain active in all the activities. I don't mind coming out to get you."

It appeared that God was not going to allow me to forget I was more than a conqueror. The move from Newtown was the fork in the road, and the signpost pointing in the direction of destiny was the Bible Club. It truly was liberating to feel my spirit dream again.

I had hit the brick wall of adolescence and could have easily gone in the direction my environment was pushing me. I could have lived out the fate that became reality for most African-American males of my generation and socioeconomic background.

But my ability to once again dream caused me to think of the impossible vision of going to college.

"Leonard, you ain't getting into nobody's college."

I could count on hearing words like these if I dared share my college dream with anybody from Brown's Trailer Park. Other words of discouragement, such as, "You're just wasting your time," would soon follow.

I knew it would be no piece of cake getting into school. However, I was armed with more than just a dream now. I was armed with the ability to accept life as a gift from God, and once I had learned to receive God's gift, the doors of promise opened wide.

It became a visionary obsession for me—the almost daily visits to the high school guidance counselor's office. I spent a major portion of my lunch break searching through the college catalogs trying to select a college that I thought would accept me. I wanted to get as far away from Laurinburg as I could get because of my desire to be independent and to see new places in North Carolina that were not bound by the grip of oppression.

Fortunately, my grades had not suffered, and I was looking forward to seeing if they would indeed carry me anywhere. I was consumed by the idea that education might just be my ticket out.

I literally devoured every college catalog I read. I read each catalog with the same hopes and dreams that I had when I played the magazine game of "This Side Is Yours" with my brothers back in Newtown.

The only thing able to tear me away from the dreams of walking on some well-manicured college campus was the voice of some guidance counselor reminding me that lunch break was over, and if I didn't want to get a tardy slip, I needed to leave.

I knew the day would come when my willingness to skip one of the only two meals of the day would pay off.

The Pfeiffer College catalog appeared to jump off the shelf. I read about Pfeiffer's attractive, historic campus and its commitment to accepting students regardless of race, gender, or nationality. I sat in the guidance office daily and learned everything I could about this college in the Western Piedmont of North Carolina. I made sure I knew everything about Pfeiffer before ever breathing a word about my intentions of attending college there.

"I'm going to Pfeiffer," I shared the news with my mama.

"Where in God's name is Pfeiffer College?" was her understandable reply. "I didn't even know you were thinking about going to college."

Fortunately, I'd grown accustomed to such comments, and my mama's words didn't affect me.

"Pfeiffer College is in Misenheimer, North Carolina," I continued, unfazed by my mama's comment. "I think I might be able to get in if my grades continue to be good."

I knew all of this must have sounded like Greek to a woman who dropped out of school because she got pregnant at age fifteen. However, despite her limited knowledge about college, I could see a sense of pride in her broad smile.

"You know we ain't never had nobody in this family finish college," she said. "If you think you can find a way to pay for it, go and try, but you know we ain't got no money to send you that far away from home," Mama added apologetically.

I countered with my knowledge from the catalog. "If I get in, I'm sure there will be grant money and scholarships available."

It felt amazingly uplifting to share the news I held inside with somebody else, and with renewed confidence I began sharing my hopes with anybody willing to listen.

"Leonard, you're going to freeze your tail off up there near the mountains," Stank said. "I don't know why in the world you want to go way up there where you ain't never been before. I heard the grand wizard of the KKK lives less than fifteen miles from that school."

The news of the KKK was not something the catalog mentioned, but I was not about to let it dampen my hopes of attending Pfeiffer.

Stank described the racial shock I would experience.

"Why you want to go up there to that White school anyway? I hear that all those children are rich White folk. I know that all those White children got money. What you going to do around all those rich children and you ain't got a pot to piss in?"

As usual, Stank was frank and characteristically blunt in his comments. It would indeed be a major cultural difference, but I was beyond that now. I was willing to do whatever it took to chase this silver lining. I was not willing to let this dream get away no matter what Stank or anybody else said.

I was not going to let anybody or anything steal my joy.

I never expected the high school guidance counselor to be my greatest temptation to let go of my dream. I thought his job was to help students achieve their dreams.

"I'm thinking about applying to Pfeiffer College in the fall," I told him.

I thought he would be overjoyed. I had no idea he would throw every obstacle he could think of in my way, trying to change my mind about college.

However, I did expect his first argument.

"Leonard, I don't think you're college material. Maybe you should just go to a community college and take up a trade."

"If you check my file, you'll see my grades are good enough for college," I answered.

"That may be true, but do you have all the required courses to get accepted into a private liberal arts college like Pfeiffer?" my guidance counselor asked. "I hope you're aware that private colleges often have higher standards."

"Yes, sir, I am aware of Pfeiffer's requirements, and I think I have all the courses they require."

His whole demeanor changed then, and he turned red as a beet. He appeared to be searching for some new response capable of getting this foolish idea about college out of my head.

"Have you taken any college entrance examination?" he finally asked.

The question delivered the desired effect as he turned to face me squarely in his swiveling office chair. His body showed the joy of a chess player calling out checkmate.

"No, sir, I have not taken a college entrance exam," I answered.

"I suggest you go back and read the catalog in order to find out what entrance examination Pfeiffer requires," he said, ending our conversation.

I searched frantically through the catalog, ashamed that I'd forgotten to look for something as important as the entrance examination requirement. How did I miss it? There it was just as plain as day in black and white—"SAT required before admission." The catalog even provided information about the cost of the test.

For the moment, this caused me to doubt my chances, but thank God, my doubt was short lived.

Later that week I marched back into his office with the confidence of a person who understood that destiny was calling. I also had enough money left from my job to pay the fee.

"I'd like to register to take the SAT in the spring, and here's my seventy-five dollar registration fee."

His jaw appeared to weigh a ton as it hit the floor. I knew what he wanted to say. "Who does this nigger think he is, questioning my authority?"

However, all he could do was take my money and register me for the test.

"Leonard, that's all you talk about—going to that dumb college," Calvin said, having grown weary of my constant conversations about

Pfeiffer. "When you get there, I bet you going to be crying to get back home."

"Calvin, you must be crazy if you think I'm ever going to want to come back here again."

I was indeed certain of one thing, and that was if I ever got out of Laurinburg, I would never look back. I saw this as the first step in that direction.

The Saturday of the test came quickly and with it the scramble to find a ride to Scotland High School. Charles McClennahan wouldn't be available because he was already in Winston-Salem for his final interview for acceptance into North Carolina School of the Arts. Therefore, my only hope rested in Stank.

I had asked Stank well in advance about his friend Charlie taking me. I had even offered to pay. Charlie just happened to be Sandra's father, and he owned a 1976 Mercury Cougar that he treated like a baby.

Evidently Stank had forgotten to ask. The responsibility for making the request became mine.

"Somebody please answer the door," I pleaded.

"Who is it?" Sandra's unique voice answered.

"It's me, Leonard," I answered.

Sandra quickly jerked the door open, thinking I was coming to see her.

"What you doing over here this early?" she asked, standing there yawning in her pink pajamas.

"I need to ask your daddy if he'll drive me to the high school so I can take the SAT." I knew Sandra could hear the anxiety in my trembling voice.

"I'll try to wake him up, but he worked all night long. Stay right here. I'll be right back," she whispered.

I hope she doesn't whisper like that when she tries to wake him, I thought.

"Who's that at my door this early in the morning?" Charlie's voice called from the other side of his bedroom door.

I could see the disappointment on Charlie's face as his eyes finally focused on me.

"Leonard, what in the world do you want?" Charlie asked while all the time looking in Sandra's direction with the wrathful, disapproving look all parents give when you're in big trouble.

I knew from that look that she would have to deal with him later for this invasion.

"Charlie, Stank wanted me to come ask you if you could please take me to the high school so that I can take the SAT for college. I'll put some gas in your car, and I'll give you something extra if you can do it," I asked with as much desperation as my voice would muster.

"I've worked all night long, but if you're willing to put gas in the car and pay me, then I'll think about."

I didn't need him to think about. I needed a ride.

Charlie walked back to his bedroom with no indication about his intentions. I stood wondering what he meant. *Didn't he realize my entire destiny was riding on his answer?* If I didn't get to the high school on time, I'd miss the opportunity to take the test, and this was my last chance because the test would not be offered again until next year.

"Come on. Let's go." Charlie spoke words that brought a deep sigh of relief that I felt run through my whole body. "I have to make a couple of stops on the way," he warned us as Stank and I climbed into the car.

I immediately became a nervous wreck, wondering if we'd make it in time as Charlie made his first stop at the gas station. *Why is he taking his sweet time?* I was definitely afraid to ask him to speed; beggars can't be choosy.

The conversation with Stank caused Charlie to drive as if they were taking a leisurely drive after church, or worse, like he was driving Miss Daisy around. I kept pretending to look at my nonexistent watch, trying to make some kind of gesture that would cause Charlie to drive faster.

Finally, I could take it no longer. "Charlie, could you please drive a little faster? I don't want to miss the test."

If he heard me, Charlie certainly didn't show it; he drove as if I had said nothing. I sat in the backseat wringing my hands and rolling and unrolling the now-demolished SAT registration form and my confirmation papers, which I would need to be admitted to the cafeteria, where the test was being given. I had anxiously rolled and unrolled the papers beyond recognition.

The car barely came to a stop before I dashed out the door, running as fast as I could toward the cafeteria of Scotland High School.

My counselor met me at the door and explained to me that I could not take the test because it had already started.

"Please let me take the test," I pleaded.

"Mr. Fairley, I'm sorry, but policy states that once the test has begun no one can be admitted."

I continued to make my plea. "But I'm only five minutes late. Please let me in. I've already applied to Pfeiffer."

"I told you I'm sorry, but I can't let you in, and I've got to get back inside so I can finish administering the test."

He closed the cafeteria doors. I stood there, looking through the glass window, watching my one opportunity at a college education slip through my fingers.

One more door closed in my face.

I turned hopelessly away from the cafeteria and started walking through the vast commons area of the high school. *What am I going to do now?* I was devastated.

I had come this far, only to have the final door to success closed in my face. And adding insult to injury, Stank and Charlie were nowhere to be found. *I guess they're gone already, thinking I'm in there taking the SAT,* I reasoned.

The only thing left to do was to start walking toward Newtown. I had made up my mind to walk to Gulf Street and try to find a ride back to the trailer park. I was hoping Allan's mother might give me a ride home. I was glad Stank and Charlie were gone. I don't think I could have ridden back to the trailer park with either of them knowing they had cost me my only way out of poverty and out of the godforsaken trailer park.

How could such a devastating thing have happened on such a beautiful day? *I can't go this way, because people will see me crying*, I told myself before turning toward the CSX railroad tracks that would take me the back way into Newtown. What a perfect symbol of the journey of my life thus far. How ironic it was that the walk from Scotland High School would take me right past the tin house we had lived in on Evans' Quarter.

I could not just walk by without stopping at the corner of Covington and King streets. It was here that I had first dared to dream that God would open doors for me. Now it appeared that I had come full circle. I was right back where I started.

I continued my conversation with myself. *I can't believe I was so stupid to believe I could go to college. My guidance counselor was right—once a nobody, always a nobody.*

The impromptu visit to Deadman's Creek led to an eruption of tears, causing temporary blindness. I just stood there looking into the water. I could not have gone another step further if I had wanted to. I was crying uncontrollably; my whole body was convulsing. I was shaking like a leaf.

The strangest thing happened while I stood there on the banks of this creek that once offered both challenge and salvation. I suddenly got the urge to pray out loud. I'd never done that before—pray out loud. After looking around to make sure nobody else was present, I let go and let God have it.

"God," I cried out. I did not even say "dear" or "heavenly Father."

"God, all my life you have teased me with the words of an old woman who could neither read nor write, but now I'm speaking for myself. Have I been a fool believing in some child's game, spending my life chasing after elusive silver linings?" I began to grow angry with each word I now yelled into God's face. "I didn't ask to be born. You should have just let me die like you started to. It wasn't meant for me to live, so why did you jump in and save my life? I would have been just fine dead in heaven instead of going through all the hell I've been through. I didn't ask you to save me. I'm tired of going hungry. I'm tired of being laughed at and run over. I'm tired of living in broken-down houses with no heat or bathroom. How much more do you expect me to take? If I'm 'more than a conqueror' why do you keep knocking me down? The harder I try believing in silver linings, the more dark clouds you send to rain on me."

I don't know what I expected to happen, but all I saw and heard were my tears falling into Deadman's Creek. I simply saw the water of a creek rushing down the middle of its banks.

"God, you've got to say something," I finally whispered, emotionally drained.

I know it sounds stupid and childish, but I was intent on standing there all night until God showed up. If this was the sin of tempting God, I was up to the test, but I wondered if God was even interested.

I would have missed it if I had not emptied myself. When there was nothing left emotionally inside of me, God showed up. I looked at Deadman's Creek with new eyes and realized something I had never thought of before. I thought about where the water flowing downstream would end up; I thought about all the obstacles that stood in its path. I thought about lessons from Mr. Isler's class that taught me that the water in creeks, lakes, and streams always made its way to one destination—the ocean. I thought about all the creeks like this one spread out over the world—creeks hidden deep in the forest yet constantly flowing and giving life. It didn't matter what happened in or around the waters of these countless creeks. The only thing the water knew how to do was to flow toward the ocean.

Grandma Gladys and all the people and places in between were the current that kept me flowing toward God's destiny. Life's waters were not meant to always stay calm. I had seen Deadman's Creek when it was calm and also when turbulent; yet it never strayed from its course. I felt like an idiot, not because I was standing there staring into a creek yelling at God, but because I had missed God's presence so many times. There was more to life than the SAT or college.

God had already been doing the hard part, and all I needed to do was trust and take the next step. I didn't exactly know what that step would be, but I was sure God would show me the way if I took the time to empty myself and look.

"If you take one step, God will take two," I had often heard my grandma say.

I turned from Deadman's Creek and continued my journey toward Newtown. I still had no clear answer, but one thing was crystal clear— I needed to complete my application to Pfeiffer College.

Surprisingly, I was no longer upset with Stank and Charlie. Deadman's Creek taught me another valuable lesson—a lesson about prayer. Prayer would be the place where I could empty myself before God, and somehow God would fill the emptiness. I could never explain how that ever happened. How could God absorb such pain and anger and transform them into a blessing? God certainly does God's best creative and redemptive work in the midst of chaos.

Monday morning I started the new school week with the resolve to do my best and simply flow toward my destiny. How I would get there became somewhat secondary, just as long as I did my best at whatever God put in front of me. The Bible Club became the banks through which my energy now flowed, and there was more than enough to keep me busy as president.

Miss Graham decided to start a scholarship fundraising drive to endow the first annual Bible Club Scholarship. The scholarship recipient would be announced during Awards Day at Scotland High School. The Bible Club was the largest club at Scotland High School, and its members formed a small army deployed to perform service projects in order to raise money. We did everything from raking yards to washing windows to collecting aluminum cans. I was a pro at finding cans. It came naturally after years of selling bottles.

The fellowship and friendships forged during our fundraising efforts sustained me through the disappointment over being locked out of the SAT. Once again, the belief in silver linings withstood the challenge of dark clouds.

In addition to organizing fundraisers, the Bible Club also hosted Christian social activities that year.

"Leonard, who are you taking to the Valentine's Banquet?" Charles asked. "You know everybody is going to be checking out who the president brings."

"I thought about asking Wanda Johnson. I think she's nice and she's pretty," I answered.

"I think Dot likes you. Why don't you take her?"

I became curious about Charles's suggestion. "I don't know. I think they're both nice. Why do you want me to take Dot?"

"I just thought you wouldn't want to take Kish's sister because they always kicked y'all butts on the football field," Charles replied.

"Man, I'm over that, and I wish Kish were still alive to see how pretty and smart his baby sister is."

Charles finally revealed his true intentions. "Well, I think one of us of ought to ask her, and since Dot likes you, that leaves me."

"I knew you wanted to ask her. Why didn't you just say so instead of beating around the bush?" I responded, acknowledging Charles's desire. "Well, now that that's settled, how are we going to get to the banquet?" I asked, knowing that as usual his car was broken down.

"I'll just ask my brother if I can drive his car."

"I know you don't mean that blue Volkswagen Beetle," I sarcastically said. "That thing ain't big enough for all four of us to get in."

"Yes, it is. You ain't that big anyway," Charles defensively answered. "I don't know why you complaining. If you have a better idea, let me know."

I did have only one choice. It was either ride in the Beetle or stay home. I had every intention of being at the Valentine Banquet. I was the president, after all.

"Okay," I said.

"I'll pick the girls up and be at your house by seven. Oh, and Leonard, make sure you wear a suit; we want to look nice for the girls," Charles ordered.

I owned one suit, a funky Carolina Blue leisure suit with elephant-size pockets and a lapel that could be used as bed linen. I had purchased it from the Asian clothing store on Main Street during my spending spree for high school.

As I expected, Charles arrived on time. Knowing that Charles was never late for anything forced me to get ready early. I immediately recognized the honk of the Volkswagen's horn. Its sound matched its size. The car seemed undersized even against the trailer I called home.

"Come on, Leonard. We don't want to be late!" Charles yelled through the open window of the car.

"You ladies look good tonight," I said to Wanda and Dot.

I never attended my high school prom, and this would be the closest thing to that experience for me. I never attended any after-school activities until becoming active in the Bible Club. The Bible Club really functioned as my social springboard and coming-out party. The demanding work of president consumed a lot of time, which was a good thing, because it took my mind off the disappointment of failing to take the SAT.

I still refused to give up my hope of attending Pfeiffer College and had mailed my application weeks before.

I didn't have time to worry or stress over whether the answer would be one of acceptance or rejection. I really did not know if they would even respond.

Therefore, it came as a sudden shock when a letter from Pfeiffer College's admissions office addressed to Mr. Leonard E. Fairley showed up in our mailbox. Once again, I relived the anxiety of possibly having one more door closed in my face.

I walked from the mailbox without the joy that should have been part of this historic moment in my life; my feelings were of doubt and foreboding. I dared not tell anybody that I had received the letter. Under any other circumstances, I would have ripped it open without a thought. I was afraid to open this letter inside the house.

"Where can I open this without anybody seeing me?" I whispered.

I instinctively turned toward the most secluded patch of woods I could find. It seemed to take forever to find the perfect spot to open the letter.

During the eternity of the search, I again began a heart-wrenching conversation with God.

"God, I'm not asking for any special attention, and I'm not asking for a favor, but I'm simply asking for an opportunity," I began, the prayer spilling from my soul with little effort. "I've been waiting on this moment all my life, and I don't want to be disappointed. It's been a long journey, and I need to know it's not been in vain. I don't know what you have in store for me, but I know it is something beyond life in a trailer park. I know it is somewhere beyond all the valleys I've journeyed through. I know you haven't brought me this far just to leave me now."

I don't know where the words came from, but just as I began to open the letter, they came. They spilled out before I even read the writing on the letter.

"I'm going to college!" I shouted with such boldness and force that it temporarily frightened me, because the words seemed to come from somebody else.

The opened letter trembled so violently in my hands that it was a wonder I could read it at all, but there it was in black and white: "Dear Mr. Fairley, we are pleased to inform you that you have been accepted into Pfeiffer College's class of 1981."

I immediately went numb. The only emotion I was able to recognize was tearful joy. The only thing that helped me recognize any emotion was the single wet teardrop trickling down the most important letter I had ever received or read in my life.

It was unbelievable. How had I gotten into school without taking the SAT?

After gaining my composure and wiping enough of the thick tears from my eyes to enable me to finish reading the letter, I discovered the miracle. Pfeiffer had accepted me based solely on my grades. The college would give me the opportunity to take the SAT with the other required placement tests once I arrived on campus.

It was certainly poetic justice that the only others witnessing this moment of quiet triumph besides myself were God and Grandma Gladys. Of course, I had no doubt that Grandma Gladys somehow had worked a deal with God in order to be standing right there with him looking at her grandson with pride.

I ran back toward our trailer with delayed excitement.

"I got into Pfeiffer!" I must have screamed all the way home, finally letting go—now willing to let the whole trailer park know what had just happened.

"Leonard, get in this house! Have you lost your mind running through this trailer park yelling like a madman?"

I jammed the letter into my mama's hand. "Look, Mama!"

In disbelief almost equal to my own, Mama read the words over and over again. I could tell the words registered when my mama reached out with her arms and engulfed me.

I had known the discipline and love of those arms, but the warmth and pride that flowed through them at this moment was totally different. The weariness was gone, and for once my mama seemed to rest in a moment of accomplishment.

My mama's words brought joy almost equal to the joy of being accepted into Pfeiffer.

"Leonard, I'm very proud of you." The words that followed were beyond that joy and brought tears to both of our eyes. "Remember, I will always love you."

The news of my acceptance spread through Brown's trailers like wildfire. The news appeared to lift the entire trailer park. We had only lived there a short time, and yet with the news of my acceptance, the downtrodden community suddenly embraced me as a favorite son. I was overjoyed to give them something to be excited about. There was not a neighbor I visited where people didn't want to know something about Pfeiffer.

Charlie tried claiming some of the glory.

"Yeah, I took him to take the SAT," he grinned as he and Stank took turns congratulating themselves.

I did not have the heart to tell them I had gotten into school despite their having made me miss the SAT. This was not a time for revenge, and although the thought did cross my mind once or twice, I did not even gloat to my guidance counselor. However, he did congratulate me upon learning of my acceptance at Pfeiffer.

The news changed everything. I would now be preparing myself to leave home.

The entire Bible Club somehow discovered I had been accepted, and the only way they could have found out was through Charles. The next Bible Club meeting was dedicated to recognizing all the seniors and the important decision about which college-bound student would be the recipient of the Bible Club Scholarship.

Miss Graham informed all the seniors planning to attend college to leave the room as the vote was taken.

"We will announce the winner at the Awards Day ceremony," Miss Graham told us as we re-entered the room. "We will continue to perform our usual fundraising activities until that time."

The work of fundraising took on new meaning now that I was a college-bound student.

True to her word, Miss Graham kept us busy with work up until the end. We finished our fundraising efforts in May just in time for the Awards Day ceremony.

The entire student body gathered in the high school auditorium for the annual announcement of students receiving scholarships and other certificates of achievement.

The principal and other school dignitaries took turns announcing the names of students fortunate enough to have received recognition. I took my place inside the auditorium with no delusions of grandeur.

It was just another opportunity to miss class. The auditorium was filled with students equally filled with the excitement of being in assembly rather than class. It was the only reason I could account for the beehive-like buzz coming from the crowd. The only thing capable of putting a stop to the constant buzz was the amplified voice of Mr. Sullivan, the principal, giving his usual monotone opening speech that we had heard a million times.

"Faculty, students, and honored guests, we welcome each of you to our campus for this special assembly," Mr. Sullivan began with all the seriousness of a presidential candidate. "We have gathered here today to honor the distinguished class of 1977. The class of 1977 has indeed distinguished itself scholastically by the number of seniors who will be continuing their education at institutions of higher learning."

I immediately straightened my slumping posture with the knowledge that I was one of those students going on to college. However, I understood that if past history was any indication, I would not be hearing my name called among those receiving scholarships.

"Charles, we might as well leave. There's no way our names will be called," I said.

"You don't know that, Leonard. Why don't you just sit still and see what happens?"

"I ain't never won nothing in my life, and I know nobody from the trailer park is going to win anything," I explained.

"Leonard, you're just as smart as anybody whose name has already been called."

"But that won't make any difference," I replied, trying to convince Charles that my chances of being called to walk across the auditorium stage and receive anything were hopeless.

Kevin interrupted our conversation. "Leonard, did you hear that?"

"Kevin, why don't you mind your own business," I replied.

"But they just called your name," he said.

"Yeah, he's right, Leonard. They just called it again," Charles said. "You better get your butt up there before they give the thing to somebody else."

I sat in total shock for what seemed like forever.

"The Laurinburg Ministerial Memorial Scholarship recipient is Leonard Fairley," Mr. Sullivan said for the third time.

I made my way timidly toward the stage to congratulatory applause. My whole body trembled as I stood on stage, shaking hands with the principal in front of Scotland High School's student body.

I barely made it back to my seat before Mr. Sullivan called my name again—this time as the recipient of the Bible Club Scholarship.

I turned and spoke to Charles. "I can't make it back up there."

"Yes, you can. Go on—you deserve it," Charles answered.

Once again, there I stood on the stage in disbelief. However, nothing prepared me for what happened next.

As I started walking back down the stage steps, I saw Mama standing there at the bottom with tears running down her face.

"I can't let all these people see me cry," I whispered to myself.

But Mama didn't care. She let it all go.

"Leonard, I'm proud of you. I know your grandma is smiling down from heaven."

I tried all I could think of to keep from crying like a baby in front of all these people. The tears were about to start flowing when I looked up at my mama's head.

"Mama, what in the world is that on your head?" I whispered as she hugged me so tight I thought I would lose what little breath I had left in my body.

I could not believe my eyes. My mama was wearing a wig. I didn't know whether to laugh, cry, or crawl under the stage in embarrassment.

I was caught in a web of emotions. I did not know a day could be so full of promise, joy, and hope. I was glad for one thing—that the assembly took place during the last class period and from here we would be going home. I don't think I could have concentrated on classwork anyway, and I was determined to know how Mama knew I was getting an award.

Before I could get off the school bus, people from the trailer park were walking up to me telling me how proud they were of me. The news was all over the trailer park thanks to Mama and Stank.

Thankfully, the wig was gone when I walked through the front door of our trailer. The first thing I asked Mama about was the wig.

"Mama, where did you get that wig? I almost didn't recognize you today at school."

"Well, you know I wasn't going to come to school looking any old kind of way. I had to look presentable for your big day," Mama explained.

"But how did you know I was going get a scholarship?" I asked.

"They wrote me a letter two weeks ago requesting my presence at the Awards Day ceremony, but they didn't tell me which scholarships you were getting," Mama answered. "I'm just so proud of you," Mama said, over and over again.

"Please don't cry again," I said.

"Leonard, you don't know how it makes me feel, after all the hell we've been through—and now to have a child going to college. It's the best thing that's happened in this family in a long time. I remember how you were born struggling to live, and now look at you. Your grandma was right. God has his hands on you."

My mama cried despite my pleading with her not to. If Mama was crying like this, then I knew Grandma Gladys must have been crying enough tears to cause a Noah-like flood in heaven.

"I know I ain't been able to give my children the best in life. I almost got y'all killed in New York, and I've been moving y'all all over God's creation not knowing if you would eat or starve," Mama said through the flood of tears. "If I could do it all over again, it wouldn't be like this. Leonard, I'm sorry I put y'all through so much. I know I'll have to pay for what I did, but today I just felt so proud and happy that at least one of y'all was trying to make something out yourself."

Mama finally fell into silent sobbing.

It was my turn now to comfort her. I had no idea that she carried such a heavy burden, blaming herself for our lot in life.

"It's all right, Mama. Don't cry," I said as I reached out and held her in arms that hopefully spoke my love. "I know it's not been easy, and I know you've done the best you could."

My words sounded so useless. Although heartfelt, I still understood that these words were so inadequate. I did not have the right words to lift such a burden.

Therefore, I simply spoke, for what seemed like the first time, words I hoped carried some release: "I love you, Mama."

Immediately, I felt the sigh too deep for words leave both our bodies. I knew then, beyond a shadow of a doubt, that this was indeed Grandma Gladys's daughter. I knew that she, too, had prayed countless nights for the safety, care, and love of her children. I knew this woman had given more than I would ever know. She didn't have the material things to give, but she gave us her soul. I realized there was something in her spirit that, although unspoken, kept me searching for silver linings.

I should have realized it the day she spoke so deeply to me about my birth and in the countless ways she allowed without interruption the reality of God's grace to be developed in me.

It had been an amazing and blessed day. It was indeed a day that reminded me once again that no matter how dark the clouds might get, there are always silver linings.

The responsibilities and details of being a senior were still to be dealt with. There were graduation invitations to be ordered. I made the realistic decision that a class ring and pictures would be too expensive. I didn't even bother ordering a class ring. As for pictures, I would just keep the proofs.

"What do I need with a class ring or picture anyway? I don't need those things as long as I have memories," I said to myself while leafing through the catalog of custom class rings. "I don't need a class ring or a picture to remind of high school."

In a way I was lying to myself as justification for not being able to afford any of those things.

The disappointment of not having these traditional items that were a vital part of the celebration and joy of graduation weighed heavily on me. Once again, the disappointment was swallowed up in my duties as president of the Bible Club. Miss Graham made sure of that with her constant array of activities for the club.

The last thing on my plate as president included the planning of our end-of-school picnic.

"Miss Graham, can we have the picnic at St. Andrews College?" I asked.

"If the weather cooperates, that's okay with me," she answered. "If the weather is good, we'll have barbecue chicken quarters on the grill."

These words made us all salivate. A picnic around St. Andrews's lake would be the perfect ending to my public education. I remembered walking there from Newtown to fish and swim at that lake, not realizing someday I would end up going to college.

Fortunately, the weather cooperated. Miss Graham set up the huge gas grill near the lake, and before long, one could smell the chicken roasting. We shared stories of all the things we were able to accomplish as a club, and the memories helped me realize I would not be attending college without the nurturing of a loving community—a community that made me ready for the journey that lies ahead.

"What was that splash?" Charles asked.

"Miss Graham, look at Kevin! He's jumped in the lake with his clothes on," I said. "I guess Kevin is glad he's graduating and will soon have his grandma out of his hair," I added, trying to explain Kevin's overexuberance.

Before Miss Graham could say "no," Charles and I followed Kevin into the lake. Why should he have all the fun? It would be my last act as president of the Bible Club, and I wanted it to be one to remember.

I camped in front of the mirror on June 9, 1977—graduation day.

I naturally reminisced about my whole life and wished that both Mable and Grandma Gladys were around to see this day. I thought about the Pine Street Patriots. Only a few of them would be graduating with me, while many of them had become what society fated them to become—just high school dropout statistics.

Still, for those who had stuck it out, even for them high school would be the extent of their education. Fate, it appeared, would finally catch up with them. Twelve years of school only prolonged the path to the likely ultimate fate of becoming a government unemployment statistic. It was a painful conclusion that waited for them. After high school would be the school of hard knocks working in factories or whatever job became available in Laurinburg, of which there were so few.

Education in the streets of hard knocks would teach them how to live from paycheck to paycheck, and often not even that necessity would be guaranteed. It was a fact of reality that the cycle of poverty could not be broken by a high school diploma alone. The piece of paper they would receive tonight would not guarantee them anything.

However, that disappointing truth could not deny the fact that high school graduation was a major event in Scotland County. It marked the only time many of these students would walk across a stage in a cap and gown to the cheers of jubilant relatives.

Parents lived for the day they would see their child complete high school, and this was especially true for the parents and grandparents who had spent countless hours on their knees praying for their children. The hope of their prayers had been to see a son or daughter live to finish high school. Parents of children in the communities I had grown up in were frightened to pray for anything beyond high school graduation; just getting a child through high school was difficult enough.

I did not know of another Pine Street Patriot graduating in the class of 1977 who would be attending college, and I certainly did not know of another trailer park child who would be doing so.

It was a painful and disappointing reminiscence, because I had grown up with the Pine Street Patriots. I had seen their creativity, their imagination, and their genius. I knew firsthand that they were just as intelligent as any honor student set to walk across the graduation stage. The years of living as outcasts became a burden too difficult to shake off, even at this joyful celebration. The hands of poverty and oppression reached out and touched this amazing milestone in the lives of my friends.

"Is there anything that cannot be affected by suffering?" I spoke to the reflection dressed in the navy blue cap and gown staring back at me from the mirror.

The only thing able to shake the depression of my reminiscing was the voice of my mama yelling at me through the closed door of the bathroom.

"Boy, what are you doing in there? If you don't hurry, you're going to miss your own graduation."

"I'm coming, I just need to make sure my cap fits over my Afro," I answered.

The familiar wail of Charles's Volkswagen beetle sounded through the open bathroom window, and my mama screamed once again.

"Leonard, you need to come out of there. Can't you hear Charles out there blowing his horn?"

"I hear him," I answered as I stepped into the living room all decked out in my navy blue cap and gown. "Don't y'all forget to make sure you come on time so you can get a good seat, and don't forget the tickets, either," I shouted on my way out the door.

"What took you so long?" Charles asked.

"You know I can't go to my high school graduation looking like a tramp," I answered.

"Mr. Sullivan told us to be there on time so we can line up and walk through the ceremony one more time," Charles warned.

"We'll get there on time."

Charles reminded me of the distance we had to travel.

"Leonard, you must have forgotten that you live out in the boondocks."

"Why don't we listen to some Earth, Wind, and Fire?" I said, hoping that would ease Charles's anxiety.

"See, I told you we'd make it in time," I said as we pulled into the St. Andrews College parking lot.

The gym was buzzing with the sounds of nervous, joyful seniors waiting for that important moment when, upon hearing their names called, they would be instant adults.

Man, there are an awful lot of people in there, I thought to myself after finding my place in line. It seemed like the whole city of Laurinburg had turned out for graduation.

I listened carefully so as not to miss the high school concert band beginning to play our cue of "Pomp and Circumstance." Line by line, more than four hundred seniors marched into the sea of people gathered in St. Andrews' gym.

Despite this being our crossover into adulthood, there certainly was still a little bit of the spirit of the child left in most of us. The commencement speaker was barely into his speech before somebody let gerbils loose into the graduation assembly. Immediately, you could hear the shrieks building across the graduating class of 1977. *Who would do such a stupid thing?* I thought. *If these are the future leaders of the world, we're in deep trouble.* However, it was kind of funny and the shrieks were starting to die down. But where did they go? The only possible place they could have gone was under the bleachers of the gym.

Thank God, the speeches were finally over, and now the tedious job of calling all those names began.

I was fortunate that my last name was Fairley and I would be among the first names called. The principal requested that all applause be kept until the entire graduating class was announced. Mr. Sullivan might as well have been speaking Greek because, after each name called, the family members of the graduate exploded in unabashed joy, and some even whistled. There was no way on God's green earth that Mr. Sullivan was going to stop families from expressing their excitement.

I knew I would soon be walking across the stage to receive my high school diploma, and I wondered if anyone would whistle for me. I thought whistling at such a ceremony was juvenile and redneckish, but for once I would have loved to hear it.

In the middle of my daydream, I heard Mr. Sullivan call my name.

"Leonard Earl Fairley," he called, and it sounded so distinguished.

I had never heard my name pronounced in such a proper and dignified manner. I was used to hearing my name called as if I were nobody. There was nothing distinguished about my name in the environment I grew up in.

I tried to walk across the stage with as much class and dignity as the sound of my name required, but all that went out the window when I heard my brother Calvin and the Pine Street Patriots whistling.

In acknowledgment of their joy, I lifted both hands in the air as I walked with dignity down the stairs on the other side of the platform. The class of 1977 was slowly losing its patience as Mr. Sullivan continued calling names. When he grew tried, Mrs. Nelson, the assistant principal, took over the duty of reading the other half of the names of the more than four hundred graduates.

The pent-up energy building in the room erupted in an explosion of joy as the last person in the class of 1977 walked across the platform. I cannot remember who it was, but for the moment, that student was the most popular person in the entire class.

I had always seen on television shows where the graduating class threw their caps into the air, but I never thought it happened in real life. Yet here we were, throwing our caps into the air. It was an amazing sight to see—so many navy blue caps floating skyward.

However, not everyone participated in the ritual. I was not about to lose my cap in all the insanity. I wanted to keep my cap as a souvenir, but I did enjoy seeing the students scrambling trying to find their caps in the mad sea of graduates.

"Charles!" I yelled through the crowd of students, parents, and relatives trying to find each other for pictures.

I found him standing with his arms around Wanda in an embrace that said, "If I don't see you anymore I hope you have a wonderful life."

The scene was the same all across the gym of St. Andrews College. Graduates were embracing friends, and before you knew it, these new adults were crying like babies. One minute, students were smiling in excitement holding up their diploma for pictures, and the next minute, tears were all over the floor. I didn't believe there could be so many tears. With all the water flowing in the gym, they could have flooded deserts and grown enough food to feed the world.

"Charles, what are we going to do tonight?" I finally got the chance to ask.

"I don't know, but I think there's an after-graduation party somewhere in town."

"If we're going to a party, I suggest we go home and change clothes," I offered.

"Okay, when we get through here, we'll go to your house and change. I brought a change of clothes with me so I can change at your house," Charles answered.

It was late by the time we reached the trailer park after the party. The only visible light was the glow from the television.

I knocked on the door, and Calvin met us at the door.

"Boy, what are you doing still up at this hour?" I asked in semi-shock.

"Mama said I could stay up and watch this movie," Calvin answered.

"Since you're still up, could you do me a favor? Can you tell Mama we're going to Pizza Hut to get some pizza?" I requested.

"Pizza Hut ain't open this late at night," Calvin replied.

"Yes, it is. They decided to stay open for graduation night and we're hungry," I explained. "Calvin, just do like I asked you and stop asking so many dumb questions."

"I want to go with y'all. I'm hungry, too, and you know it ain't nothing in this house to eat," Calvin replied.

"Boy, you've got some nerve thinking we're going to let you hang out with us tonight."

I was an adult now, and I didn't want to be caught dead with a child, especially tonight.

Charles said, "Leonard, it ain't going to hurt nothing. Let him come."

I looked at Charles in disbelief.

"What's wrong with you, Charles? He ain't nothing but a kid. This is our night. Why you want to spoil it by letting him tag along?" I responded, in disregard for Calvin's feelings. "Besides he ain't got on no clothes or shoes."

"I can find something to put on real quick," Calvin said.

"I don't mind him coming," Charles added.

I knew this was an argument I'd lose; it was Charles's car, and I couldn't tell him who could ride in his car.

I angrily relented. "Well, what you waiting for, go on and put on some clothes before we change our minds."

I could see the excited smile on Calvin's face in the soft glow of the television's light.

We arrived at Pizza Hut and placed our order. The restaurant was packed with other graduates and their families. Finally our pizza arrived.

"This pizza sure is good," Calvin said between greedy bites.

"I'm glad you like it," I said sarcastically. "Calvin, whose shoes you got on?" I asked as I lowered my head to take a sip of sweet tea.

"I couldn't find my shoes so I grabbed the first pair I could find," he answered.

"Don't you know you got on Mama's shoes?" I whispered so only Charles and Calvin would hear.

Charles broke out in uncontrollable laughter, and the entire restaurant started staring at us.

Calvin had done it again. The daredevil had struck again, even at my high school graduation.

Graduation was now over, and my focus would turn to preparing to actually go off to college.

Once again, the summer brought with it the job I had grown to love—painting schools for the CETA program with Mr. Isler. It felt so surreal to be painting classrooms where I had once been a student, particularly at Covington Street and Central schools. It seemed like such a long time ago since my self-esteem had been challenged, molded, and shaped in these places. *What child will be sitting here next year looking out the window daydreaming about the future as I once did?* I thought. I had spent countless days doing just that, hoping against hope that my grandma was right about silver linings. *What child of poverty would be sitting here struggling to make sense out of the injustice of the double standard of poor and rich?*

Michael Harrington brilliantly describes the double standard of poverty in his landmark books, *The Other America* and *The New American Poverty*.

No child ought to be sitting in a classroom trying to live with such a travesty of justice, I angrily thought as I stood there with my paintbrush. *They should be learning new things, for God's sake, not listening to the grumble of an empty stomach. They should be thinking of recess, not about how they're going to hide the holes in their shoes or clothes.*

One of my greatest hopes of a college education was that it would give me the tools to do something to change the lives of people who were never given a chance. However, I had no idea what area of study would equip me for such an overwhelming task.

But I had to get to college first, and I just couldn't go without the necessary college essentials. I was starting from scratch. I would need to buy everything, from bedcovers to sheets to toiletries. I would even have to buy enough underwear to last me a year.

The people in Roses Department Store must have thought I had lost my mind when I walked up to the checkout counter with a trunk and thirty-two pairs of Fruit of the Loom underwear.

I answered the astonished look on the clerk's face.

"I'm going to college," I blurted out loud enough for people standing in every checkout line to hear.

The clerk just looked at me and started a conversation as she rung up each item including, unfortunately, the underwear separately.

"What school you going to, honey?" she asked, as I wished she would speed up.

"I'm going to Pfeiffer College," I answered.

"Where in the world is that?" she continued.

"It's in Misenheimer, North Carolina," I politely answered.

"That still don't help me much," she replied.

"It's between Albemarle and Salisbury," I replied.

The conversation helped me feel less nervous about all these people looking at my underwear. I was glad to get out of that store with my pride intact.

The summer was also an opportunity for me to see another side of religion. Something told me I wouldn't get out of Laurinburg without another test.

"Leonard, I want you to go with me to this tent revival," Charles requested.

"What kind of revival is it?"

"It's in Bennettsville, South Carolina," he answered.

Although I'd been active in the Bible Club at high school, I still hadn't had much dealing with the church. Therefore, my curiosity was up.

"Okay, I'll go with you," I answered.

It was enough to make me lose my religion and what little faith I had in the church.

The tent was located in a neighborhood that was a carbon copy of Newtown, except this was South Carolina. The tent was packed on the Wednesday night we decided to attend. It was easy to see what kind of people these were. I had lived my entire life around people like these. These were people looking for any form of help—people looking for God to drop a big hand out of the sky and change their status in life.

The crowd gathered that night included single mothers on welfare and elderly people receiving monthly Social Security checks. It included sick people looking for healing that doctors had failed to provide and people with no health insurance, thus unable to attend a doctor's office.

These were the people of the Bible belt who had nothing else to believe in but God.

The apostle, as he was called, was already into the service as Charles and I walked into the big tent perched in the middle of a vacant lot in the middle of downtown Bennettsville. Before we could find a place to sit down, a woman jumped up and started speaking in tongues, and the old Hammond organ, played by an equally ancient-looking woman, seemed to infuse spirit into the entire congregation. People started to fall onto the dirt floor of the tent, rolling around in the sweet ecstatic release of what was called "being slain in the spirit." More and more people began speaking in tongues until they almost drowned out even the deep voice of Apostle Johnson.

Before long, the drum and a guitar joined the spirit-zapping organ, giving the people even more energy. The wailing and cries grew louder, and I thought it would never end.

Apostle Johnson was drenched in sweat, but he appeared to never tire as his message, whatever it was, got lost between the "Amens," "Hallelujahs," and "Thank you, Jesus!" of the now frantic crowd.

If this was the release the people came looking for, they wouldn't leave disappointed. Apostle Johnson was not about to let that happen. He seemed to know instinctively when the people were ready for the next phase of the service. In one fluid, unnoticed movement of his wet body, Apostle Johnson motioned to the organist to tone it down, and when the organ slowed, the people did the same, right on cue.

The apostle spoke with sincerity and seriousness.

"God told me there's somebody here tonight looking for a healing. It's a mother and daughter. The healing you're looking for, mother, is for your daughter," he said, scanning the crowd.

Suddenly from the back of the tent came a mother and daughter.

Apostle Johnson walked off the platform and met the mother and daughter in one of the aisles of the big tent. The mother shyly whispered into his ear.

"The Lord wants to heal this child's hearing tonight, but we've got to be obedient to God first," Apostle Johnson said as he turned the young child toward the congregation.

The little girl was a beautiful child with big doll-like eyes. I could not think of anyone sitting in the tent that night who would not want such a beautiful child to be healed.

Apparently, Apostle Johnson knew it as well.

"We've got to be obedient to God tonight," he bellowed out once again to the waiting crowd. "The Lord told me that ten people were going to give one thousand dollars tonight, and five would give five hundred. If we expect the Lord to be faithful to us, we've got to be faithful to God."

The mother looked out at the crowd with pleading eyes—eyes that said to the congregation, "Please, be faithful tonight so that my daughter can be healed."

I could not believe what I was seeing and hearing. The line gradually started to grow as people started walking up to a table guarded by two strong-looking ushers. In amazement, I watched people start placing money in the two baskets on the table. I knew these were people who could least afford to make such a sacrifice, but they wanted so badly to be obedient to God.

Once again, the organ player began to whip the people into a spiritual frenzy, and the speaking in tongues started again in earnest as well. The little girl seemed lost and frightened as people started being "slain in the spirit" right in front of her. It was apparent the people felt their obedience included "making a joyful noise unto the Lord."

Apostle Johnson started his prayer as the shouts of the people gradually turned into a unified hum. He proceeded to put his fingers into the little girl's ears, as her mother assured her it was all right and that Apostle Johnson only meant to help her.

Releasing his fingers from her ears, he whispered into her ears loud enough for us to hear, "In the name of Jesus, ears open up."

It made no difference how many times he said those words; the child still didn't respond.

What was wrong? Hadn't the people been obedient enough?

I got up and walked out of the tent in tears.

"Leonard, do you want me to take you home?" Charles asked.

The silent tears now turned into an audible sorrow and disgust.

"Yeah, I'm ready to go and I don't ever want to come back here again," I replied with the force of all my pain.

"I'm sorry I brought you out here."

"It ain't your fault, Charles," I replied.

We drove back to the trailer park without another word spoken between us. The pain of our mutual disappointment and anger was too deep for words.

It took me almost the entire summer to get over how the so-called apostle had used God. The scene caused me to rebel against my Grandma Gladys's prophecy that God's call was on my life. I wanted nothing to do with a God who allowed people like Apostle Johnson into his service.

I attempted to do everything I could to get what I'd witnessed out of my head. Once again, the ragamuffin community of Brown's Trailer Park helped me through it. I simply wrapped myself deeper into preparing for college.

I was busy packing my newly purchased trunk when Sandra walked into our house.

"Leonard, what you doing?" she innocently asked.

"I'm packing for school," I answered.

"Boy, that sure is a lot of underwear," Sandra said. "I hope you don't make a mistake and pack some of Stank's big ole underwear."

The clothesline out back swung back and forth in the wind, drying the jeans, shirts, and of course, Stank's underwear.

I don't recall who made the dare.

"Sandra, I double dare you to go put on a pair of Stank's drawers hanging on the clothesline and run around the trailer in them."

Sandra ran outside toward the clothesline, giggling hysterically.

"I can't believe she's actually going to do it," I said.

"She's doing it," Shelia yelled as we all made our way toward the back door.

It was indeed a sight that brought tearful laughter to our eyes watching Sandra run around the trailer in underwear five times too big for her. I hadn't found much to laugh about after the scene at the tent revival, but Sandra, in her own silly way, brought back the laughter.

I still hadn't changed my mind about God's calling on my life. I still didn't want to have anything to do with such a God.

But Sandra brought joy back to me. The joy of college was once again heard in my voice.

However, I still wondered if my faith in silver linings would still persist under the intense scrutiny of higher education.

The much-anticipated day to leave for the campus of Pfeiffer College arrived faster than I thought it would or should. Without question, I was excited about going, but I had no idea what to expect. It had been easy talking about going to college, but I was learning it was another thing to actually wake up to the reality of it happening.

Charles pulled up into the thick sand next to our trailer on time as usual. Together, we had mapped out the desired route to take weeks ago, but even that seemed a distant memory. It had been just a yellow highlighted destiny on a map, but now it was about to become a physical, spiritual, and emotional destiny. I was about to find out what Dorothy felt like when she left Kansas and ended up in the Land of Oz. Nothing would ever be the same again, and I could feel it as we loaded my trunk into the car.

Charles understood, because he, too, would be making such a journey in a few days. Therefore, he allowed me to spend a few minutes with Mama before we departed.

I had not practiced or talked about this moment much, and maybe that's why I spoke with such raw emotion.

"Mama, I'm scared to leave."

"I know," she answered. "I've known it for a long time, but I wanted to give you space to deal with it on your own. It's hard to leave what you've been use to for so long," Mama tenderly said.

"But Mama, I always thought I'd be happy to finally have a dream come true," I explained. "I've dreamed of going to college. Why do I feel like this now?"

"Leonard, dreams are built from your surroundings. It don't matter how bad things look or what side of the tracks you come from."

There was something familiar about the sound of her voice. Of course I had spent my whole life hearing it, but there was something different about it this time. I remembered only one other time I had heard her talk like this. Her voice sounded almost identical to the way it sounded on the day she told me about my premature birth.

"Leonard, there is something I've got to tell you before you leave," she said with a catch in her throat. "God brought you into this world, and God kept you."

"Yeah, Mama, I know all that. Grandma never let me forget it. Remember?"

"That's true, Leonard, but there's something else you must realize," she said. "God raised you, too. I tried the best I could, but I got sense enough to know that my best couldn't have gotten you to this point. I prayed that God would keep all my children, but you seem to have lived in that prayer."

Somehow, I was beginning to understand what Mama was saying. I could see God's finger in it all. Nothing had been random. God had used both the good and bad to mold and shape me. Nothing I had ever experienced was a wasted moment. Perceptions become the reality, and reality yields behavior, and behavior yields destiny.

Grandma Gladys made sure that I would see not only the dark clouds but also the light shining behind them. Indeed, that is what had been happening in every experience I could remember.

I was learning to look at things with different eyes. I was looking at things through the eyes of a grandma who truly lived life with the mind of Christ. It was the mind of Christ that gave her the wisdom to keep me alive. Somehow she'd done everything in her power to pass that mind on to me, and her death had not stopped the learning.

I could hear Grandma Gladys in my mama's voice. She was making sure I would take the belief in silver linings with me to college.

I stood there talking to Mama for a good hour, and by now everybody was gathered in the tiny front room of our mobile home waiting to say goodbye. Immediately, I understood that in this trailer stood every experience of my life, and if college was to mean anything, I needed to take every life experience with me.

We were not a hugging, touchy-feely kind of family, but for once in my life, I needed to touch all the history standing in that room—the history of jumping creeks, the history of struggling together, the history of first loves. I would need to carry all of that with me.

Therefore, I hugged everybody to make sure that I would leave nothing behind. I understood that these were the true silver linings that nothing could ever take away.

I climbed into Charles's car and began a journey forever blessed with silver linings.

"I wouldn't take nothing for my journey," Mama Gladys would sing. My journey, up until this point, had not been one of smooth sailing, but I was glad to have taken it. As the car left behind the trailer park and eventually Laurinburg, I knew that I could also sing, "I wouldn't take nothing for my journey."

My journey was rich, and I was certain that its richness would be able to sustain me. The journey was just beginning, and I would now need to trust the community that had nurtured me.

I was looking forward to the new places that silver linings would take me.

About the Author

Leonard E. Fairley has served as resident bishop of the South Carolina Annual Conference of The United Methodist Church since September 1, 2024. Previously he served as resident bishop of the Kentucky Annual Conference and Red Bird (now Central Appalachia) Missionary Conference from 2016-2024, and as interim bishop for the North Carolina Annual Conference from Sept. 1, 2021, to Jan. 1, 2023.

Fairley graduated from Pfeiffer College and Duke University's School of Divinity. He has been awarded honorary doctoral degrees from Union College in Columbia, Kentucky, and Kentucky Wesleyan College.

Before his election as bishop, he served the North Carolina Annual Conference since 1984. His last appointment was serving as superintendent of the Capital District, the largest district. He served at

St. Peters UMC in Hamlet, North Carolina, and Soapstone UMC in Raleigh, North Carolina, before becoming the Rockingham district superintendent. He served in that role for seven years before returning to the local church in 2012 as lead pastor at St. Francis UMC in Cary, North Carolina.

Fairley served on numerous boards and agencies in the North Carolina Conference, among them as Conference Vitalization Consultant, chair of Congregational Development, vice chair of both the Council on Finance and Administration and Conference Board of Church and Society, the North Carolina Conference Transition Team, the Conference Board of Ordained Ministry, the Conference Episcopacy Committee, and as a General and Jurisdictional conference delegate.

He has participated on mission work teams in Costa Rica, Jamaica, Montserrat, Zimbabwe, Haiti, Honduras, Serbia, and with the Appalachia Service Project.

In addition to this memoir, Fairley has published a book of poetry, *Who Shall Hear My Voice*. He also was a contributing writer to *The Day the Earth Moved Haiti: From Havoc to Healing*.

He was married to Priscilla Ann Russell until her death in 2013. In January 2018, God surprised him with new love, and in September of that year, Fairley married Dawn Sparks. Dawn had lost her soulmate, Rev. David Sparks, in 2015. Between them, the Fairleys have four adult children and eleven grandchildren.

www.ingramcontent.com/pod-product-compliance
Lightning Source LLC
Chambersburg PA
CBHW021140160426
43194CB00007B/636